Perfect Days on the...

FRENCH RIVIERA

Map Included

www.marco-polo.com

Contents

For chapters: See inside front cover

TOP 10

Not to be missed!

Our TOP 10 hits – from the absolute No. 1 to No. 10 – help you plan your tour of the most important sights.

1 MONACO'S CASINO ➤ 92

Charles Garnier's magnificent casino building is the ultimate symbol of luxury on the achingly glamorous French Riviera.

2 NICE'S MUSEUMS ➤ 44

The Musée Matisse is one of Nice's museum highlights. Henri Matisse bequeathed his entire private collection to the city, a place where he spent many winters during his life.

3 VILLA EPHRUSSI ➤ 68

Baroness Béatrice Ephrussi de Rothschild realised a common dream by building her own palace on the Cap Ferrat peninsula. The villa with its magnificent grounds are spectacular proof that money and taste can go hand in hand.

4 SAINT-TROPEZ ➤ 142

Stars and wannabes turn this town with its harbour and beaches into a jetset playground each and every summer.

5 ÈZE ➤ 70

This settlement filled with stone houses and cobbled streets is a textbook example of a *village perché* – a hilltop village perched high above the sea.

6 MUSÉE PICASSO ➤ 114

This museum in the Grimaldi family's former castle in Antibes boasts a world-class art collection and a glorious sculpture garden with views of the sea.

7 CANNES ➤ 116

Cannes has much more to offer than its film festival and the palatial hotels on the Promenade de la Croisette – the meandering streets leading up to the fortress in the Old Town retain a village feel to this day.

8 THORONET ABBEY ➤ 146

This unostentatious, 12th-century Cistercian abbey is a classic example of Provence's Romanesque architectural style.

9 ÎLES DE LÉRINS ➤ 119

Both the Île Ste-Marguerite and the monastic island of St-Honorat are little oases of calm that are perfect for taking long strolls through landscapes steeped in culture.

10 FONDATION MAEGHT ➤ 121

Catalan architect Josep Lluís Sert built one of the world's most beautiful private museums in St-Paul-de-Vence for the collectors Marguerite and Aimé Maeght. It's stuffed with works by Miró, Braque, Giacometti and Chagall.

THAT FRENCH RIVIERA

Find out what makes the French Riviera tick and experience its unique flair – just like the locals themselves.

SHOPPING AT THE MARKET

If they don't have something at the markets on the French Riviera, it simply isn't worth having! Browse around the fresh vegetables, ripe fruit, aromatic cheeses and tasty herbs in the market halls of **Cannes (Marché de Forville** ➤ 135) or **Antibes** (➤ 135) and in **Nice's** Old Town (✚ 188 D3).

SWIMMING IN THE CITY

The beach running along Nice's **Promenade des Anglais** (✚ 188 A4–B3) is a good 10km/6mi long. Even during the height of summer, you'll find enough space for a refreshing dip in the sea. And good news if you don't like salt on your skin: most of the public beaches have showers.

HIKING ON THE COAST

The old coastal **Customs Officers' Paths** (*sentier des douaniers* or *sentier littoral*) are currently experiencing a renaissance. One of the most beautiful leads from **L'Escalet** to **Cap Lardier** on the **St-Tropez peninsula**. Whatever the

Colourful and inviting: Nice's markets

FEELING

Busy at all hours of the day and night: Nice's famous Promenade des Anglais

That French Riviera Feeling

Snorkellers near Porquerolles

season, you'll find some empty beaches for a swim along the way.

BOULES

All you need for the French national pastime of **pétanque** is a simple **strip of gravel**. Head to the **place des Lices** in **St-Tropez** (➤ 143) to spot the occasional celebrity throwing some steel balls at the little *cochonnet* ('piglet'). Join in and have a go yourself!

CYCLING ON THE ISLAND

There are only a very few cars on the island of **Porquerolles** (➤ 150) near **Hyères**, so rent a bicycle, get in the saddle and start exploring! It's home to some breathtaking **cliff-lined coasts** and idyllic bays that are just perfect for a swim.

ADMIRING SOME ART

The French Riviera has magnetically attracted artists for more than a century. The **Musée d'Art Moderne et d'Art Contemporain** (*Mamac*) in Nice (✚ 188 D2) has one of the most exciting collections of contemporary art around. It boasts a large number of pieces by **Niki de Saint-Phalle** and works from the 'School of Nice' by the likes of Ben, Yves Klein and **Martial Raysse**. It's free to get in.

SLEEPING IN A CANOPY BED

You don't have to stay at grand hotels to enjoy the luxury of a canopy bed. You'll also find them in such smaller lodgings as the **Auberge du Vieux Château** next to the church in **Cabris** (➤ 131). The views from this medieval village sweep over the hilltop town of **Grasse** and right down to the Mediterranean sea.

DINNER BY THE WAVES

Dine by the sea in Nice and listen to the the sound of the waves as you eat your meal. The **Plage Beau Rivage**, a private beach, (➤ 60; also open in winter) offers a good restaurant and a place to sunbathe in the heart of the city.

The Magazine

THE JETSET PLAYGROUND

A fabled land of unending sunshine, azure seas and sparkling light where winter never came was the talk of 19th-century European high society. It was dubbed the Côte d'Azur – also known as the French Riviera.

Towards the end of the 18th century this was still a poor and remote area of France. The first British traveller to be seduced by the mild winter climate was the writer Tobias Smollett, who visited Nice in 1763 and wrote about its warmth in *Travels in Italy and France* (1765). Later, in 1834, a British nobleman and politician, Henry Lord Brougham, was forced by a cholera epidemic to stop in the little fishing village of Cannes, where he found the scenery and climate so beguiling that he bought a plot of land and built a villa.

Sailing – just one of many popular pastimes near Saint-Tropez

A Winter Retreat

Other Britons followed, and the French Riviera rapidly became one of the most fashionable winter destinations for the well-heeled of the world, with sovereigns, statesmen, aristocrats, wealthy bourgeois and courtesans all paying it a visit. No less than Queen Victoria, the Aga Khan, Empress Eugénie (Napoléon III's wife) and King Leopold of Belgium held court here, and artists and writers flocked to the region, inspired by the magical light and scenery. It marked the start of what is known as the *belle époque*.

By 1860 it was Europe's most sophisticated winter retreat, ideally located between the newly fashionable resorts of Monaco and Cannes. The high society taste for luxury gave rise to the most exuberant and daring architectural projects, as owners vied with each other to create the most flamboyant villa. Railways, palatial hotels, semi-tropical gardens and the fabled Promenade des Anglais in Nice were built to meet their needs.

Monaco – the poorest state in Europe until 1850 – boomed in 1865 with the opening of the glamorous Monte-Carlo Casino, and fortunes were won and lost by the famous and the fashionable. Then, in 1887, the poet and Dijonnais vineyard owner Stephen Liegeard gave the region the glamorous, evocative name that confirmed its success – La Côte d'Azur ("The Azure Coast").

Palais du Prince, Monaco

A Russian Romance

Since the Russian Revolution of 1917, the French Riviera has been a popular destination for Russian aristocrats and émigrés, including such luminaries as Ivan Bunin (the first Russian to win the Nobel Prize for literature, in 1933) and artist Marc Chagall (➤ 45). It was in the Russian Orthodox Church in Nice that, by an Imperial Manifesto, Alexander III was officially proclaimed heir to the Russian throne, and Russian architects left their mark on the coast with such masterpieces as the Fernand Léger museum in Biot (➤ 127) and the dazzling Cathédrale Orthodoxe Russe St-Nicolas in Nice (➤ 53).

The beautiful Château des Ollières, now a luxury hotel (39 avenue des Baumettes, Nice), was built by Prince Lobanov Rostowsky. However, on being recalled to Moscow he gave it to his mistress as a gift of love.

THE BEAUTIFUL ERA

The development of the Cote d'Azur came at the height of *la belle époque* – the beautiful era. The style is a fusion of the most daring and ornamental architectural features, everything from turrets, domes and cupolas; faïence and fresco; glass chandeliers, marble and gilt – the more opulent and extravagant the better.

Many villas and hotels built in this style survive on the French Riviera, including the Négresco (➤ 48) and the Cathédrale Orthodoxe Russe St-Nicolas (➤ 53) in Nice; the Villa Grecque Kérylos and its elegant rotunda (➤ 73) in Beaulieu; the Villa Ephrussi de Rothschild on Cap Ferrat (➤ 68); the Monte-Carlo Opéra and Casino (➤ 92) and the Carlton Hotel in Cannes. Built in 1912, its twin cupolas were modelled after the breasts of the famous dancer and courtesan La Belle Otero.

Summer Holidays

The area flourished throughout the *belle époque*, but it was not until the "Roaring Twenties" that the region became a summer resort, made fashionable by such trendsetting American socialites as composer Cole Porter and writer F Scott Fitzgerald (► 19). Under their racy influence swimming came into vogue, and glamorous French fashion designer Coco Chanel started a new fashion craze after holidaying here – the suntan. Soon the French Riviera was the haunt not only of millionaires and royalty, but also of fashion divas, film stars and the greatest artists,

Carlton Hotel, Cannes

writers and thinkers of the time, including Renoir, Matisse, Picasso, Hemingway, Camus, Sartre and Huxley.

Today the French Riviera continues to draw galaxies of celebrities to its shores, including Brigitte Bardot, Elton John and Claudia Schiffer. Despite the advent of mass tourism and low-fare airlines, its resorts remain chic and exclusive with their "see-and-be-seen" promenades, their beautiful sun-soaked beaches and their bustling harbours of millionaires' yachts. After nearly two centuries the aptly named Côte d'Azur ("Azure Coast"), with its enticing, electric blue sea, remains the home of the rich and famous and one of the most glamorous playgrounds in the world.

A–Z of LOCAL CUISINE

Dining on the French Riviera is a magical experience. The local cuisine combines the voluptuous flavours of the Mediterranean with brilliant, sun-drenched colours and alluring fragrances to create a veritable feast for the senses.

- **Aïoli** is a delicious garlic mayonnaise, often served with shellfish.
- Try the region's world-famous **bouillabaisse**, a rust-coloured fish stew with up to 12 different kinds of fish, or try ***bourride*** – poor man's fish soup, for smaller appetites, but also delicious.
- The **cheese** course is always a treat – try the delicious local chèvre (goat's cheese) called ***banon***, served wrapped in chestnut leaves.
- Hearty **daube de boeuf** (a beef stew with red wine, cinnamon and lemon peel) is especially warming in winter months.
- **Estocaficada** (stockfish stew) is ubiquitous dishes in coastal restaurants.
- Petit **farcis** (savoury stuffed courgettes, tomatoes and artichoke hearts) feature frequently as a filling starter.
- Boeuf **gardian** is a spicy bull's beef stew with olives, originally from the Camargue, but served throughout the region.
- Many dishes rely on an aromatic blend of wild **herbes de Provence** – bay, marjoram, basil, thyme, rosemary, and sometimes lavender flowers.
- **Ideal gifts** to take home include the local jams (*confitures*). Look out for such unusual flavour combinations as wild apricot and rosemary, or mandarin and thyme.
- **Fish dishes** reign supreme in the Mediterranean, with *loup* (bass) the most popular catch. Try it grilled *au fenouil* (over a fire of fennel twigs) and flambéed with aniseed-based pastis.
- **Moules frîtes** (mussels with french fries) are always good value.
- Nice's signature dish, the classic **salade Niçoise**, is made with tuna, egg, black olives, lettuce, green beans, tomatoes and anchovies.

Selection of olives for sale in the Old Quarter of Nice

- **Olives**, olive oil, herbs, garlic and tomatoes form the basis of Riviera cuisine.
- Look out for **pissaladière** (a delicious olive and onion pizza) in the resorts close to the Italian border.
- Crystallised fruits, including quince, apricots, melon, pears and figs, are a speciality here. Look out also for **quince paste** (*pâte de coing*).
- **Ratatouille** is a traditional Provençal dish of stewed tomatoes, onions, courgettes, aubergines and sweet peppers. It is served as a meal on its own with French bread, or as a side dish.
- A simple treat is ***socca*** (a thin pancake made with chickpea flour). Try it in Vieux Nice.
- Local black or green olives make tasty **tapenade** (olive paste with capers and anchovies), delicious served on crusty bread.
- Don't be put off if you are presented with a plate of shiny, black, sea-weed-draped sea **urchins** (*oursins*) – they are a great delicacy here!
- The tiny village of Tourettes-sur-Loup grows violets primarily for the perfume industry, but you can also find **violettes glacés** (crystallised violets) and even violet jams, syrups, oils and liqueurs.
- Eleven per cent of France's **wine** comes from Provence and the French Riviera. Look out for the little-known rosé wines of Draguignan and the Bellet wines of Nice.
- **Le Louis XV** (▶ 104), Alain Ducasse's fabled restaurant in Monaco, is the jewel in the crown of gourmet temples on the French Riviera.
- From market stalls and local cafés to trendy brasseries and Michelin-starred restaurants, wherever you eat, you will be served by **zealous** gourmands passionate about their food. After all, *la cuisine Provençale* is among the world's finest regional styles.

PERFUME

Flowers have made Grasse the International Capital of Perfumery. The fields around are cloaked with jasmine, rose and tuberose flowers and the air is heady with their scent.

The French Riviera is resplendent with flowers, from the extravagant gardens of luxury villas along the coast to the stripy fields of purple lavender and the fragrant wild flowers and herbs of the bucolic hinterland. For over 400 years the fragrance-filled town of Grasse has been the centre of the French perfume industry, which is responsible for two-thirds of the nation's production.

During the 16th century it was a tannery town and glove-makers began to use local flowers to perfume leather gloves – a fashion made popular by Catherine de Medici. As a consequence, acres of flowers were planted and the fields around Grasse are still cloaked with jasmine, rose and tuberose flower – the three key ingredients in the art of perfumery – as well as lavender, mimosa and jonquil. Grasse is now the International Capital of Perfumery, with over 30 perfumeries.

> "I sleep in nothing except Chanel No 5"

The Art of Perfumery

To learn more about the history and alchemy of this ancient industry, visit the new olfactory museum in the Musée International de la Parfumerie (➤ 125), a treat for the senses. Covering 3,000m^2 (1.86mi^2), it offers a range of exhibitions and activities including workshops where you can blend your own signature perfume. The beautifully scented La Bastide

Spectacular fields of lavender fill the landscape during the summer months

du Parfumeur in Mouans-Sartoux is a 1.6ha (four-acre) botanic garden teeming with plants traditionally cultivated around Grasse for the perfume industry (May–Sep daily). There are also guided tours around the three greatest perfume houses in the world – Fragonard, Galimard and Molinard (► 125) – which still use traditional methods.

Le Nez

Grasse has 30 major perfumeries in and around the town. Each employs a head perfumer, known as *"le nez"*. The "nose" identifies the origins of all the plants using his highly developed sense of smell and ever increasing repertoire of scents. With the aid of smelling testers he composes fragrance harmonies of varying notes – rather like a musician. There are 300 "noses" in the world, half of whom work in France, and around 50 in Grasse. It is their job to blend the different essences to create new fragrances. A top "nose" produces just three or four perfumes a year.

Classic Perfumes

There are many classic perfumes that are still fresh and as popular now as when they were first developed. Created by one of the top noses of Grasse, Coco Chanel launched Chanel No 5 in 1925. Still loved by many, it was famously associated with Marilyn Monroe.

FILM SET

Ever since the Lumière brothers filmed *Train Entering La Ciotat Station* in 1895, the south of France has been at the forefront of cinematic development, and many of its towns and villages have featured in films by the legendary French directors Pagnol, Truffaut, Godard and Vadim.

Ridley Scott shooting his movie *A Good Year* on the French Riviera

Director Godard and film legend Brigitte Bardot at the Studios de la Victorine

By the 1920s Nice was the capital of French cinema, with nearly 200 films being made at the celebrated Studios de la Victorine in just one decade. Actors, actresses and directors flocked to the French Riviera to make their fortune, first in silent films and then the early "talkies", during what's known as the Golden Age of Classic Film.

The Hollywood Greats

The legendary American film actress Grace Kelly came here to star alongside Cary Grant in *To Catch a Thief* (1955), directed by Alfred Hitchcock. During the filming she met Prince Rainier III and the rest is history: she didn't act again, but chose to concentrate on her duties as Princess, wife and mother until her fairy-tale life came to an abrupt end in a tragic car accident on the Moyenne Corniche (➤ 74) in 1982. (A neighbouring road, the Corniche Littorale from Nice to Cannes, featured in Frederick Forsyth's classic 1973 film, *The Day of the Jackal.*)

Sex goddess Brigitte Bardot is another glamorous name associated with the French Riviera. She made her screen debut in 1952, aged 18, in *Le Trou Normand.* In the same year she married celebrated film director Roger Vadim. Already a magazine celebrity and pin-up by 1956, her 17th film, *Et Dieu Créa La Femme,* was an international success. Her sexy walk as she strolled around St-Tropez made Bardot, Vadim and the port world-famous, and marked the start of a new, permissive era. As *Time* magazine once wrote: "Brigitte Bardot exuded a carefree, naïve sexuality that brought a whole new audience to French films." Brigitte Bardot still lives in St-Tropez to this day.

Unforgettable: Grace Kelly and Cary Grant in *To Catch a Thief*

Brad Pitt at a screening of his movie *The Tree of Life* in Cannes

Film Fame

Among the best-known movies shot in the region is *Tender is the Night* (1962), based on F Scott Fitzgerald's famous autobiographical novel of the same name. It portrays the reckless hedonism of the Riviera during the 1920s and '30s, when notorious American socialites F Scott and Zelda Fitzgerald frequented the palatial Hôtel du Cap Eden Roc on Cap d'Antibes.

Jean de Florette

The prolific Provençal writer Marcel Pagnol had always dreamed of turning his novels into films to pay tribute to his beloved countryside, and in 1935 he founded his own production company and studios in Marseille. His most enduring novel, *L'Eau des Collines* (The Water of the Hills), is best known in its adaptation into the highly acclaimed films *Jean de Florette* and *Manon des Sources*, which tell the moving story of how two 1920s provincial farmers systematically destroy the happiness of a man from the city (played by Gérard Depardieu).

In the 21st century the allure of the Riviera as a film set shows no sign of tarnish and the Côte still has a starring role. Director Ridley Scott's film *A Good Year* based on the Peter Mayle novel is a romantic comedy set in sunny Provence where a high-flying London banker gives it all up for love and the lure of the south. More sinister love is portrayed

Abdellatif Kechiche's movie *Blue is the Warmest Colour* won the Palme d'Or in 2013

Actress Zhang Yuqi at the pr… of *The Great Gatsby* in 2013

in the 2007 film adaptation of Süskind's best-selling novel *Perfume: The Story of a Murderer* – about achieving the ultimate perfume from the murdered bodies of rather a lot of beautiful girls. Much of the film is shot in Provence and the story features Grasse as the "holy grail" of perfume (➤ 12–13).

On a much lighter note, *Mr Bean's Holiday*, also released in 2007, charts the bumbling exploits of the Rowan Atkinson character in a French farce similar to the genre of Jacques Tati's *M. Hulot's Holiday*. Delightfully daft Mr Bean wins a trip to Cannes for the Festival, creating mayhem and mishap and ends up having his video diaries shown at the Festival.

The Cannes Festival

Now known simply as the Festival de Cannes, this glittering event was founded in 1939 as an independent alternative to the Venice Film Festival which, at the time, was run by Mussolini's Fascists. The outbreak of war led to the postponement of the first festival until 1946 but, with the exceptions of 1948 and 1950, it has taken place ever since for two weeks in mid-May and celebrated its 60th anniversary in 2007. The top prize is the Palme d'Or (golden palm) awarded for Best Film. Winning this coveted title does not guarantee the film will become a blockbuster, as many are more of the art-house genre, but the Cannes winners are often the year's most talked-about films. The winner of the Palme d'Or in 2011 was Terrence Malick's *The Tree of Life*, Michael Haneke's *The White Ribbon* (2009) and *Amour* (2012) and in 2013 it went to *Blue Is the Warmest Colour (La Vie d'Adèle)* by Abdellatif Kechiche. Title holders have included *La Dolce Vita* (1960), *Blow Up* (1967), *Taxi Driver* (1976), in 1979 *Apocalypse Now* and *Die Blechtrommel (The Tin Drum)*, *Paris, Texas* (1984), *Farewell My Concubine* (1993) and *Pulp Fiction* (1994)

> "Brigitte Bardot brought a whole new audience to French films"

Party Time

Most of the action takes place at the famous red-carpeted Palais des Festivals, and mostly by invitation-only but there are film screenings open to the public and the Cinéma de la Plage has outdoor screenings. From high-octane to highbrow art-house, the world's biggest film festival is teeming with glamorous celebrities, wheeler-dealers, paparazzi and all-night partying.

ON LOCATION

Movies that use the Provence-Côte d'Azur region as a subject or a stage:

Mare Nostrum 1926
The Magician 1926
To Catch a Thief 1955
Et Dieu...créa la femme (And God Created Woman) 1956
Bonjour Tristesse 1958
Tender is the Night 1962
The Troops of St. Tropez 1964
La Cage aux Folles 1978
Never Say Never Again 1983
Jean de Florette 1986
Manon des Sources 1986
Horseman on the Roof 1995
The Transporter 2002
A Good Year 2006
Perfume: The Story of a Murdererer 2006
Mr Bean's Holiday 2007
Monte Carlo 2011
Renoir 2012

ART and ARTISTS

The French Riviera continues to inspire world-famous and aspiring artists who keep coming here for the vibrant colours and the warm, southern light. Generations of artistic geniuses – including Impressionists, Fauvists, Surrealists and contemporary masters – have found inspiration and *joie de vivre* on the coast.

Impressionism

The Impressionists broke away from classical art disciplines. The luminosity of the Riviera fed their souls and palettes and inspired them to create a new response, an impression, of this extraordinary natural world.

Claude Monet is generally regarded as leading the Impressionist school, and with his fellow artists organised an exhibition of their work in 1874. One of Monet's paintings had the title "Impression: Sunrise". The press immediately seized on this, derisively labelling them "Impressionists". In the quest for spontaneous impressions of nature, Monet studied the effects of light and colour on the Mediterranean coast. Pierre Auguste Renoir, a friend of Monet's, was also fascinated by Impressionism, and they are probably the Impressionists that most often painted scenes of the Riviera. Renoir lived in Domaine des Colettes, in Cagnes-sur-Mer, until his death in 1919.

"When I understood that every day I would see the same light, I could not believe my luck"

Fauvism

Just as both Monet and Renoir were from northern France, so too was Henri Matisse. Seduced by the "Mediterranean luminosity" he exclaimed "When I understood that every day I would see the same light, I could not believe my luck". Matisse was the leader of Fauvism – the first of the

The Chagall Museum in Nice is dedicated to the life and work of Marc Chagall

major avant-garde movements, characterised by vibrant colours and distorted landscapes. The name evolved when a critic singled out as the only exhibit of merit a Renaissance-like sculpture in the midst of an exhibition of these works of brilliant colours and tortured shapes, exclaiming "*Donatello au milieu des fauves!*" (Donatello among the wild beasts!) This appealed to the artists, who adopted the name for their movement

ARTISTS' GARDENS (ART EN PLEIN AIR)

The Fondation Maeght's sculpture garden (➤ 121) is a must-see for all art aficionados, with its playful collection of fountains, statuary, mosaics and mobiles by such luminaries as Chagall, Braque, Calder, Giacometti and Moore. The amusing gardens of **Château de la Napoule** (➤ 123) are worth a visit too, with their animal-shaped topiary and bizarre "demon" statues created by eccentric American millionaire sculptor Henry Clews in 1919. The mixture of past and present in the gardens of the **Villa Ephrussi de Rothschild** (➤ 68) is extraordinary. It is here that Graham Sutherland, among others, took pleasure in drawing the exotic flowers and plants. The most moving artist's garden on the French Riviera is the **Renoir Garden** (and Museum, ➤ 128) – a simple grove of ancient gnarled olive trees where the painter would sit in his wheelchair for hours, his brushes strapped to his rheumatic fingers. The garden today still resembles a Renoir landscape.

***Le Bonheur de Vivre (The Joy of Life)*, a pioneering work by Matisse**

which included Matisse, Derain, Braque, Bonnard, Léger, Picabia and Chagall. The sites favoured by the Fauves, including the resorts along the French Riviera, were frequently the same ones that had been celebrated by the Impressionists. Often called the quintessential Fauve work, Matisse's *Le Bonheur de Vivre* (*The Joy of Life*) is a huge canvas portraying a primitive, rough landscape with wild, nude women – a synthesis of nature and human form. Although short-lived (1905-8), Fauvism was extremely influential in the evolution of 20th-century art.

Cubism to Post-Impressionism

Other interpretations were discovered and explored, and Braque, along with Picasso, founded the Cubist movement in 1907. Both were great admirers of Paul Cézanne, inspired by his attempt to capture a structured visual language. Picasso moved to the French Riviera after the War where he lived until his death in 1973, leaving behind countless artistic expressions of the *joie de vivre* that he derived from the area.

Picasso painted his *Jeune Femme assise dans un Fauteuil* in 1970

While so many adopted the area out of love, Paul Cézanne was a native – he was born in Aix-en-Provence in 1830. Often called the father of modern art, his was the greatest single influence on both Pablo Picasso and Henri Matisse. He briefly joined the Impressionists then worked in isolation – and had a most profound effect on the art of the 20th century. Those less perturbed by titles and labels recognised that what united them was not a name, but the determination to assert their artistic independence. Paul Gauguin wrote, "I am an Impressionist artist, that is to say, a rebel". His friend, the Post-Impressionist Vincent Van Gogh, joined him in the south, where he created all of his greatest, heavily symbolic paintings.

Contemporary Art

Expressionists were more attached to primitive art – artists such as Erwin Sutter (1897–1976) whose work *Rue de la Foutette* (Bibliotheque Municipale Grasse) depicts his inner torment in the heavily outlined, simplified forms. Nice also produced its own school of artists, the Nouveaux Réalistes, in the 1960s. The Museum of Modern and Contemporary Art (MAMAC) is a fascinating showcase of works by them and other avant-garde movements including Fluxus, Pop Art and American abstract painters. With more museums and galleries than any French city outside Paris, Nice is an art house. Along Line 1 of the new Nice-Côte d'Azur tramway, works designed by 15 world-famous artists line the route, forming an outdoor museum of contemporary art.

The MAMAC provides a good overview of modern and contemporary art

FESTIVALS

Festivals are a way of life on the French Riviera – there are 170 of them every year: seasonal, cultural, historic, musical, sporting, culinary, religious and even profane.

A flower parade in Nice

- The Feast of the Epiphany (6 Jan) marking the 12th day of Christmas, commemorates the Three Kings with crown-shaped pastries.
- In February, Bormes-les-Mimosas (➤ 153) holds the Corso Fleuri, a dazzling procession of floral floats, majorettes and brass bands. Menton (➤ 76) has fêted its lemons every February since 1934. The biggest pre-Lenten celebration is the Nice Carnival (www.nicecarnaval.com).
- March has unusual festivals, including Nice's Festin des Cougourdons, a festival of dried, sculpted gourds, and the Fête des Violettes in Tourrettes-sur-Loup (➤ 168), when the village is carpeted with fresh violets.
- In April, go to the mountains for the Ski Grand Prix marking the end of the season at Isola 2000 (www.isola2000.com) – it is 90 minutes drive from Nice.
- May – the Monaco Grand Prix (➤ 108) is the only Formula One circuit on public roads, once described as "trying to ride a bicycle round your living room". The glitterati arrive for the Cannes Film Festival (➤ 18) .
- July and August are filled with music festivals, ranging from the Rencontres de Musique Mediévale at the Abbaye du Thoronet (➤ 146) to the Nice Jazz Festival (www.nicejazzfest.com), a week-long event of jazz, blues, fusion and urban funk in the Jardin Albert 1er (between Place Masséna and the Promenade des Anglais; ➤ 38).
- In the autumn months highlights include a Chestnut Festival during October in Collobrières (➤ 154); and a firework display for the Fête du Prince – Monaco's national day (19 November).
- Around Christmas time there are fairs and feasts such as the Fête des Vins in Bandol and the Foire aux Santons (Provençal speciality of clay figures, including nativity scenes) – in Fréjus.

Finding Your Feet

First Two Hours

Arriving in Nice

By Air

- **Nice-Côte d'Azur** (tel: 08 20 42 33 33; www.nice.aeroport.fr) is the major airport for eastern Provence and lies on the coast 6km (4mi) west of Nice. Direct flights are available from mainland Europe, but many long-haul destinations require you to change planes in Paris. Terminal 1 serves the majority of international flights, with airlines including British Airways, bmibaby and Aerlingus. Terminal 2 serves Air France, British Midland and easyJet.
- The easiest way to **get into Nice** is by **bus**. Lignes d'Azur (www.lignesdazure.com) runs three bus routes from the airport into central Nice. **Bus 23** runs from Terminal 1, Stand 6, into the heart of the city every 20 minutes. **Express Bus 98** goes to the **bus station** (*gare routière*) in centre of Nice via the Promenade des Anglais. It departs from Terminal 1, Stand 1, or Terminal 2, Stand 5. **Express Bus 99** goes to the Nice **train station** (*gare SNCF*). It departs from Terminal 1, Stand 1 or Terminal 2, Stand 4. It's 20 minutes by bus to central Nice. To catch any of these routes, you will need to purchase a Lignes d'Azur day pass (€6).
- Purchase **bus tickets and passes** from ticket machines, or at the office opposite the bus stand outside Terminal 2. See www.nice.aeroport.fr or www.lignesdazur.com for more information. Remember to **validate** your ticket in the machine on the bus, or you may incur a fine.
- The local **TER** (*Trains Express Régionaux* or Regional Express) **train station**, Nice St-Augustin, is a short walk from Terminal 1. Trains run from here to the *gare SNCF* in central Nice.
- **Taxi** ranks are situated outside both terminals, and a taxi into Nice costs between €22 and €32. The cost increases between 7pm–7am and on Sundays and public holidays. Have your cash ready (there are ATMs inside the terminals) as taxis accept payment in cash only.
- **Car-rental** desks on the arrivals level are open until 10pm. After this time you can rent cars from the car-rental zone at Terminal 2, behind the P5 car park. Nice is a 15- to 30-minute drive from the airport on the **N7**.
- A free **shuttle bus** runs between the two terminals every 7 to 10 minutes.

By Train

- Train services within France are run by the state railway company, the Société Nationale des Chemins de Fer (**SNCF**; tel: 08 92 35 35 35; www.sncf.fr).
- Nice is easily reached from Paris in 6 hours on a **TGV (Train à Grande Vitesse)** high-speed train – change at Lyon or Marseille. TGVs run five times daily in summer, twice daily in winter. **CORAIL** trains provide regular long-distance services (*Grandes Lignes*) and **TER** provide the local service (*Lignes Régionales*). Nice train station has 11 regular connections from other European countries and 20 daily connections with large cities in France.
- A **car-train service** is available between major French cities in which vehicles are conveyed at the same time as their owners, who travel in *couchettes* (sleeping cars). It is advisable to book this service well in advance through SNCF (www.sncf.fr) as car space is limited and the service is very popular.

- For more **information in English**, and to purchase **rail passes** online, go to Rail Europe (www.raileurope.co.uk; or www.raileurope.com in the US).

By Road

- Nice interconnects with major European cities via an **extensive motorway network**. The city is linked by the **A8** (La Provençale) to Aix-en-Provence in the west and the Italian border in the east.
- It takes approximately 9 hours to drive from **Paris to Nice** by motorway.
- From the motorway, **access to the city centre** is via five exits: promenade des Anglais (exit 50), St-Augustin (51), St-Isidore (52), Nice-Nord (54) and Nice-Est (55).
- **Long-distance bus routes** within France are generally slightly less expensive than the trains, but much slower. Eurolines operates services to Nice (tel: 08 92 69 52 52, within Nice tel: 04 93 80 08 70; www.eurolines.fr).
- **Nice Tourist Offices:** ✉ 5 promenade des Anglais ☎ 08 92 70 74 07; www.nicetourism.com 🕒 Mon–Sat 8–8, Sun 9–7 (high season); Mon–Sat 9–6 (low season). ✉ Gare SNCF, avenue Thiers ☎ 08 52 70 74 07 🕒 Mon–Sat 8–8, Sun 9–7 (high season); Mon–Sat 9–7, Sun 10–5 (low season). ✉ Aéroport Nice Côte d'Azur, Terminal 1 ☎ 08 92 70 74 07 🕒 Daily 8–9 (high season); Mon–Sat 8–9 (low season).

Arriving in Monaco

By Air

- **Access to Monaco** by air is via the International Nice-Côte d'Azur Airport. The 17km (11mi) from the airport to Monaco can be covered by road, or a 6-minute **helicopter** flight departing daily every 20 minutes, and costing from €105 per person each way www.heliairmonaco.com.
- **Rapides Côte d'Azur** (tel: 08 20 42 33 33; www.rca.tm.fr) runs bus 110 every hour from both airport terminals. It takes about 45 minutes to reach the city centre (€20 single, €30 return).
- A **taxi** from the airport will take about 35 minutes, and cost about €80.

By Train

- Monaco is connected with France and the rest of Europe via a **TGV** line that runs between Paris and Monaco (5 hours 45 minutes), and by the slower **TERs**, connecting Monaco with towns and cities in the local area.
- **International rail connections** with Monaco include the Train Bleu, an overnight service from Paris to Ventimiglia, and the Ligure, which runs from Marseille to Milan. The Metrazur stops at all towns along the French Riviera up to the Italian border, with more regular services in summer.

By Road

- Monaco is linked to France, Italy, Germany, Switzerland, Belgium and the UK by a network of **motorways**. Coming from Italy, take the Monaco-Roquebrune exit (58); from France, take the Monaco exit (56).
- The three **corniche roads** (➤ 72) are the most scenic routes between Nice and Monaco, although the A8 may be faster, especially in summer.

By Sea

- The main harbours are **Condamine** (or Port Hercule) and **Fontvieille**. Both can handle yachts. Intercontinental liners anchor in Monaco Bay.
- **Monaco Tourist Office** ✉ 2a boulevard des Moulins, Monte-Carlo ☎ 04 92 16 61 66; www.visitmonaco.com

Finding Your Feet

Arriving in Cannes

By Air

- **Several regular buses** operate between Cannes and Nice-Côte d'Azur International Airport, 27km (17mi) away. Lignes d'Azur bus 200 departs every 30 minutes from Terminal 2, Stand 3 (€4 day pass). Rapides Côte d'Azur (tel: 0 82 04 32 33 33; www.rca.tm.fr) runs bus 210 from both terminals (€20 single, €30 return).
- A **taxi** from the airport to Cannes costs about €67–€85.
- A **helicopter** service between the airport and Cannes is available, and costs approximately €114 per person one way. It departs every 30 minutes, with a free shuttle between the heliport and the centre of Cannes.
- The smaller **Cannes-Mandelieu Airport**, 8km (5mi) outside Cannes, can be accessed by private planes and charter flights.

By Train

- The **Cannes train station (gare SNCF)** in the town centre can be reached by TGV, TER and CORAIL services. See www.sncf.com or Rail Europe (www.raileurope.co.uk; www.raileurope.com) for more information. International trains to Cannes include the Train Bleu from Paris to Ventimiglia, and the TEE (Trans Europe Express).

By Road

- Approach Cannes from the **A8** motorway, and take the Cannes Est exit (42).
- **Cannes Tourist Office** ✉ Palais des Festivals, 1 boulevard de La Croisette ☎ 04 92 99 84 22; www.cannes.travel

Arriving in St-Tropez

By Air

- The nearest airports are **Toulon-Hyeres** (52km/37mi), **Nice-Côte d'Azur** (65km/40mi) and **St-Tropez/La Mole** (20km/12mi). La Mole airfield has domestic and international flights, including regular flights to Geneva, Basel-Mulhouse-Freiburg, Munich, Paris and Nice.
- A **taxi** from Nice airport to St-Tropez costs about €250.
- Sodetrav runs a bus service from the airport to St-Tropez (€19.30; www.sodetrav.fr).

By Train

- St-Tropez does not have its own railway station, however a regular **bus service** runs between St-Tropez and the nearest railway stations at St-Raphaël and Toulon.

By Road

- From Marseille–Aix **A8 motorway** take the exit at the Cannet des Maures junction, then proceed on the D558 for 38km (24mi).
- From Nice take the **A8 motorway** and exit at the le Muy junction, then proceed on the D25 for 40km (25mi).
- There is a **coach service** from Nice to St-Raphaël with Variose d'Autocars (tel: 04 98 11 37 60).
- **St-Tropez Tourist Office** ✉ Quai Jean-Jaurès ☎ 04 94 97 45 21; www.ot-saint-tropez.com

Getting Around

You could get around the French Riviera in a helicopter if you were so inclined, but the local train line is very efficient and a number of buses are also available. A car is useful if you plan to explore smaller villages away from the main resorts.

Domestic Air Travel

- **Helicopter** travel is becoming increasingly popular in the area, particularly between Nice airport and glamorous Monaco. Several companies offer this service, including Héli Air Monaco (tel: 04 93 21 34 95; www.heliairmonaco.com) and Azur Hélicopter (tel: 04 93 21 48 60; www.azurhelico.com). There are information desks for various companies outside the arrivals of Nice airport, Terminal 1.

Trains

- **High-speed TGV trains** (www.tgv.co.uk) connect Paris with many towns along the French Riviera, including Toulon, Hyères, Les Arcs, Draguignan, St-Raphaël, Antibes, Cannes, Nice, Monaco and Menton.
- **Regional TER trains** (www.ter-sncf.com) connect many towns on the French Riviera (up to the Italian border). They're punctual and reliable.
- **Bicycles** can be taken onto all suitable trains outside the peak hours (Mon–Fri 7am–9am and 4:30pm–6:30pm).
- **Tickets** can be bought at stations, but if there is no ticket office or it is closed you can pay the conductor on the train. You must stamp your ticket in the orange machine on the platform before boarding the train at the start of your journey to **validate** it. If the platform doesn't have a validation machine, the conductor will help.

Buses

- **Several bus** services connect key towns along the French Riviera, but reaching smaller villages can be problematic.
- On Sundays and official holidays, services are **often limited**.
- Timetables are available at the bus station or through bus company offices. The **bus station** (*gare routière*) is usually situated at the central town square, close to the railway station (*gare SNCF*).
- **Tickets** can usually be bought on board, but may also be available from kiosks (*tabacs*) around the town. Remember to validate your ticket in the machine on the bus.
- **Lignes d'Azur** (tel: 08 10 06 10 06; www.lignesdazur.com) is the city bus service for Nice and the surrounding area, including the airport. The bus station is at boulevard Jean Jaurès. The long-distance bus station (*gare routière*) is next door.
- **Lignes d'Azur bus tickets** can be bought on the bus; at Bel Canto, 29 avenue Malausséna (Mon–Sat); at the Grand Hotel, 10 avenue Felix Fauré (Mon–Sat), and at various *tabacs* around Nice. Single tickets: €1.50; multi tickets: €20 (20 trips) or €10 (ten trips); day passes: one day €5, seven days €15.
- **Compagnie des Autobus de Monaco** (www.cam.mc) serves Monaco, with six routes covering the Principality. Routes 1 and 2 are most useful for visitors, linking Monaco Rock with Monte-Carlo.
- **Tickets** can be bought on the bus and are available as singles, in packs of four or eight, or as a day pass.

Finding Your Feet

- In Cannes, **Bus Azur** run services (6am–8:30pm) covering the city and surrounding towns. Information can be found at the **bus station** in place Cornut Gentille, next to the town hall (tel: 08 25 82 55 99). **Sillages** runs services from Cannes north into the hills around Grasse (tel: 08 00 09 50 00/04 93 64 88 84; www.sillages.eu).
- **Bus Azur** €1 for a single ticket, and packs of ten or weekly passes are also available for about €9.50. You can buy single tickets on the bus, but all others must be purchased from the bus station.
- St-Tropez does not have a bus service within the town itself. **Sodetrav** (tel: 08 25 00 06 50; www.sodetrav.fr) buses run around the Golfe de St-Tropez from the town's *gare routière*, just outside the parking du Port. They also provide services to markets in the area and to the rail stations at Toulon and St-Raphaël. Tickets can be bought on the bus.
- **Raphaël Bus** (tel: 04 94 83 87 63) runs services within St-Raphaël and along the Corniche de l'Esterel between St-Raphaël and La Trayas.

Tram

- Measuring over 9km (5.5mi) in length, a new tramway connecting the Nice-Nord and Nice-Est motorway exits with the place Masséna in the city centre was opened in 2007. In 2013, it was extended to reach Pasteur Hospital (*Hôpital Pasteur*) in the north. The line running east-west from the harbour to the airport with two underground stations won't be ready until 2020. Single tickets: €1.50; ten tickets: €10.

Taxis

- **Taxis** charge a pick-up fee and then charge per kilometre (0.6mi) driven, plus extra for items of luggage and travel in the evening, 7pm–7am, or on Sundays. All taxis use a **meter** (*compteur*), and taxi stands in towns and cities are marked with a square blue sign. If you phone for a taxi, the meter will be set the moment it sets off to pick you up.
- Some taxis accept bank cards, but most will **accept cash only**. It is usual to give a tip of around 10 per cent.

Driving

- Summer brings many tourists to the French Riviera. **Traffic jams** are a problem at this time of year, particularly on the coast.
- An excellent system of motorways/expressways (***autoroutes***, marked with an "A" onmaps and road signs) fans out from Paris, making it fairly straightforward to drive between destinations. **Tolls are charged** on most *autoroutes*. The majority of major foreign credit cards (including MasterCard and Visa, etc.) are accepted at nearly all of the pay stations (*péage*) along these roads.
- There's a comprehensive network of other roads across the country, including main highways (***route nationale***, marked N), lesser highways (***route départementale***, marked D) and minor country roads.
- If **bringing your own car** to France, you must always carry the following documentation in addition to your passport: a full, valid national driver's licence, a certificate of motor insurance and the vehicle's registration document (plus a letter of authorisation from the owner if it is not registered in your name). Third-party motor insurance is the **minimum requirement**, but fully comprehensive cover is strongly advised. Check that your **insurance** covers you against damage in transit, and that you have adequate **breakdown cover** (for information contact the AA; tel: 0800 444 500; www.theAA.com, or your own national breakdown

organisation). You must also display an **international sticker** or distinguishing sign plate on the rear of the car by the registration plate. **Headlights** of right-hand-drive cars must be adjusted for driving on the right.

Renting a Car

- Cars may be rented by drivers **21 or over** who have held a full driver's licence for a year, but some companies require a minimum age of 25. The average **maximum age** limit is 70, and you will be requested to show your licence and passport or national ID card. For UK drivers it is advisable to have your paper licence as well as your plastic card.
- Most major **car rental firms** such as Europcar, Avis and Hertz have outlets at airports, main railway stations and in large towns and cities throughout France. Most will let you return your car to other cities and even countries, but agree this will need to be arranged and agreed when you make your booking; there may be a surcharge.
- Due to high taxes, renting a car in France can be **expensive**. Fly-drive packages arranged through a tour operator or airline could be less expensive. SNCF has train and car-rental deals from mainline stations.
- Most **rental agreements** will include: unlimited mileage, comprehensive insurance cover, theft protection and 24-hour emergency roadside assistance, although some agencies may charge you mileage over and above a certain distance.
- Make sure you have **adequate insurance** and are aware of what you are covered for in the event of an accident. Always check the small print as some low-cost operators have an extremely **high excess charge** for any damage to the vehicle.

Driving Know-How

- Drive on the **right-hand side** of the road (*serrez a droite*).
- Drivers must be **18 or over**, and you'll need to be 21 or over to rent a car.
- **Speed limits** are 50kph/31mph on urban roads, 90kph/56mph outside built-up areas (80kph/49mph in rain), 110kph/68mph on dual carriageways/divided highways and non-toll motorways (100kph/62mph in rain), and 130kph/80mph on toll motorways (110kph/68mph in rain). Visiting drivers who have held a licence for less than two years must follow the wet-weather limits **at all times**, even when it's dry. Drivers from within the EU who **exceed the speed** limit by more than 25kph/15mph may have their licences confiscated by the police on the spot.
- At roundabouts/traffic circles, *Cédez le passage* or *Vous n'avez pas la priorité* signs indicate that traffic already on the roundabout has priority.
- **Do not overtake** where there is a solid single line in the centre of the road.
- **The blood alcohol limit** is 0.5 percent (US blood alcohol content 0.05).
- **Fuel** comes as unleaded (95 and 98 octane), lead replacement petrol (LRP or *supercarburant*), diesel (*gasoil* or *gazole*) and LPG. Many filling stations **close on Sundays** and at 6pm during the week.
- The **French highway code** is available at www.legifrance.gov.fr. For information on road signs, see www.permisenligne.com
- **New legislation** came into force from 1st July 2008 requiring all drivers to carry a minimum of **one reflective jacket and a warning triangle** with an on-the-spot fine for failure to do so of between €90 to €135. Reflective jackets and warning triangles can usually be purchased at the port.

Accommodation

A wide variety of accommodation is available on the French Riviera. The region boasts some of the most exclusive and expensive places to stay in France, but don't be put off – more affordable options are also up for grabs. Accommodation ranges from hotels through to French *chambres d'hôte* (B&Bs), *gîtes, auberges* and campsites.

Types of Accommodation

Hotels

- Hotels in France are regularly inspected and are **classified into five categories**: (1*–5*, plus Palace). They must display their rates (including tax) both outside the hotel and in the rooms. Charges are usually per room rather than per person, and breakfast is generally charged separately. If you're travelling with a family on a budget, note that for a little extra, many hotels will put another bed in your room (*lit supplémentaire*).
- International chain hotels and motels are the easy option, but lots of far more interesting alternatives are available at similar prices. If you're keen on experiencing a slice of authentic French *hotellerie*, some of the best accommodation can be found at the nation's hundreds of small, family-run inns and hotels known as **Logis de France**. Dotted throughout the country, most boast their own restaurant serving good, local food. Logis have their own system of classification that uses 'fireplaces' instead of stars. For listings, visit www.logis-de-france.fr.
- There are some great **luxury hotels** if you want to treat yourself. The traditional *belle époque* hotels have a cachet which is hard to beat. For something with a more modern twist, look at designer hotels such as Hi Hôtel in Nice (► 58). In most luxury hotels, health and beauty treatments are provided in state-of-the-art spas. Smaller, but no less expensive, are the boutique hotels, with just a few rooms styled by fashion gurus.

Bed & Breakfast

- **Chambres d'hôtes** are the French equivalent of Bed & Breakfasts. They offer rooms to rent in farmhouses, castles and a selection of other private residences. The largest association is **Gîtes de France** (www.gites-de-france.fr), which grade their wide variety of rooms with a system of *épis* (ears of corn). Maison d'Hôtes de Charme (www.iguide-hotels.com) also offer elegant private accommodation. Alternatively, try such other nation-wide bodies as Fleurs de Soleil (www.fleursdesoleil.fr) and Clévacances (www.clevacances.com), or contact local tourist offices - they'll supply you with the addresses of guestrooms nearby.
- The **breakfast** that comes with private guestrooms – usually a selection of breads and homemade jams – is frequently a more generous affair than you'll get at a hotel. Some guestrooms also offer a **table d'hôtes** arrangement, whereby the price includes an (often lavish) evening meal with drinks that guests enjoy with their hosts.

Self-catering

- **Gîtes** are self-contained cottages, villas and apartments, often with swimming pools, widely available all across France. They offer particularly good value for families, providing simple and decent accommodation (bring or rent your linen), with a certain rustic charm.

- Many of the most charming *gîtes* are administered through the **Gîtes de France** organisation, which inspects and grades them according to comfort and facilities (www.gites-de-france.fr). Tourist offices also generally hold this information.

Youth Hostels and Budget Options

- **Budget beds** are available at a number of youth hostels (*auberges de jeunesse*) along the Cote d'Azur. Most will charge a small **extra fee** if you are not a member of **Hostelling International** (www.hihostels.com) in your home country. For a list of youth hostels available in the area, contact the French federation of youth hostels, Fédération Unie des Auberges de Jeunesse (tel: 01 48 04 70 40; www.fuaj.org).
- A growing number of budget hotels and **cheap deals** can be booked **online** though sites such as Octopus Travel and Expedia.

Camping

- Sites are **inspected and graded** with a star system like that of the hotels, and range from basic, providing electricity, showers and lavatories to luxurious holiday centres, with swimming pools and other family sports activities, restaurants and bars, and kids' clubs. Many have pre-pitched tents with separate sleeping and living space and mobile homes on site, all complete with cooking equipment, fridges and beds.
- Campsites can become very crowded, particularly during July and August. It is a good idea to **book well ahead** during the high season, which runs from April to October. Contact the National Federation of Campsites (tel: 01 42 72 84 08; www.campingfrance.com).
- Camping or overnight parking of caravans and motorhomes is **not permitted** on the beach or at the roadside. Check with the local town hall first if you plan on *camping sauvage* (away from official campsites), as it is often forbidden, especially in areas at risk of forest fires.
- If you haven't booked and need to find a campsite, the **local tourist office** should be able to advise you, and in case of an emergency, police stations can also let you have a list of local campsite addresses.

Finding a Room

- It is essential to **reserve your accommodation** well in advance for July and August, when it is almost impossible to find accommodation if you haven't booked ahead. Local tourist offices can tell you where rooms are available, and will be able to provide you with a list of accommodation with prices. In villages without a tourist office, you're likely to find the greatest concentration of hotels in the main square or centre of town.
- When you **check in**, you'll need to complete a registration form and show your passport. Ask to see the room first, especially in cheaper accommodation, where payment is often taken in advance.

Seasonal Rates

- **Higher prices** may be charged between April and October along the French Riviera. You can be sure of paying more in July and August.

Accommodation Prices

Expect to pay per double room per night

€ under €80 **€€** €80–€150 **€€€** over €150

Food and Drink

The French create superb gastronomic feasts, and take enormous pride in their food. Eating out is one of the best ways to experience French culture and hospitality. Try the local dishes and order in French – it's part of the fun.

Eating

- You'll find a decent **restaurant**, if not several, in every town, where the glasses are polished, the linen starched, the waiters knowledgeable and the service impeccable. Expect to **reserve your table in advance, dress smartly, and allow plenty of time** for the full gastronomic experience. Michelin stars and Gault et Millau *toques* help to identify the top eating places. Top restaurants have a *menu dégustations* with selected signature dishes and accompanying wines at a fixed price.
- **Brasseries** and **bistros** are **informal** establishments where you can sample traditional local dishes, such as *bouillabaisse*. Brasseries are generally open longer hours than other restaurants, and bistros tend to be small and friendly family-run restaurants with a modest wine list.
- Anything described as **Provençal** style means it is cooked with olive oil, garlic, tomatoes, onion and herbs. **Niçois** style involves olive oil, garlic, tomatoes, onion, herbs, olives, capers, anchovies and tarragon.
- Lunchtime menus tend to offer the **best value**, when a *menu du jour* (daily menu) of two or three courses with wine costs much less than an evening meal. *Prix fixe* (set price) three- or four-course meals also offer good value.
- Restaurants mostly keep to **regular opening hours,** noon–2:30 and 7:30–10, although some may stay open longer in summer. They sometimes close for Sunday dinner and all day Monday, and some close completely between November and Easter.
- **Service** should be **included in the bill** (*l'addition*) – look for the words *service compris*, or *s.c.* If the service is exceptional, you could leave your loose change in a bar, or a tip of around 5 per cent in a restaurant.
- Since 2008 all restaurants are **non-smoking** (*non-fumeur*).

Drinking

- In cafés you will be charged more for your drink if sitting outside. Locals tend to **stand at the bar** where it is cheaper. Cafés and bars serve coffee, soft drinks, alcohol, snacks and informal meals and often tea.
- Cafés and bars can open as early as 7am **to serve breakfast**, and close any time between 9pm and the early hours of the next morning. Licensing hours vary according to the individual establishment.
- A *carafe d'eau* (tap water) is usually supplied **free of charge** when you order food. Bottled water (*eau*) comes as *gazeuse* (carbonated) or *non-gazeuse* (still). Beer (*bière*) is usually light European lager. White and red wine (*vin blanc, vin rouge*) is widely available. If in doubt, try the house wine (*vin ordinaire* or *vin de table*) by the carafe (*pichet*).
- The **legal age** for drinking alcohol is 16. Children aged 14 to 16 may drink wine or beer if accompanied by an adult.

Restaurant Prices

Expect to pay per person for a three-course meal, excluding drinks:

€ under €25 **€€** €25–€60 **€€€** over €60

Shopping

The towns along the French Riviera offer all kinds of shopping, ranging from the chic boutiques of Monaco to the atmospheric local markets you'll find in little villages. Any purchase is an indulgence, whether you're buying haute couture or choosing the chocolatiest cake in a *pâtisserie*, but let's face it: this glamorous stretch of coastline is hardly the place for self-discipline.

Where to Go

- **Markets** (*marchés*) are a quintessentially French experience, and a wonderful way to sample the local produce and atmosphere. Large cities hold markets daily, and smaller towns will have at least one a week. They generally operate from around 7am to noon. There are also *marché nocturnes* (night markets) at cours Saleya in Nice and at Fréjus Plage most evenings in the summer. The people selling the food are usually the people who made it too, and they can tell you all about their produce. In addition to food markets, there are often markets selling books, antiques, flowers, glassware and pottery.
- **Food shops** usually open from Tuesday to Saturday, between 7 or 8am and 6:30 or 7:30pm, and may close for lunch. Some may open on a Monday afternoon, and most bakeries open on Sunday morning. With the exception of supermarkets, **food stores** tend to specialise in one kind of product, and in each town you will find a *boulangerie* (bakery), *pâtisserie* (cake shop), *charcuterie* (delicatessen) and *poissonerie* (fishmonger).
- **Supermarkets** and **hypermarkets** generally open from 9am to 9 or 10pm, Monday to Saturday; the main names include Auchan, Carrefour, Casino, Champion and E Leclerc. Here you will find the *boulangerie, boucherie* and *charcuterie* under one roof.
- Boutiques selling **fashion**, shoes and lingerie, designer babywear and maternity clothes are in abundance. The most upmarket of these are in Monaco, Nice, Cannes and St-Tropez. Department stores (*grand magasins*) can also be found in the larger cities.

What to Buy

- Provence is known for its excellent **produce**: fresh herbs, olive oil, lavender, honey, garlic, truffles and wine are among its specialities, and any market in the French Riviera will have a proliferation of these. Locally, snaffle up delicious ***marrons glacés*** (glazed chestnuts) in Collobrières, drench yourself in **perfume** from Grasse, and buy quality **glassware** from Biot, ***faïence*** (fine glazed ceramics) from Moustiers-Ste-Marie, **sculpture and art** from St-Paul-de-Vence and **haute couture** from Monaco.
- **Grasse** is famous for its perfume, made from flowers grown on the nearby hillsides. This is where most of the best-known **French perfume** originates. You won't find Chanel or Dior here, but at the Musée International de la Perfumerie you'll be able to create your own signature perfume or there is plenty of the less expensive, but high-quality local perfume to try.
- **Biot** is well known for the ceramics and glassware it produces. You can visit a glass-blowing workshop to see the wares being made.
- There are various options for buying **wine**. Hypermarkets usually stock an excellent range of French wines at a good price.
- Experience a shopping spree of the highest order in **Monaco**, where the biggest names in fashion display their latest offerings at the sweep of **luxury stores** along the avenue des Beaux-Arts.

Entertainment

Whether you are interested in classy casinos, chic nightclubs or film and jazz festivals, this area has a wealth of entertainment, encompassing everything from hedonistic nightspots to humble village festivals.

Music

- **Jazz** aficionados flock to the area in July when the French Riviera hosts two of Europe's major jazz festivals. They generally overlap, allowing you to sample the best of both. **Jazz à Juan** (➤ 126) attracts some of the greatest names in jazz and swing to the pine groves of Antibes–Juan-Les-Pins, while the lively **Nice Jazz Festival** (➤ 26) takes place in Nice's Cimiez gardens over five days.
- Menton hosts an annual **chamber music** festival (➤ 77) in August in the baroque square of the Parvis de la Basilique St-Michel Archange, in the heart of the Old Town.
- Cannes holds a **classical music** festival, Nuits Musicales du Suquet (Suquet Musical Nights), over ten days in mid-July.
- **Sacred music** is performed at summer concerts in the Cimiez monastery and in churches in Nice.

Film

- Hollywood descends upon Cannes in May, during the annual 12-day **film festival** (➤ 18). The biggest screenings and parties are strictly invitation only affairs, but there are some public screenings as well.

Nightlife

- A lively **club scene** thrives in the major resorts along the coast. Tourist offices, music stores and cafés will have flyers. Clubs often don't get started until midnight, and stay open until dawn. Dress well to make it past the bouncers-cum-fashion-police at the door, and be prepared to pay an extortionate amount for your drinks. The admission charge usually includes your first drink.
- The inextricably linked **café-bar** is the place for a drink in the evening, particularly in smaller towns. Every bar worth its salt will have tables outside during the summer. In cities, bars open as early as 7am to serve breakfast and stay open until the early hours of the morning. Out of season and out of the cities, bars may close as early as 9.
- Monte-Carlo's **casino** (➤ 92) is part entertainment, part spectator sport: a great place to blow your savings, or at least watch the drama unfolding around the high rollers. Be prepared for an **admission fee** and to dress smartly, or you will be restricted to playing the poker machines in the outer section. Tables open around 8pm and close around 4am. Only foreigners (over 18) are allowed to play, so you'll need your **passport**. Locals, even the royal family, are barred from gambling.
- There is a vibrant **gay bar and club scene** in Nice and St-Tropez (www.gay-provence.org). Check out local listings magazines for details of what's on where.

Sport

- Motor racing fans will look forward to Monaco's glamorous **Grand Prix** which takes place in May (➤ 108).

Nice

Little Treats

Simple Pleasures

Head to René Socca (➤ 59) in the Old Town to try a piece of *socca*, a **flatbread made from chickpea flour.**

An Overview

Head up Castle Hill (Colline du Château) high above the harbour and the **Promenade des Anglais** (➤ 49) to enjoy views of the sun sinking beneath the horizon.

Swimming on the 8th Floor

Cool off from the city with a dip in the rooftop pool at the **Splendid Hôtel** (➤ 57).

Getting Your Bearings

Nice is France's main tourist centre, the most visited city after Paris, and the French Riviera's largest, most vibrant resort. Friendly and informal, it radiates a unique atmosphere that is hard to define, although many have tried, labelling it the "Queen of the Riviera", "Capital of the Côte d'Azur", "Nizza la Bella", "The Big Olive" and "Mediterranean Chicago". "Nice" just doesn't seem to cover it.

Overlooking Nice and the azure Baie des Anges

Over the centuries the city has enjoyed a colourful history. Founded by Greeks and settled by Romans, it thrived in the Middle Ages under the Counts of Provence who were followed by the Italian Dukes of Savoy. Unified with France only as recently as 1860, it still retains a strong Italianate character and is a seductive mix of the best of France and Italy, with its own dialect (*lenga nissarda*) and delicious cuisine. Nice is also blessed with more museums and galleries than any French town outside Paris. Its Mediterranean charm has long provided inspiration to artists, with its pastel-painted buildings and terracotta roofs,

TOP 10

Don't Miss

At Your Leisure

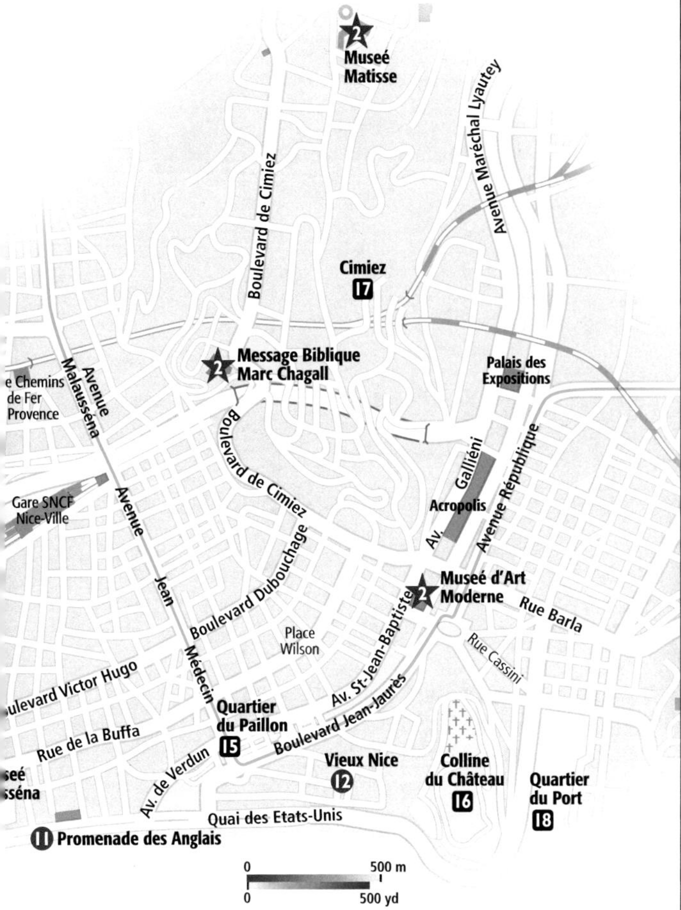

Museé Matisse
Avenue Maréchal Lyautey
Boulevard de Cimiez
Cimiez 17
Message Biblique Marc Chagall
Palais des Expositions
Avenue Malausséna
e Chemins de Fer Provence
Gare SNCF Nice-Ville
Boulevard de Cimiez
Av. Gallieni
Acropolis
Avenue République
Avenue Jean Médecin
Boulevard Dubouchage
Museé d'Art Moderne
Rue Barla
Rue Cassini
Place Wilson
Av. St-Jean-Baptiste
ulevard Victor Hugo
Quartier du Paillon 15
Boulevard Jean-Jaurès
Rue de la Buffa
Av. de Verdun
Vieux Nice 12
Colline du Château 16
Quartier du Port 18
seé sséna
Quai des Etats-Unis
11 Promenade des Anglais
0 500 m
0 500 yd

cradled by the vine-clad foothills of the Maritime Alps and fringed by a vivid blue sea bathed in magical, incandescent sunlight. Even the palatial hotels, designer boutiques and crowded terrace cafés exude a carefree *joie de vivre*. No wonder Nice has been voted the city where the French would most like to live. As Sandy Wilson remarked in his musical comedy *The Boy Friend* (1954): "Other places may be fun, but when all is said and done, it's so much nicer in Nice."

Vieille Ville

Nice

Two Perfect Days

If you're not sure where to begin your travels, this two-day itinerary recommends a practical and enjoyable tour of Nice, taking in some of the best places to see. For more information see the main entries (➤ 44–56).

Day One

Morning

Start the day at ⓬ **Cours Saleya** (➤ 50) one of France's best fruit, vegetable and flower markets, where the air is fragrant with lavender, mimosa, olives, *socca*, strawberries, citrus fruits and *herbes de Provence*. Then explore the dark, narrow alleys of ⓬ **Vieux Nice** (➤ 50), with its lively cafés, flower-festooned squares, small boutiques and galleries.

Lunch

The lively, narrow streets of Vieux Nice are full of tiny restaurants. For a light bite, **Lou Pilha Leva** (➤ 59) serves Niçois fast-food enjoyed *toute ensemble* with local shoppers on outdoor benches. For dessert, **Fenocchio** (➤ 59) is a must – they sell the best ice cream on the French Riviera.

Afternoon

Set off to the stylish residential district of Cimiez, to the remarkable ★ **Musée Matisse** (right, ➤ 44),

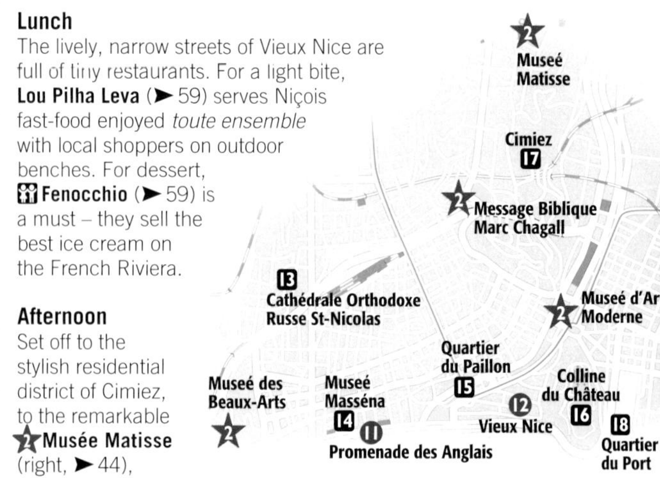

housed in a handsome 17th-century villa in an olive grove, with works spanning the artist's entire life. Nearby, the ★2 **Musée national Message Biblique Marc Chagall** (➤ 45) is also well worth a visit, with its series of monumental canvases and dazzling stained-glass windows evoking biblical scenes.

Evening

Reserve a table at **Aphrodite** (➤ 58) to experience Niçoise cuisine at its best, then while away the balmy evening sipping chilled Provençal wines on the café terraces lining the cours Saleya.

Day Two

Morning

Stroll along the fashionable palm-lined waterfront – the **11 Promenade des Anglais** (left; ➤ 48) – past exuberant mansions and follies created by English lords and Russian aristocrats, and the world famous Hôtel Négresco, built in the classic wedding cake-style architecture of Nice's heyday, the *belle époque*. A short uphill detour from the seafront leads you to the ★2 **Musée des Beaux-Arts** (➤ 45), with its impressive fine arts collection from the 17th to the 20th centuries.

Lunch

Return to the city centre for a platter of Nice's finest shellfish at **Le Grand Café de Turin** (➤ 59).

Afternoon

Just a stone's throw away, ★2 **Musée d'Art Moderne et d'Art Contemporain** (➤ 46) showcases works of the "Nice School", 20th-century multimedia iconoclasts whose extraordinary constructions spoof society and the precious highbrow world of art. Alternatively, make the climb up **16 Colline du Château** (Castle Hill, ➤ 54) for sweeping views over the bustling **18 Quartier du Port** (➤ 55) and the curvaceous, glittering Baie des Anges.

Evening

Buy tickets for the **Opéra de Nice** (➤ 62), a rococo extravaganza in red and gold that's home to the Nice Opera, the Philharmonic Orchestra and the Ballet Corps. Round off a perfect evening with a sumptuous meal at **L'Acchiardo** (➤ 58) in Nice's Old Town.

2 Nice's Museums

The quality of light and intense colours of the French Riviera have long attracted artists to this part of France. As a result, Nice has a strong artistic heritage and the largest number of galleries and museums of any French city outside Paris. Some of the best include the Musée des Beaux-Arts, featuring fine art from the 17th to the 19th centuries within a grand villa; the Musée d'Art Moderne et d'Art Contemporain (MAMAC), a legacy of the French and American avant-garde artists drawn to the area in the 1960s; and the individual galleries of Matisse and Chagall, who both lived here and left behind important collections of their works.

Musée Matisse

Henri Matisse (1869–1954), who spearheaded the Fauvist movement in the early 20th century, wintered in Nice from 1917 until his death in 1954, and bequeathed his entire personal collection to the city. Together with a second, even bigger, donation from his wife in 1960 (including more than 100 personal effects from his studio in the nearby **Hôtel Regina**), it formed the basis of an extensive collection that celebrates the life, work and influence of this great artist.

The Musée Matisse is in Les Arènes park, set in the middle of a large olive grove in the **Cimiez** district of Nice (➤ 54). The museum incorporates the striking red 17th-century villa where Matisse actually lived, which houses the permanent collection, and a modern underground building where three temporary exhibitions are held each year.

The permanent collection allows visitors an overview of Matisse's entire working life, starting with copies of Old Master paintings, through an era of sober, dark-toned paintings of the 1890s (including his first personal painting, *Nature Morte aux Livres*, and *Intérieur à l'Harmonium*) and his Impressionist and Fauvist phases (*Jeune Femme à l'Ombrelle* and *Portrait of Madame Matisse*). The bright colours and simple shapes of his maturity are best portrayed in his decorative, post-war paper cut-outs, silk-screen hangings and works such as *Nature Morte aux Grenades* and the well-known *Nu Bleu IV* (*Blue Nude IV*).

The museum also boasts 57 bronze sculptures by Matisse, almost all his sculpted work, and the world's largest collection of his drawings and engravings, including his illustrations for Irish writer James Joyce's novel *Ulysses*, and his powerful sketches and stained-glass models for the remarkable Chapelle du Rosaire at Vence (➤ 129). Matisse is buried in the nearby **Cimiez cemetery.**

TAKING A BREAK

There is a **café** in Les Arènes park near Musée Matisse. Alternatively, pack a picnic with supplies from the cours Saleya **market** and enjoy it in the park.

Musée National Message Biblique Marc Chagall

Down a side road at the foot of Cimiez hill, this striking modern museum was especially designed by André Hermant to exhibit Chagall's "Biblical Message", a series of 17 monumental canvases created between 1954 and 1967, vividly evoking the Garden of Eden, Moses and other biblical themes. Other works were donated to the museum after Chagall's death in 1985, making this the largest and most important permanent collection of his work.

Chagall was a highly individualistic Russian-Jewish painter who drew his main themes from the Old Testament and Russian-Jewish folklore. Born in Vitebsk (in present-day Belarus) in 1887, he spent the war years in America, before moving permanently to St-Paul-de-Vence in 1950. He opened the museum here himself in 1973.

Known for his dreamlike paintings featuring violin-playing goats and people floating in the sky, Chagall's paintings here are vast and expressive canvases vividly portraying biblical stories (*messages bibliques*) and Jewish subjects, including his childhood *shetel* (*Jewish village*) home. Also in the collection are Chagall's mosaic of Elijah and beautiful blue stained-glass panels depicting the creation of the world.

Musée des Beaux-Arts

This prestigious museum of fine arts is housed in a handsome 19th-century mansion, once home to a Ukrainian princess, at the western end of the beach. The collection here began with a donation by Napoléon II, and focuses on European fine arts from the 17th to the 19th centuries. Highlights include paintings of the Riviera by Edgar Degas, Alfred Sisley and Raoul Dufy, sculptures by Auguste Rodin and paintings by Italian Old Masters.

The main attraction of the museum is a collection of works by the Impressionist café-society artist **Raoul Dufy** (1877–1953), moved from the former Musée Dufy on the waterfront because the salt air was affecting the paint.

Musée des Beaux-Arts

Of particular note are the early Fauve works, the 1908 *Bâteaux à l'Estaque* (a cubist painting predating Cubism).

One gallery is given over to 18th-century Niçois artist Carle Van Loo (1705–65), and the main staircase is adorned with the works of Jules Chéret (1836–1932), a popular *belle époque* lithographist, who introduced colour advertising posters to France in 1866. The École Française is well represented, with works by Degas, Boudin and Sisley. There are also important Impressionist and Post-Impressionist works by Bonnard, Vuillard and Van Dongen (including his famous *Tango of the Archangel* – which evokes the Roaring Twenties on the Riviera).

Musée d'Art Moderne et d'Art Contemporain (MAMAC)
This remarkable museum traces the history of French and American avant-garde from the 1960s. Nice was at the centre of *nouveau réalisme* – the French counterpart to pop art – in the 1960s, and the collection at the Musée d'Art Moderne et d'Art Contemporain (MAMAC) includes works by the movement's most prominent artist, Yves Klein, as well as that of other artists from the time who lived and worked in the town, such as pop artists Andy Warhol and Roy Lichtenstein.

The MAMAC building, designed by Yves Bayard and Henri Vidal, is itself a bold piece of modern art, with four octagonal, grey-marble towers linked together by glassed-in walkways.

Collections are exhibited in rotation and reflect the main avant-garde art movements of the last 40 years in France and America. The primary focus is on French *noveau réalisme* and the artists of the second École de Nice, such as Raysse, César, Arman, Ben, Tinguely and Yves Klein. Many of their works parody society and the highbrow art world. Also look out for artworks from the support-surface movement (where artists sought to reduce painting to its materialistic reality, concentrating on the frame and the texture of the canvas), and a collection of Christo's drawings

Musée d'Art Moderne et d'Art Contemporain (MAMAC)

INSIDER INFO

You can visit **all of Nice's municipal galleries and museums by purchasing a single ticket** (48 hours: €10; 7 days: €20; en.nicetourisme.com/Museums). If you're also planning to visit places other than Nice, however, it's worth buying a **French Riviera Pass** (one day: €26; two days: €38; three days: €56). This not only gets you into the Chagall Museum and the Musée Matisse in Nice, but also the Fernand Léger Museum in Biot, the Oceanographic Museum in Monaco, the Villa Kérylos in Beaulieu and the Villa Ephrussi in Saint-Jean-Cap-Ferrat.

In More Depth: Nice has spent a lot of time and money renovating the **Villa Masséna** (35, promenade des Anglais). The building, surrounded by a small but beautiful park, houses paintings, photos and sculptures documenting the history of the city from the 18th to the early 20th century. The **Villa Arson** (20, avenue Liégeard) is a centre for contemporary art that's supported by Ben Vautier and other old masters of the second Nice School. It's home to a university (located in the 18th-century villa) and a complex of buildings in the Bauhaus architectural style. It's also well worth seeking out the **Asian Arts Museum** (405 promenade des Anglais) and the **Anatole Jakovsky International Museum of Naïve Art** (avenue de Fabron).

and wrapped "packages" from the 1960s. American Abstraction, Minimalism and pop art are also represented.

The **rooftop terrace** of MAMAC has unsurpassed views of Nice, as well as Klein's *Mur de Feu* (Wall of Fire) which is illuminated on special occasions.

TAKING A BREAK

Have a convenient coffee in MAMAC's **Café des Arts**. If you fancy something more substantial, enjoy a seafood lunch nearby at **Le Grand Café de Turin** (► 59). For a cheap bite, join the locals lining up for a snack at Nissa Socca on rue Ste-Réparate (► 60).

Musée Matisse
188 off C1 · 164 avenue des Arènes
04 93 81 08 08; www.musee-matisse-nice.org · Wed–Mon 10–6
15, 17, 20, 22, 25. Bus 15 free between the Matisse and Chagall museums, tickets are available from the museum's sales desk · See: Insider Info

Musée des Beaux-Arts
188 A3 · 33 avenue des Baumettes · 04 92 15 28 28
Tue–Sun 10–6 · 3, 6, 9, 10, 11, 12, 22, 23 · See: Insider Info

Musée d'Art Moderne et d'Art Contemporain (MAMAC)
188 D2 · Promenade des Arts · 04 97 13 42 01; www.mamac-nice.org
Tue–Sun 10–6 · 1, 2, 3, 4, 5, 6, 7, 8, 9, 10, 14, 16, 25, 30, 88, 89
See: Insider Info

Musée National Message Biblique Marc Chagall
188 C1 · Avenue du Docteur Ménard
04 93 53 87 20; www.musee-chagall.fr · Jul–Sep Wed–Mon 10–6; Oct–June Wed–Mon 10–5 · 15 (free between Chagall and Matisse museums) · €8

11 Promenade des Anglais

The elegant Promenade des Anglais and the opulent buildings of the *belle époque* (beautiful era) that line it have an air of sophistication reminiscent of the halcyon days of Nice, when it was a haven for the European aristocracy in search of a more agreeable climate. The lavish architecture and sparkling blue bay continue to draw people today, with runners and rollerbladers all coming here to enjoy the fresh sea air and the wonderful view.

An evening stroll along the Promenade des Anglais

Originally the promenade was a simple coastal path only 2m (6ft) wide. Today it is a broad, noisy, seafront road, and the white wedding-cake-style architecture of the luxury ***belle époque* hotels**, such as the stately Négresco, are juxtaposed with ugly concrete apartment blocks. Despite all this, the promenade is still an attractive spot for a stroll, and on fine days is full of people sauntering, sitting in the sun or rollerblading.

The wide promenade follows the brilliant azure coastline for 6km (4mi), and will take a few hours to walk all the way up and back, although it is also possible to rent bicycles or rollerblades to cover the distance (➤56). To the north lies a web of busy pedestrianised streets, brimming with restaurants, bars and chic boutiques. The Promenade des Anglais officially ends at the Jardin Albert Ier, but the walkway can be followed as far east as quai des États-Unis, and around quai Rauba-Capéu to Vieux Port.

Hôtel Négresco

Of the many splendid *belle époque* buildings along the Promenade des Anglais seafront, the best known is the magnificent domed Hôtel Négresco (➤8). The hotel was built in 1912 for the Romanian Henri Négresco, once a gypsy-violin serenader, who went bankrupt eight years later. Nevertheless, it remains a famous Riviera landmark, a National Historic Monument and one of France's most magnificent hotels. Its guest list is legendary, including Churchill, Chaplin, Piaf, Taylor and Burton, Picasso, Dali and the Beatles. The American dancer Isadora Duncan died outside the hotel in 1927, when her trailing scarf caught in the wheel of her Bugatti and broke her neck.

From the outside the pink-and-white turreted façade resembles a wedding cake more than a hotel. You may have trouble finding the main entrance because it is in a small back street. Incidentally, the whole hotel was built backwards to protect guests from the then unfashionable sun.

Jeanne Augier ran the hotel – home to gourmet restaurant *Le Chantecler* (➤ 59) – from 1957 until his 90th birthday in 2013, and managed to resist all temptations to place it in the hands of foreign investors throughout. As well as functioning as a traditional hotel, the Négresco is also an eclectic museum of modern art and décor. Its interior is full of surprises, ranging from the world's largest Aubusson carpet to gaudy, gold, glittery bathroom suites. The décor is inspired by the royal palace at Versailles, and the lavatories are more lavishly ornamented than any you are likely to see. Meals in La Rotonde restaurant (➤ 60) are served in the original cabins of an 18th-century merry-go-round. With prices starting from €285 per night, the Négresco might not be Nice's most reasonably priced hotel, but it's certainly one of a kind.

The Hôtel Négresco

TAKING A BREAK

Inside the Négresco, **Le Chantecler** (➤ 59) or the more affordable **La Rotonde** (➤ 60) make for memorable dining.

Promenade des Anglais
188 A4–B3
52, 59, 60, 62, 94, 98, 99

Hôtel Négresco
188 B3 37 promenade des Anglais 04 93 16 64 00
52, 59, 94, 98, 99

INSIDER INFO

Extend your stroll to include the road leading around the headland towards the port in the east. Known in the local dialect as **quai Rauba-Capéu** or "Hat Thief", this windy spot is a great place to watch the sun set. Insider Tip

Exploring further: Stairs and an elevator lead from the quai des États-Unis to Colline du Château (➤ 54) above, from where there are wonderful **views** of the whole city. Insider Tip

12 Vieux Nice

The best way to discover Nice is to get lost in the tangle of dark, narrow streets that make up historic and atmospheric Vieux Nice (Old Nice). Also known as the Vielle Ville (Old Town), this is most colourful part of the city, full of life, festooned with flowers and laundry, and brimming with cafés, hidden squares and bustling markets.

In this jumble of lanes there are the usual bars, restaurants and souvenir shops, but you can also stumble across side streets leading into quiet, undiscovered corners. In the back streets, designer boutiques, atmospheric galleries and intimate Niçois restaurants rub shoulders with no-nonsense workers' cafés and run-of-the-mill stores catering for the daily needs of the locals. The **rue du Marché**, **rue de la Boucherie**, **rue du Collet** and **rue Pairolière** have the atmosphere of a covered market, with food stalls full of tempting produce. Insider Tip For early risers, a visit to the pungent **fish market** on place St-François is an interesting and rewarding experience.

At the heart of Vieux Nice is **cours Saleya**, buzzing day and night with **alfresco** restaurants, bars, and the vibrant fruit, vegetable and flower markets that take place here each day. Nearby are two interesting small baroque churches: the **Église de l'Annonciation**, one of the oldest churches in Nice; and the **Chapelle de la Miséricorde,** which is noted for its elaborate rococo interior and a gem of baroque art.

Vieux Nice also has several quirky art galleries, including the **Galerie de la Marine** and the vaulted **Galerie des Ponchettes**, which was formerly used as an arsenal for the Sardinian navy then as a fish market until Matisse persuaded the local authorities to renovate it in 1950. Both stage temporary exhibitions, changing every three months.

Nice's fountains also come in handy for more practical-minded citizens...

Cours Saleya

This spacious, sunny square is the scene of

DID YOU KNOW?
The **Bay of Angels** took its celestial name from the story of Réparate, Nice's 15-year-old patron saint, who died a martyr in Caesarea in Palestine. One evening in the year AD 250, fishermen in the bay saw a frail boat containing her lifeless body on a bed of flowers. Guided by two angels and a dove, the boat was bringing Réparate home to Nice.

one of France's best fruit, flower and vegetable markets, taking place here every morning, except Monday, which is reserved for antiques dealers. The colourful stands overflow with locally grown produce, including flowers, olives, honey, tomatoes, aubergines, citrus fruits and *herbes de Provence* – a veritable feast for the senses.

Arrive at dawn and you will find the Riviera's top chefs choosing their *plats du jour* (dishes of the day) from the tempting food displays. During the day it is fun to watch the world go by from the pavement terraces of the bars and restaurants that line the famous market, or to try a light snack from the market stalls. Look out for *pissaladière* (onion tart with anchovy and olives) and *beignets de courgettes* (frittered courgette flowers) or try some *socca* (traditional Niçois chickpea pancake) . At night cafés and restaurants come into their own, making this one of Nice's most animated nightspots.

Cathédrale Ste-Réparate

In place Rosetti, the main square of Vieux Nice, is the lovely baroque Cathédrale Ste-Réparate, built by local architect Jean-André Guibera in 1650 and dedicated to the city's patron saint St Réparate whose relics lie within the cathedral.

The building is dominated by an 18th-century bell tower and a magnificent emerald dome of Niçois tiles. The carefully proportioned façade, with its arcaded entrance, decorative niches and medallions, dates from 1825 and has recently been enhanced with colour.

Inside, visitors are confronted by a profusion of baroque marble, stucco and gilt. Note the ornate marble high altar and choir balustrade, the walnut panelling in the sacristy (acquired from Nice's Dominican convent), and the painting *Dispute du Saint-Sacrement* in the right transept, attributed to the school of Raphael.

Palais Lascaris

In a narrow back street at the heart of the Old Town, behind a façade of ornate balconies and pilasters adorned with garlands of flowers, lies the beautiful Palais Lascaris. This Genoese-style palace was originally four separate houses, bought in 1648 by the powerful Lascaris-Ventimiglia family. The city of Nice purchased the property in 1942 and has since restored this noble building.

In the entrance hall the family coat of arms is engraved on the ceiling, bearing the motto "Not even lightning strikes us". On the ground floor there is a reconstruction of a pharmacy dated 1738, with an unusual collection of porcelain vases. A grandiose balustraded staircase, decorated with 17th-century paintings and statues of Mars and Venus, leads to sumptuous reception rooms containing elegant chandeliers, Flemish tapestries, 17th- and 18th-century furniture and a *trompe-l'oeil* ceiling.

TAKING A BREAK

For simple, inexpensive, local food, **Bar René Socca** (➤ 59) at the top of the Old Town is a friendly place for a light meal or to sample the local specialities. For dinner, just around the corner from Bar René, **La Table Alziari** (4 rue Francois Zanin; tel: 04 93 80 34 03), owned by the respected Alziari family of olive-oil fame, serves traditional Provençal food.

---

188 C/D3

Cours Saleya Market
188 C3 Cours Saleya
Fruit and vegetable market: Tue–Sun 6–1 pm. Flower market: all day except Sun pm. Flea market: Mon am
All buses go to the *gare routière*, near Vieux Nice

Cathédrale Ste-Réparate
188 D3 Place Rossetti
04 93 92 79 10 Daily 9–12, 2–6
Free No shorts or sleeveless shirts

Palais Lascaris
188 D3 15 rue Droite 04 93 62 72 40
Wed–Mon 10–6; Closed Tue
See: Insider Info ➤ 47

Galerie de la Marine
188 C3 59 quai des États-Unis
04 93 91 92 90 Tue–Sat 10–12, 2–6, Sun 2–6. Closed Mon and public hols
See: Insider Info ➤ 47

Galerie des Ponchettes
188 C3 77 quai des États-Unis
04 93 62 31 24
Tue–Sun 10–6; Closed Mon and public hols
See: Insider Info ➤ 47

Shopping in Cours Saleya Market

INSIDER INFO

- When selecting your fruits and vegetables at cours Saleya, use a **tin** given to you by the vendor. To really look like a local, take along a basket or your own shopping bag.
- Get to cours Saleya **in the morning** when people are out buying food from the market. For **a cheap breakfast**, buy some pastries and fresh fruit and grab a coffee from one of the cafés along the street.

At Your Leisure

Colourful cupolas adorn the Russian Orthodox church in Nice

13 Cathédrale Orthodoxe Russe St-Nicolas

This magnificent pink-and-grey Russian Orthodox church, crowned by six gleaming, green, onion-shaped cupolas, was built by Tsar Nicolas II in 1903 in memory of Alexander II's son Nicolas, who is buried in the grounds. The young, consumptive Tsarevich Nicolas was brought to Nice in search of good health in 1865, but to no avail. The luxurious villa in which he died was later demolished to construct the cathedral and a mortuary chapel.

The interior takes the form of a Greek cross and is brimming with precious icons, frescoes and treasures. The lavish **iconostasis** separating the sanctuary from the nave features a striking icon of Our Lady of Kazan, painted on wood and set in silver and precious stones. The church still conducts regular services in Russian.

188 A2 Avenue Nicolas II
06 63 28 98 99
Tue–Sun 9–noon, 2–6 Free
No shorts or sleeveless shirts

14 Musée Masséna

This museum of art and history is situated in the **Palais Masséna**, which was built in 1901 by Prince Victor Masséna, the great-grandson of Nice-born Marshal Masséna, Napoléon's ruthlessly ambitious military genius. The building was bequeathed to the city of Nice on the condition that it became a museum devoted to regional history.

The wide-ranging historical exhibits include paintings by members of the early Nice School, a library containing over 10,000 rare books and manuscripts, and a fearsome collection of 15th- and 16th-century weaponry. A section reserved for local traditions includes a display of regional costumes, furniture, *faïence* pottery and craftwork.

188 B3 35 promenade des Anglais and 65 rue de France
04 93 91 19 10 Wed–Mon 10–6
52, 59, 94, 98, 99, 60, 62
See: Insider Info ➤ 47

15 Quartier du Paillon

The once fast-flowing and often dangerously high River Paillon was canalised in the 1830s and began to vanish under the pavements. It now trickles below Nice's showcase gardens – lush Jardins Albert Ier, fountain-filled place Masséna, leafy

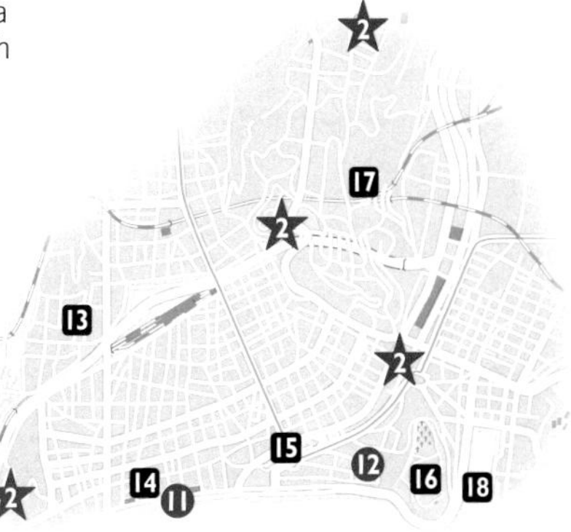

place Général Leclerc and the delightful hanging gardens of the promenade du Paillon.

The Paillon district's main focal point is **place Masséna**, a stately 19th-century square of red-ochre buildings built across the path of the river. Many important streets fan out from here, notably **avenue Jean Médecin** (Nice's main shopping street) and **rue Masséna** (a lively pedestrian zone). A balustraded terrace and steps to the south lead to the Old Town.

Colourful fishing boats and yachts line the port at Nice

To the north the covered course of the river provided space for several grand civic projects built in recent years: a row of cultural complexes including the MAMAC building; the **Théâtre de Nice** and the eye-catching **Acropolis** convention centre, an eyesore of concrete slabs and smoked glass.

Théâtre de Nice
188 D2 promenade des Arts
04 93 13 90 90 All buses

Acropolis
188 D1/2 1 esplanade Kennedy
04 93 92 83 00 All buses, Tram T1

16 Colline du Château

The seafront promenade ends at Colline du Château (Castle Hill). Surprisingly, there is no château here, but a high headland rising up between the beach area and the port. The hilltop is a park with cool, shady gardens and fantastic views over the crowded port (► 56), colourful Vieux Nice below, and the voluptuous curve of the Baie des Anges.

It was on this imposing site that Nice originated as the ancient Greek acropolis of Nikaïa. Archaeologists have discovered Roman and medieval remains, although the medieval fortress and other buildings that stood here were destroyed by the French in the early 18th century, when Nice belonged to Savoy.

The best approach is up the steps from **quai des États-Unis**, or by elevator from nearby **Tour Bellanda**. Descend eastwards along montée Eberlé and rue Catherine Ségurane to the elegant, arcaded **place Garibaldi**, which is named after the great 19th century Niçois revolutionary Giuseppe Garibaldi (hero of Italy's unification), whose statue stands in the square.

188 D3
Colline du Château 04 93 85 62 33
Elevator operates June–Aug daily 9–8: April–May, Sep 10–7: Oct–March 10–6
Free

17 Cimiez

Cimiez is a district of luxury villas and palatial residences on the low hills overlooking the city. A monument dedicated to Queen Victoria outside her favourite winter residence, the **Hôtel Regina**, serves as a reminder that Cimiez was frequently visited by royalty in the past. It is still considered to be Nice's smartest residential quarter.

The Cimiez district is the site of **Roman Nice**. As early as 140 BC the Romans built a town on the hills of Cimiez called Cemenelum which, by the end of the second century AD, had 20,000 inhabitants. There are Roman ruins and a museum at the Parc des Antiquités, an archaeological site now laid out as a pleasant little park that's known locally as **Les Arènes**.

The remains of a small amphitheatre (Arènes) were excavated here. The oval arena itself, still within the ruins of its original Roman walls, now hosts open-air concerts, including Nice's jazz festival in July. Beside the park, the small, modern **Musée Archéologique** displays objects found here and elsewhere in Nice and illustrates the city's history from the Bronze Age to medieval times.

Nearby is the **Musée Matisse** (➤ 44). Both museums back on to an old olive grove that is the venue for the international Nice Jazz Festival (➤ 22) in July.

At the eastern end of the grove is the **Monastère Franciscain de Cimiez** (Franciscan Monastery) and the church of Notre-Dame-de-l'Assomption. The Franciscans have used the church and monastery since

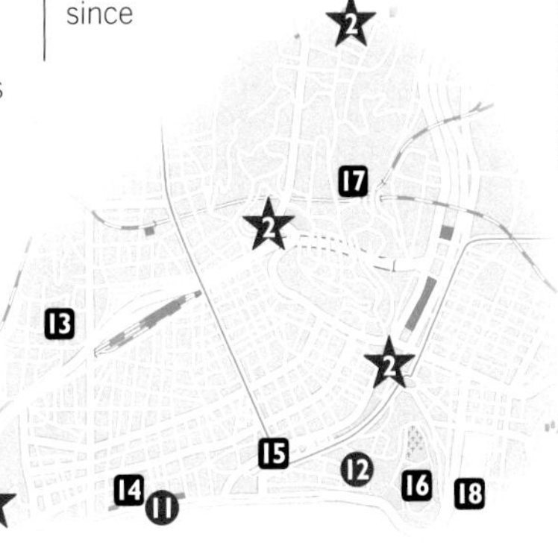

1546. Inside are two masterpieces by Louis Bréa, a leading painter of the Nice School, and an impressive carved altarpiece. Dufy and Matisse lie buried in the adjacent cemetery.

188 off C1

Parc des Antiquités & Musée Archéologique
160 avenue des Arènes (entrance: avenue Monte-Croce)
04 93 81 59 57 Wed–Mon 10–6
15, 17, 20, 22, 25 See: Insider Info ➤ 47

Monastère Franciscain de Cimiez
Place du Monastère, avenue Bellanda
04 93 81 00 04 Mon–Sat 10–12, 3–6; Closed Sun and public hols
15, 17, 20, 22, 25 See: Insider Info ➤ 47

18 Quartier du Port

For centuries there was no port at Nice. Local boats simply moored in the lee of the castle rock, while larger ships anchored in the harbour

A statue of Queen Victoria in one of the city's parks

at Villefranche. It was only in 1750 that Charles-Emmanuel III, Duke of Savoy, saw the potential trading benefits, and excavated a deep-water port at the mouth of the Lympia River.

Today the port is busy with craft of all kinds, from tiny traditional fishing barques to car ferries from Corsica. It is flanked by striking red-ochre, 18th-century buildings and the neo-classical church of Notre-Dame-du-Port. An interesting area for a evening stroll, you will also find some popular restaurants in this part of town.

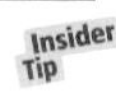

The port is best approached via a windy headland, **quai Rauba-Capéu**, past a colossal monument commemorating the 4,000 Niçois who died during World War I. On a hill to the east of the port, the **Musée de Terra Amata**, built on the site of an excavated fossil beach, documents prehistoric life in the region dating back 400,000 years.

188 E3 1, 2, 7, 9, 10, 14, 20, 30, 32

Musée de Terra Amata

25 boulevard Carnot 04 93 55 59 93

Tue–Sun 10–6: Closed some public hols

81, 100 Free

Monastère Franciscain (Franciscan Monastery) in Cimiez

FUN AND GAMES THROUGHOUT THE YEAR

- Kids will love cycling or rollerblading along the Promenade des Anglais. **Rent cycles and blades** from Roller Station (49 quai des États-Unis; tel: 04 93 62 99 05).
- In December, part of the place Masséna is converted into an **outdoor ice-skating rink.** Skates can be rented opposite the rink. There is also a permanent **indoor ice-skating rink** (*patinoire*) at the Jean Bouin Palais de Sports Centre (place Don Bosco) just north of MAMAC.
- **Colline du Château** has plenty of room for children to run around, and a good-sized playground.
- The **beach** is a good place to cool off in the hot weather and has a pebbly seashore, perfect for skimming stones.

Where to...
Stay

Prices
Expect to pay per double room, per night:
€ under €80 **€€** €80–€150 **€€€** over €150

Hôtel Acanthe €

Simple accommodation with relatively small but clean rooms located in a great position opposite the Jardins Albert 1 (situated close to Vieux Nice and the Promenade des Anglais). Serves a basic continental breakfast.

188 C3 2 rue Chauvain 04 93 62 22 44; www.hotel-acanthe-nice.cote.azur.fr

Hôtel Aria €€

Set in the heart of the Musicians' quarter among art deco and *belle époque* architecture (a good 10 mins' walk north of the Promenade des Anglais), this 1890 building has light, airy rooms. Some are classically furnished, others are in the Provençal style, and still more overlook a pretty little square.

188 B2 15 avenue Auber
04 93 88 30 69; www.hotel-aria-nice.com

Hôtel Armenonville €€

A 20th-century mansion with a lovely flower garden is the setting for this attractive two-star hotel. Some rooms have terraces looking out over the garden below. All rooms are bright, clean and comfortable, with charming touches of antique furniture. Breakfast can be enjoyed in the garden.

188 A3 20 avenue des Fleurs
04 93 96 86 00; www.hotel-armenonville.com

Auberge de Jeunesse de Nice €

This youth hostel in the wooded hills of Mont Boron, 10km (6mi) from the city and the beach, has beautiful views of Nice. Accommodation is in dormitories with six to eight beds. There is a communal room with a TV, kitchen, laundry service and internet access. Breakfast is included. Credit cards are not accepted.

186 C2 Route Forestière du Mont-Alban
04 93 89 23 64; www.fuaj.org

Splendid Hôtel & Spa €€€

This four-star hotel with multilingual staff lies less then ten minutes' walk north of the Promenade des Anglais. The outdoor pool up on the eighth floor is open to hotel guests from May to October. It's right next to the breakfast room, the bar and the restaurant. There's also a spa area on the ground floor.

Insider Tip

188 B3 50, avenue Victor Hugo
04 93 16 41 00; www.splendid-nice.com

Hotel Les Cigales €€€

This charming, noble old residence with a very pretty façade is located just five minutes from the sea and the Casino. Warm sunny colours complement the spacious rooms and there is an attractive solarium terrace.

188 B3 29 rue Dalpozzo
04 97 03 10 70; www.hotel-lescigales.com

Comté de Nice €

A simple but sparklingly clean hotel near the station with rooms at reasonable prices. You'll find a public car park and the Libération tram station right round the corner – the latter is just three stops away from Place Masséna.

188 B1 29, rue de Dijon
04 93 88 94 56;
www.hotelcomtedenice.com

Hi Hôtel €€€

This modern designer hotel has quirky furnishings, an organic 24-hour canteen, a *hammam* (Turkish bath) and a pool on the roof. Yoga classes and massage are available. This is a new take on luxury hotel accommodation and an experience in itself..

188 A3 · 3 avenue des Fleurs · 04 97 07 26 26; www.hi-hotel.net

Hôtel Négresco €€€

Built in 1913, the Négresco and its signature dome are key parts of the French Riviera and have landmark status. The interior is an ode to fine art, ranging from the Renaissance to the modern. The sumptuous rooms maintain the atmosphere of the French Riviera from its early 20th-century heyday. The hotel has a private beach.

188 B3 · 37 promenade des Anglais · 04 93 16 64 00; www.hotel-negresco-nice.com

Palais de la Méditerranée €€€

This palace with a casino was a legend in the early 20th century, but fell out of use and stood empty for 25 years. Its magnificent art deco façade now contains 187 lavish bedrooms and suites, a pool and a spa, bars and a restaurant.

188 B3 · 13 promenade des Anglais · 04 92 14 77 00; www.lepalaisdelamediterranee.com

Hôtel Windsor €€–€€€

Around half of this hotel's 62 rooms have been designed by contemporary artists. Its owner, Odile Payen, entrusts the furnishing of new rooms to creative types each year. The belle époque villa also includes a garden with a pool, a spa area, a bar and temporary art exhibitions in the foyer.

188 B3 · 11 rue Dalpozzo · 04 93 88 59 35; www.hotelwindsornice.com

Where to...
Eat and Drink

Prices
Expect to pay per person for a three-course meal, excluding drinks:
€ under €25 **€€** €25–€60 **€€€** over €60

L'Acchiardo €

One of the few authentic café bar/restaurants remaining in Vieux Nice, serving simple, nourishing dishes at reasonable prices, and probably the best fish soup in Nice. (Insider Tip)

188 D3 · 38 rue Droite · 04 93 85 51 16 · closed Sat–Sun dinner

L'âne Rouge €€–€€€

This Michelin-starred restaurant has a menu full of exciting flavours, but the seafood dishes are particularly creative and tantalising. The wine list includes an excellent range of the best local vintages. The restaurant itself is warm and inviting, with a large fireplace. Sit on the flower-filled terrace in summer to enjoy the view of the port.

188 E3 · 7 quai des Deux-Emmanuel · 04 93 89 49 63; www.anerougenice.com · Fri–Tue 12–2:30, 7:30–10; Thu 7:30–10. Closed Feb

Aphrodite €€€

The imaginative culinary creations of young chef David Faure are a seductive blend of classic French and local cuisine. The artistry of his delectable desserts would grace any modern art gallery.

184 C2 10 boulevard Dubouchage
04 93 85 63 53;
www.restaurant-aphrodite.com
Closed Sun, Mon; 2–20 Jan;

Bar René Socca €

The classic Old Town destination for *socca* – simple flat breads made from chickpea flower – and other specialities from Nice.
188 D2 2 rue Miralheti
(corner of rue Miralheti and rue Pairolière)
04 93 92 05 73 Tue–Sun 9–9

Le Boccaccio €€

Set in the Masséna pedestrian area, this stylish restaurant occupies two floors and has a huge terrace. The décor is reminiscent of a 16th-century galleon. The *bouillabaisse* is superb but fish, meat and pasta dishes also feature.
188 C3 7 rue Masséna
04 93 87 71 76
Daily lunch, dinner

Les Brasseries Georges €€

A brasserie-style restaurant in a converted art deco theatre with the kitchen in full view on the stage. Late-night menu up to midnight.
188 C3 4 rue Sacha Guitry
04 93 13 38 38 Daily

Le Chantecler €€€

Nice's leading restaurant – a Michelin-starred bastion of French gastronomy housed within the Negrésco and a truly memorable dining experience.
188 B3 Hôtel Négresco, 37 promenade des Anglais 04 93 16 64 00 Wed–Sun 12:30–2, 7:30–10. Closed 4 Jan–4 Feb

L'Estocaficada €€

The regional dishes in this atmospheric bistro are made from ingredients fresh from the market, and are ideal for a snack or a full-blown meal, washed down with a reasonably priced Provençal wine.
188 C3 2 rue de l'Hôtel de Ville
04 93 80 21 64 Closed Sun–Mon

Fenocchio €

Don't miss the best ice creams on the Cote d'Azur, in imaginative flavours ranging from lavender and olive to tomato and basil.
188 D3 2 place Rosetti 04 93 80 72 52

Le Grand Café de Turin €€

This cosy café serves Nice's best shellfish in huge portions. Order oysters by the dozen, *coquillages* by the kilo or, if you're feeling really brave, a plateful of sea urchins (*oursins*).
188 D2 5 place Garibaldi
04 93 62 29 52 Daily

Lou Pilha Leva €

Lou Pilha Leva in the local *patois* means "you take away". At the heart of Vieux Nice, this hole-in-the-wall serves piping hot plates of *socca, pissaladière, beignets, farcis, pizza* and other Niçois specialities. Ideal for a snack lunch. Cookery lessons are available with the chef and proprietor, Brigitte Autier; for details see www.pitacou.fr
188 D3 10 rue du Collet
04 93 13 99 08
Daily 8am–11pm (8pm in winter)

La Maison de Marie €€

A good place for a romantic candlelit meal in the evening, this restaurant is centrally situated, yet sheltered from the hustle and bustle of rue Masséna by a peaceful, paved courtyard. In fair weather a couple of tables are set out on the terrace. The menu includes such Mediterranean treats as sardines stuffed with pine nuts, and lamb with a herb crust.
188 C3 5 rue Masséna
04 93 82 15 93; www.lamaisondemarie.com
Daily noon–2, 7–11

La Mérenda €€

An irresistible menu of Niçois specialities lovingly prepared by Dominic le Stanc, former chef of the Hôtel Négresco's famous Chantecler restaurant, and a name synonymous with the very best in

Provençal cuisine. Le Stanc left the Chantecler to run this tiny rustic restaurant with his wife. With only 12 tables and no telephone, booking a place can be difficult (best to call in well in advance), but the food is worth the effort.
188 C3 4 rue Raoul Bosio
Closed Sat–Sun, public hols, 4–17 August

Nissa Socca €

Named after the speciality of Nice, the *Nissa* (Nice) '*socca*' – chickpea flour pancakes – reign supreme in this tiny eatery. So, too, do *pizzas*, *pissaladière*, *gnocchis* and *ravioli*. Popular with the locals and tourists.
184 B1 7 rue Ste-Réparate
04 93 80 18 35 closed Sun; Jan

Plage Beau Rivage €€

This restaurant at the Hotel Beau Rivage serves Mediterranean cuisine right on the beach in a quiet location beneath the Promenade des Anglais that's shielded from the noise of the street. It's an ideal place to relax to the sound of the sea at midday (when the prices are at their most reasonable), or enjoy a light evening meal after a dip.
188 C3 107, quai des États-Unis
04 93 80 34 03;
www.plagenicebeaurivage.com Daily

La Rotonde €€€

La Rotonde is the Riviera's most original brasserie. A circular restaurant with kitsch merry-go-round décor, complete with flashing lights, automata and painted wooden horses. Under the roof of the famous Hôtel Négresco, but more reasonably priced than the hotel's prime restaurant, Le Chantecler.
188 B3 37 promenade des Anglais
04 93 16 64 00
Daily 7am–11pm. Closed 24 Dec

Le Safari €€

This bistro in Vieux Nice is hugely popular, and in good weather its terrace bulges with people. On offer are authentic local specialities (salad of chopped fresh artichokes with olive oil and lemon, crudités with warm anchovy sauce) and a great choice of freshly baked pizza.
188 D3 1 cours Saleya
04 93 80 18 44; www.restaurantsafari.com
Daily noon–2:30, 7–11

Terres de Truffes €€

This unique restaurant specialises in seasonal truffles and is the ideal place to sample dishes made with truffles. Even the desserts are made with these precious gastronomic jewels. A carefully selected wine list complements the menu.
188 C3 11 rue St-François-de-Paule
04 93 62 07 68 Mon–Sat

L'Union €

Leave the crowds of tourists and head to Borriglione, the university quarter where time ticks at a different pace. This eatery serves such specialities as stuffed vegetables (*petits farcis*), tripe (*tripes*), beef stew (*daube*) and gnocchi. People play *boules* on the terrace in summer.
188 off C1 1 rue Michelet 04 93 84 65 27; www.unionrestaurant.fr Daily

La Villa Corleone €€€

This restaurant in the hotel district (less than ten minutes' walk from the sea) is evocative of Nice's Italian history. Its Sicilian specialities, pasta and fish dishes are stupendous. Even the pizza from the wood-fired oven is a genuine pleasure. Whatever you do, make sure to book in advance.
188 B3 48 boulevard Victor Hugo
04 93 76 78 23; www.la-villa-corleone-nice.fr
Mon–Sat noon–2:30, 7–10:30

La Route du Miam €–€€

It's worth travelling out to this eatery in the north of town to taste its hearty cuisine from southwest France. Dishes include duck filled with foie gras.
188 B3 1 Rue Molière
06 16 36 33 22
Tue–Sat 7:30pm–10:30 (Book ahead)

Where to... Shop

Avenue Jean Médecin is the main shopping street in Nice and has big department stores. There are little boutiques and galleries scattered around Vieux Nice, but the highlight of shopping here is the lively market at cours Saleya.

MARKETS

The **Marché Saleya** (cours Saleya, open Tue–Sun 7am–1pm) is a fruit and vegetable market with the best of Provençal produce, including locally grown olives, tomatoes and basil. The **Marché aux Fleurs**, Nice's colourful flower market, also takes place here daily, except on Mondays the **antiques market** takes its place (open 8–5). In summer, an **arts and crafts** market is also held here (June–Sep, Tue–Sun 6pm–midnight), selling both Provençal crafts and global handicrafts.

PROVENÇAL GIFTS

Confiserie Florian sells delicious sweet treats at Nice's harbour (14 quai Papacino; tel: 04 93 55 43 50; daily). The house specialities include candied fruits (oranges, lemons, etc.) and flower petals (including violets and roses).

Faïence, the famous white pottery with delicate, hand-painted designs from the tiny Provençal village of Moustiers-Ste-Marie, can be found at **Fayences de Moustiers** (18 rue du Marché; tel: 04 93 13 06 03).

FOOD & DRINK

Buy freshly pressed olive oil from **Moulin à Huile d'Olive Alziari** (14 rue St-François-de-Paule; tel: 04 93 85 76 92, open Tue–Sat 8:30–12:30, 2:15–7), an old family shop, established in 1868, that presses its own olive oil and sells *olives de Nice* by the kilo. The olive oil on sale here comes from a mill in Nice's northwest corner, which you can visit by appointment.

Chocolats Puyricard (40 rue Pastorelli; tel: 04 93 85 34 30) produces handmade chocolates that are considered the finest chocolates in France. The tiny **Pâtisserie Cappa** (7–9 place Garibaldi; tel: 04 93 62 30 83; daily) has a selection of mouth-watering cakes and pastries. Try the *tourte de blettes*, a local tart with apples, raisins, pine nuts and rum. **Espuno** (35 rue Droite; tel: 04 93 80 50 67) is one of France's premier bakeries and makes an excellent *fougasse* (a type of bread cooked in hot ashes). **Maison Auer** (7 rue St-François-de-Paule; tel: 04 93 85 77 98) is a traditional maker of crystallised fruit, and a good place to sample this local speciality.

For wine, **Caprioglio** (16 rue de la Préfecture; tel: 04 93 85 66 57) in Vieux Nice has a price range to suit all purses – from *vin de table* to the top French *crus*.

Domaine Massa (596 chemin de Crémat; tel: 04 93 37 80 02) is an old farm hidden in the hills behind Nice that cultivates two distinctly Niçois products – carnations and Bellet wine. Phone in advance for a tasting.

ART & PHOTOGRAPHY

There are many galleries in Vieux Nice. **Galerie Boutique Ferrero** (2 rue du Congrès; tel: 04 93 88 34 44) specialises in modern art. **Atelier Galerie Dury** (31 rue Droite, 04 93 62 50 57) has artworks by Christian Dury.

The photography of **Jean-Louis Martinetti** (17 rue de la Préfecture; tel: 04 93 85 61 30) captures the essence of Nice and makes a wonderful souvenir.

Where to... Go Out

NIGHTLIFE

There are a number of good wine bars in Vieux Nice, but many close by midnight. A few stay open later, including **Le Staccato** (4 rue du Pont Vieux; tel: 04 93 13 84 35) which is open until 2:30am and hosts live jazz in its cosy cellar during winter.

Performances by national and international DJs have made the twin nightclubs of **High Club** and **Studio 47** (45 promenade des Anglais; tel: 04 93 96 68 00; Fri–Sun 11pm–5am) two of the hottest venues in Nice. The smaller, smarter Studio 47 is designed for over-25s.

Wayne's Bar (15 rue de la Préfecture; tel: 04 93 13 46 99; daily noon–2am) has been a favourite among locals for a number of years. It features wild parties with a young, international crowd. Le Bar des Oiseaux (5 rue Saint-Vincent; tel: 04 93 80 27 33; Wed–Sat 7:30pm–11pm), a bar-restaurant near the theatre, is a real institution. They have live music every Friday and Saturday evening.

Le Before (18 rue du Congrés (near sea); tel: 04 93 87 85 59), is an ambience lounge serving *apéro dînatoire* (apéritifs with food). Open from 6pm to crack of dawn. **La Bodeguita del Havana** (place Masséna; tel: 04 93 92 67 24) is a bar, restaurant and nightclub, with salsa music, South American food and a good atmosphere. **Le liqwid** (11 rue Alexandre Mari in Old Nice; tel: 04 93 76 14 28) is an ultra-hip restaurant/club. The DJ spins a quality mix and good beats will keep the sleepless going till dawn.

Nice's **Casino Ruhl** (promenade des Anglais; tel: 04 97 03 12 22) boasts all the usual glamour with its dinner cabarets and private gaming rooms. The **Palais de la Méditerranée** (13 promenade des Anglais; tel: 04 92 14 68 00) has a casino, a luxury hotel, a gourmet restaurant and a variety of shows behind its art deco façade.

CINEMA

Cinémathèque (Acropolis, 3 esplanade Kennedy; tel: 04 92 04 06 66, open Oct–June, Tue–Sat 2–10, Sun 3–5) shows original old films, as well as all the latest releases. **Cinema Rialto** (4 rue de Rivoli; tel: 08 36 68 00 41, open 11–11) shows films in their original language.

FESTIVALS

The Nice Carnival and Nice Jazz Festival (➤ 26) are two of the biggest in town.

MUSIC & THEATRE

The **Auditorium du Conservatoire national de region** (24 boulevard de Cimiez; tel: 04 92 26 72 20, open Mon from 6pm, except school hols) has open rehearsals every Monday. The standard is high and entry is free. The **Opéra de Nice** (9 rue St-François-de-Paule; tel: 04 92 17 40 00; www.opera-nice.org, open Tue–Sat) stages opera, classical music and ballet.

The **Palais Nikaia** (163 route de Grenoble; tel: 04 92 29 31 29; www.nikaia.fr) is the region's largest multi-purpose venue and draws the great international stars. A special bus is provided for concerts (line 95). **Theatre de Verdure** (Espace Jacques Cotta, promenade des Anglais; tel: 04 97 13 37 55) is located in the heart of a garden and accommodates up to 3,000.

More mainstream theatre can be seen at **Théâtre National de Nice** (promenade des Arts; tel: 04 93 13 90 90; www.tnn.fr), with classic and contemporary plays.

Around Nice

Little Treats

Contrasting Vistas
You can see across to the Principality of Monaco and its high-rises from the **clifftop village of Roquebrune** (➤ 74/75).

A Rose by any Other Name…
Rare floral varieties will delight all of your senses in the rose garden at the **Villa Ephrussi de Rothschild** (➤ 68).

Renaissance Man
The **museum in Menton** (➤ 76) showcases the multifaceted life and work of the director, actor, painter and poet Jean Cocteau.

Getting Your Bearings

The dramatic stretch of azure coast between Menton and Nice, with its chic towns, glorious beaches and backdrop of snow-capped mountains, was the original piece of coastline to which the name "Riviera" was applied, when it first became fashionable as a winter destination in the 19th century. The towns here still evoke *belle époque* grandeur.

The sea and coastline from Èze's lofty Jardin Exotique

Today the resorts of this incredible stretch of coastline have virtually fused together into one giant, bustling megalopolis from Menton to Cannes. But each resort has managed to maintain its identity: genteel Menton, an old Italo-Provençal resort of art nouveau villas and citrus trees on the Italian border, is considered by many to be the most attractive town on the French Riviera; Cap Ferrat – the "Peninsula of Billionaires" – with its sumptuous villas amid subtropical foliage, is arguably the most desirable address on the Riviera; while jet-setting Monaco (► 83–104) is its most sophisticated holiday playground.

The resorts are linked by three famous cliff roads, called Les Corniches, which hug the contours of the coast at varying levels, traversing the most mountainous stretch of the French Riviera with their hair-raising bends, sudden tunnels and breathtaking views. Two medieval hilltop villages dominate the coast here: La Turbie with its massive Roman monument, and picturesque Èze, clinging to a mountaintop 427m (1,400ft) above sea level, with dizzying views of the coast. By contrast, the interior is surprisingly unpopulated, with its fertile valleys and ancient villages perched on the hillsides, a perfect retreat from the touristic frenzy of the coast.

Opposite: Augustus' Trophée des Alpes towers above La Turbie

TOP 10

- 3 Villa Ephrussi de Rothschild ➤ 68
- 5 Eze ➤ 70

Don't Miss

- 19 The Corniches ➤ 72
- 20 Menton ➤ 76

At Your Leisure

- 21 Gorbio ➤ 78
- 22 Peille ➤ 78
- 23 Peillon ➤ 79
- 24 Coaraze ➤ 80

Around Nice

Two Perfect Days

If you're not sure where to begin your travels, these itineraries recommend practical and enjoyable days out around Nice, taking in some of the best places to see. For more information see the main entries (➤ 68–80).

Day One

Morning

Drive the ⓳ **Corniche Inférieure** (➤ 72) from Nice via Villefranche-sur-Mer to St-Jean-Cap-Ferrat to visit the beautiful rose-pink ★3 **Villa Ephrussi de Rothschild** (➤ 68), with its sumptuous period interiors, impressive art collection and beautiful gardens.

Lunch

The elegant **coffee shop at Villa Ephrussi** is ideal for lunch or some light refreshment. The *gâteaux* are especially delicious.

Afternoon

Walkers will enjoy the **shaded coastal path** around the cape. The numerous coves are ideal for a lazy afternoon spent swimming and sun-bathing. Or be a real local and promenade along the waterfront in the **port of St-Jean-Cap-Ferrat**, where there are inviting waterfront bars, cafés and restaurants, serving chilled drinks, perfect pastries and outside tables for people watching.

Evening

Return to **Villefranche-sur-Mer** (➤ 72) for a meal at one of the waterside eateries beside the yacht harbour. Try **La Mère Germaine** (➤ 85) for exceptional seafood.

Day Two

Morning

Take the dramatic ⓳ **Moyenne Corniche** (➤ 74) route and zigzag your way to the teetering

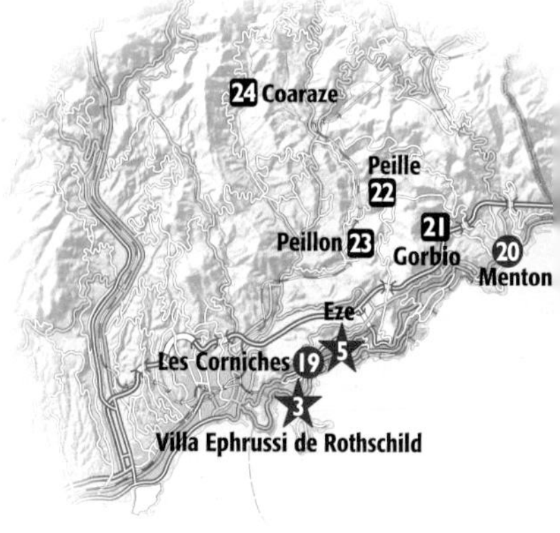

village of **5 Èze** (right; ➤ 70), breathtakingly perched on the cliff edge high above the Riviera. Leave your car and explore the narrow, stepped alleys and flower-filled, cobbled pathways, full of tiny craft shops and boutiques hidden in caves within the rocks. Visit the exotic garden (right) with its cacti and vivid tropical flowers, and the perfume factories at the foot of the hill.

Lunch

Considering its tiny size, Èze has more than its fair share of fine restaurants – perfect for a long, lazy lunch. Splash out on a lavish meal at **La Bergerie** (➤ 83) or **La Chèvre d'Or** (➤ 83). For budget travellers, **Le Cactus** (➤ 83) serves cheap, tasty crêpes in a tiny, vaulted restaurant in the old gateway.

Afternoon

Continue eastwards by car onto the scenic **19 Grande Corniche** (➤ 74). Admire the dazzling coastal views over Monaco from La Turbie, then proceed to the beautiful seaside town of **20 Menton** (below; ➤ 76), France's warmest resort. If you enjoy driving you may wish to follow a lengthy, winding detour at La Turbie (along the D53 and D22), to visit the tiny "twin" hilltop villages of **22 Peille** (➤ 78) and **23 Peillon** (➤ 79). The scenery along this stretch is truly wild and spectacular. On arrival in Menton explore the delightful Old Town, with its medieval houses painted in ice-cream shades, or relax in the fragrant gardens of Palais Carnolès (Europe's largest citrus fruit garden). Art aficionados should not miss the Musée des Beaux-Arts, Musée Jean Cocteau and the Salle des Mariages (➤ 77).

Evening

Dine at **Mirazur** (➤ 84), a restaurant in Menton with two Michelin stars.

3 Villa Ephrussi de Rothschild

This rose-pink belle-époque palace, surrounded by immaculate formal gardens and wonderful sea views, was constructed by the flamboyant Baroness Béatrice Ephrussi de Rothschild in 1912 as a place to hold banquets, entertain guests and house her extensive art collection.

Beatrice de Rothschild (1864–1934), wife of wealthy banker Maurice Ephrussi, was a woman of seemingly unlimited means who had a passion for travel and fine art. She created her dream villa here in the glorious style of the great palaces of the Italian Renaissance, and set it in immaculate gardens. The villa took a series of 40 architects five years to build, some of the architects lasting only a few hours before their dismissal. Located on exclusive Cap Ferrat, with sea views on all sides, the villa claims one of the most beautiful outlooks on the Riviera.

The Baroness died in 1934, leaving the villa to France's Académie des Beaux-Arts. Visitors can now wander around the beautiful gardens and the ground floor of the villa, although you have to take a guided tour to see the collections on the first floor.

The **interior of the villa** is lavishly decorated with rare furniture (including some pieces that once belonged to

The extravagant pink villa and gardens of Villa Ephrussi de Rothschild, St-Jean-Cap-Ferrat

INSIDER INFO

- On the first floor is the **Salon des Singes** (Monkey Room), with monkey friezes on the walls and porcelain monkeys on display, reflecting the Baroness's particular fondness for monkeys. Entrance to this room and the rest of the first floor will cost an additional fee.
- Watch at least the first part of the 18-minute film, which evokes the splendour of daily life on the Riviera during the *belle époque*, and then goes on to retrace the history of the house and the collection. Insider Tip

Getting there: Via **public transport**, the villa is 800m from Beaulieu-sur-Mer station or take bus 81 or 100.

Marie Antoinette), set off by rich carpets, tapestries and an eclectic collection of rare *objets d'art*, and one of the world's most beautiful collections of Vincennes and Sèvres porcelain. There are around 5,000 works of art in the collection here, ranging from French period furniture and tapestries to Renaissance religious art, fine 18th-century porcelain, and art from the Far East, including a display of pink jade and rare Chinese chests. Despite being filled with priceless works of art, the villa has retained the atmosphere of an occupied residence.

The **gardens** are divided into nine distinct areas, following Spanish, Florentine, Stone, Japanese, Exotic, Rose, Provençal, French and Sèvres (porcelain) themes. The main (French) garden is landscaped to resemble a ship's deck with a Temple of Love on the bow and Musical Fountains that play every ten minutes. The Baroness even decreed that her gardeners dress as sailors while tending the gardens.

TAKING A BREAK

The villa has an elegant **tea room** with wonderful views of the Bay of Villefranche from its large windows. Open from lunch until closing time, it serves a range of salads and pastries.

---

187 D2
St-Jean-Cap-Ferrat
04 93 01 33 09; www.villa-ephrussi.com
Mid Feb to Oct daily 10–6; July–Aug 10–7; Nov to mid-Feb Mon–Fri 2–6, Sat, Sun 10–6
€12.50

5 Èze

Without a doubt one of the region's most strikingly situated and best-preserved hilltop village, Èze affords truly breathtaking views.

The hilltop village of Èze

The town is often referred to as the Nid d'Aigle (Eagle's Nest) because of its remarkable location, sitting atop a 430m (1,375ft) spike of rock beside the Moyenne Corniche, half-way between Nice and Monaco, where the mountains meet the coast. The village is exceptionally picturesque, with narrow medieval lanes and steps, and several vantage points looking straight down onto the sparkling sea below.

The settlement records of Èze date back as far as the 11th century, although the site has been occupied since the Bronze Age. The village was fortified in the 14th century and belonged to the Counts of Savoy for hundreds of years. In 1792, following the creation of the Alpes-Maritimes region, Èze became part of the Principality of Monaco. It was only after 1860, when locals voted in the village chapel for annexation to France, that peace finally came to Èze.

On entering through the only gateway in the **ancient ramparts**, you will be struck by the tall, golden houses and the labyrinth of tiny vaulted passages with cobbled alleys and stairways. These climb steeply up to the ruins of a once massive **Saracen fortress**, destroyed by the French at the beginning of the 18th century, giving dazzling views out to sea. The ruins are surrounded by an exotic garden (**Jardin Exotique**), bristling with more than 400 kinds of magnificent cacti, succulents and rare palms.

Be sure to take time to explore the flower-filled passageways within the medieval village, where there are deluxe château-hotels, fine restaurants and little shops hidden in caves within the rock – tiny treasure troves of antiques, ceramics, pewter and olive wood. Insider Tip

At the foot of the hill two Grassois perfume factories, **Galimard** and **Fragonard**, contain interesting museums in which the secrets of perfume production are explained. Nearby, the **chemin de Nietzsche** (a narrow path once frequented by the German philosopher, see Inside Info below) zigzags steeply down to the beach and the former fishing village of Èze-Bord-de-Mer, a more modern town and popular coastal resort.

TAKING A BREAK

There are some lovely places to eat in Èze, but as this is a tourist honeypot, most of them are quite expensive. In the old village, **Le Nid d'Aigle or Le Cactus** (➤ 83) are both good options. There are also a number of cafés and restaurants close to the tourist office on **place du Général de Gaulle**.

Exploring the narrow passageways in Èze

187 D3

Tourist Office
Place du Général de Gaulle
04 93 41 26 00;
www.eze-riviera.com
May–Sep Mon–Sat 9–7, Sun 2–7;
Oct–April Mon–Sat 9–6:30,
Sun 9:30–1, 2–6:30

Jardin Exotique
rue du Château 04 93 41 10 30
Jul–Aug daily 9–7:30; June, Sep
9–7; 9–4:30 rest of year €6

INSIDER INFO

- The **summit of the Jardin Exotique**, 429m (1,408ft) above the sea, is a wonderful vantage point, and has a viewpoint indicator marking out places of interest that can be seen from the top of the garden.
- The **café terrace** of the Château Èza hotel has one of the best views.
- The **Fragonard** perfume factory just past the village on Moyenne Corniche has a shop selling a large range of perfumes. More Fragonard products and homeware can be found at Fragonard Maison – it's located on avenue du Jardin Exotique at the entrance to the village.
- Vehicles cannot enter the old village. There is a large **parking area** at the foot of the village and a lift for disabled visitors.
- For a better understanding of how remote and inaccessible Èze was before the invention of the car, come here on foot. A precipitous **path up from the shore** is named after the 19th-century philosopher Friedrich Nietzsche, who, living by the sea, often took this strenuous walk up to the medieval village.

19 The Corniches

Three famous cliff roads, the Corniche Inférieure, the Moyenne Corniche and the Grande Corniche, traverse one of the most scenic stretches of the Riviera from Nice to Menton via Monaco. The landscapes you'll see here are so enchanting that you won't even mind the frequent busy traffic.

Fishing boats anchored at Villefranche-sur-Mer

Corniche Inférieure (N98)

Villefranche-sur-Mer

This small fishing village, with boats bobbing about in the harbour, has changed little since it was founded in the 14th century as a customs-free port (hence its name). Considering its proximity to Nice and Monte-Carlo, Villefranche remains surprisingly unspoiled. Its beautiful bay, one of the world's deepest, is fringed with warm-hued houses, atmospheric waterfront bars, cafés and restaurants.

A maze of steep stairways and cavernous passageways climb from the harbour through the Old Town. Dark and eerie **rue Obscure**, a narrow, vaulted 13th-century street, has sheltered the inhabitants of Villefranche from bombardments throughout history right up to World War II.

In a sturdy 16th-century **citadel** on the waterfront is the Mairie (town hall) and two *musées* with work by local artists and some by Miró and Picasso.

The 14th-century **Chapelle St-Pierre** on the quay, once used to store fishing nets, was decorated in 1957 with frescoes by Villefranche's most famous resident – poet, playwright and film director Jean Cocteau. His luminous paintings depict St Peter living among the local fisherwomen and gypsies.

Cap Ferrat

Cap Ferrat, like Cap d'Antibes and Cap Martin, has long been a favourite haunt of the world's rich and famous. Considered the most desirable address in the Riviera, the Cap is smothered in huge, impenetrable villas hidden amid sumptuous, subtropical gardens. Among the properties here is the lavish **Villa Ephrussi de Rothschild** (➤ 68).

Despite its wealth and exclusivity, Cap Ferrat is quite open to visitors and has a tourist office in the peninsula's small main town, St-Jean-Cap-Ferrat, an approachable, sleepy place with a few restaurants and cafés along the port. Away from the harbour, the streets and houses are far less grand than the mansions elsewhere on the peninsula. Walking paths link much of the Cap and the tourist office will be happy to point you in the direction of the little harbour or the trails that are marked out around the 14km (9mi) coastline, with wonderful sea views.

Beaulieu-sur-Mer

True to its name, Beaulieu is a "beautiful place", and is also one of the warmest resorts on the Riviera, sheltered by a natural amphitheatre of hills. It had its heyday in the late 19th century when many celebrities stayed here, including the then Prince of Wales, Empress Sissi of Austria, Piotr Ilyich Tchaikovsky and Gustav Eiffel. This prosperous little town has a glamorous casino built in the 1920s, an elegant Edwardian Rotonde (today a local history museum), *belle époque* villas and a palm-lined promenade on the sheltered Baie des Fourmis.

The town's most curious attraction is the extraordinary **Villa Grecque Kérylos**, sitting on the tip of the northern headland. This seaside villa was built in 1908 by archaeologist Théodore Reinach, and is a perfect reproduction of a Greek villa from the 2nd century BC. No expense was spared in the villa's lavish interior of marble, ivory and bronze. Reinach lived here for almost 20 years, eating, dressing and behaving as an Athenian citizen.

From Beaulieu-sur-mer the Corniche Inférieure continues up the coast through Monaco (➤ 87), and ends at Roquebrune-Cap Martin (➤ 74).

The marina, St-Jean-Cap-Ferrat

The 10th-century Carolingian castle overlooks the rooftops of Roquebrune-Cap-Martin

Moyenne Corniche (N7)

Èze

Èze, the most strikingly situated and best-preserved Provençal hilltop village, stands high on a rocky pinnacle ten minutes' drive from Nice and Monaco. It has spectacular views over the Riviera as far as Corsica.

Insider Tip From the top of the Jardin Exotique at Èze (▶ 71), there is a view of all three corniches.

Grande Corniche (D2564)

La Turbie

The teetering village of La Turbie sits on a ridge in the hills above Monaco. The monument for which this village is famous, the **Trophée des Alpes**, is situated at the loftiest point of the old Roman highway (the Via Julia), 480m (1,575ft) above sea level. This enormous monument, originally 50m (165ft) high and 38m (125ft) wide, was built in 6 BC to commemorate Augustus' conquest of the Alpine tribes. It was used as a fortress in the Middle Ages, largely dismantled under the orders of Louis XIV in 1705, and further destroyed in the 19th century when its stonework was quarried to build a nearby church. However, enough of the monument survived to enable its partial restoration in later years. The present structure stands 35m (115ft) high and has a long inscription on its base listing the conquered local tribes.

The gardens surrounding the trophy have fantastic panoramic views and a small museum documenting the trophy's restoration. The nearby baroque **Église St-Michel-Archange** contains works attributed to the schools of Veronese, Raphael, Bréa, Ribera and Murillo.

Roquebrune-Cap-Martin

Roquebrune-Cap Martin is divided into two areas: old Roquebrune, an attractive medieval hilltop village, and the smart coastal resort of Cap Martin.

Old **Roquebrune** is a fascinating tangle of ancient flower-filled lanes, stairways and vaulted passages, which cluster around its **castle**, the oldest feudal château remaining in

France and the sole example of Carolingian style. Built in the 10th century to ward off Saracen attack, it was later remodelled by the Grimaldis, and restored in 1911 by Lord Ingram, one of the first wave of wealthy tourists drawn to stylish Cap Martin. Other visitors to **Cap Martin** included Queen Victoria, Winston Churchill, Coco Chanel and architect Le Corbusier, who drowned off the cape in 1965 and lies buried in Roquebrune cemetery. A coastal path in his honour circles the cape, past sumptuous villas shrouded in dense foliage (➤ 164).

---

187 D3

Villefranche-sur-Mer Tourist Office
Jardin Francois-Binon 04 93 01 73 68; www.villefranche-sur-mer.com

Château de Roquebrune
P1 William Ingram 04 93 35 07 22
June–Sep daily 10–1, 2:30–7, 10–12:30, 2–5 rest of year €5

Chapelle St-Pierre
Quai Courbet, Port de Villefranche 04 93 76 90 70
Summer Wed–Sun 10–12, 3–7; winter Wed–Sun 10–12, 2–6.
Closed mid-Nov to mid-Dec €2.50

Beaulieu-sur-Mer Tourist Office
Place Georges-Clemenceau 04 93 01 02 21; www.beaulieusurmer.fr
Jul–Aug Mon–Sat 9–12:30, 2–7, Sun 9–12:30;
Sep–June Mon–Fri 9–12:15, 2–6, Sat 9–12:15, 2–5

Villa Grecque Kérylos
Beaulieu-sur-Mer 04 93 01 47 29; www.villa-kerylos.com
Mid-Feb to Oct daily 10–6; July–Aug 10–7;
Nov to mid-Feb Mon–Fri 2–6, Sat–Sun 10–6 €11

La Turbie Tourist Office
Place Detras 04 93 41 21 15; www.ville-la-turbie.fr

Trophée des Alpes
18 avenue Albert 1er
04 93 41 20 84; www.la-turbie.monuments-nationaux.fr
Mid-May to mid-Sep Tue–Sun 9:30–1, 2:30–6:30;
10–1:30, 2:30–5 rest of year €5

INSIDER INFO

- Coming from Villefranche-sur-Mer to St-Jean-Cap-Ferrat, a **shaded coastal path** winds around Cap Ferrat past countless enticing inlets (ideal for a refreshing dip) towards St-Jean, where you can have lunch by the harbour. Insider Tip
- The top two corniches are notoriously accident prone, so if you are in a hurry it is better to take the **A8** *autoroute*, which carves its way through the mountains behind the three coast roads from Nice as far as the Italian border. Insider Tip

20 Menton

Lying just 1.5km (1mi) from the Italian border, it comes as no surprise that Menton is France's most Italianate resort, a lovely jumble of tall, pale ochre houses at the foot of a sheltering mountain backdrop.

The baroque church of St-Michel in Menton's Old Town

Until the mid-19th century, when the Riviera became a fashionable and wealthy winter resort, Menton was a little-known fishing port belonging to the Grimaldi family. In 1860 it was annexed by Napoléon III. Its warm climate made it a popular winter resort with the Russian and English aristocracy, including Queen Victoria, who visited here in 1882. *Fin de siècle* hotels resembling palaces started to spring up throughout the town and exotic Edwardian gardens were planted, some of which are still beautifully maintained today. After World War I, Menton lost out to its more glamorous neighbours – Nice, Cannes, St-Tropez and Monaco – although the faded elegance of the *belle époque* is still apparent.

By contrast, the **Old Town** is a hotchpotch of ancient pastel-coloured houses dissected by terracotta-paved steps, alleys and tiny squares. The Italianate air of many of the buildings here provides an insight into the period before Menton became French. Climbing the narrow rue Longue towards the place de la Concepcion, you will find two magnificent baroque churches with finely ornamented façades: **St-Michel** and the **Chapelle des Penitents Blancs**. Between them is the **parvis St-Michel**, a mosaic square of black and white cobbles depicting the Grimaldi coat of arms. This square provides a delightful setting for the summer Chamber Music Festival (► 86).

At the top of the Old Town is a fascinating **cemetery** with sweeping sea views, once described by writer Guy de Maupassant as "the most aristocratic in Europe". Other notable sights include the **Palais Carnolès**, the 18th-century summer residence of the Princes of Monaco, now home to Menton's Musée des Beaux-Arts (seek out works by

Raoul Dufy and Graham Sutherland among its collection of fine art), and the two museums dedicated to the town's most famous son, **Jean Cocteau** (1889–1963). Cocteau also decorated the remarkable **Salle des Mariages** (registry office) in the Hôtel de Ville with a range of romantic and spiritual images of matrimony.

Menton is France's sunniest town, with an annual 300 days of sun. The town is bursting with semitropical gardens created by wealthy Edwardian horticulturalists. Most of the parks and gardens are in the prosperous Garavan district, in the foothills behind the town near the Italian border. The best are the **Jardin Botanique du Val Rahmeh**, the **Jardin Serre de la Madone** and the Valencian **Jardin Fontana Rosa**, dedicated to writers by Spanish author Blasso Ibánez. These gardens catch the sun even in winter, and enabled aristocratic gardeners to cultivate exotic plants from around the world (➤ 16).

Menton is also the "lemon capital of the world"; its surrounding slopes are covered in **citrus groves**. The garden around the Palais Carnolès claims to be the largest citrus fruit garden in Europe. The Biovès garden in the town centre, bordered with palms and lemon trees, is the venue of Menton's **Fête du Citron** (Lemon Festival) in February.

TAKING A BREAK

The **Café du Musée** boasts an attractive setting in architect Rudy Ricciotti's **Cocteau Museum**. It serves drinks and light meals and has a terrace outside.

---

187 E3

Tourist Office
8 avenue Boyer 04 92 41 76 76; www.tourisme-menton.fr
Jun–Sep daily 9–6; Oct–May Mon–Sat 8:30–12:30, 2–6, Sun 9–12:30

Musée Jean Cocteau
2 quai Monléon 0489 81 52 50; www.museecocteaumenton.fr
Wed–Mon 10–6 €6; includes entry to the nearby Bastion Museum (quai Napoléon III; tel: 04 93 57 72 30; Wed–Mon 10–noon, 2–6 €3)

Salle des Mariages
Hôtel de Ville, place Ardoïno 04 92 10 50 00
Mon–Fri 8:30–12:30 (last visit 11:30), 1:30–5 €2

INSIDER INFO

- The **Fête du Citron** (Lemon Festival) starts on Shrove Tuesday and lasts for 10 days.
- A **chamber music festival** is held in August in the parvis St-Michel (➤ 86).
- Take a stroll through the **local market** (Marché Municipal), at Halles Municipales just behind the quai de Monléon, for an authentic experience of food shopping in France (daily 5am–1pm). 
- The Service du Patrimoine, based at 5 rue Ciappetta (Hôtel d'Adhémar de Lantagnac, 24 rue St Michel; tel: 04 92 10 97 10), runs **guided tours** of Menton and its gardens.

At Your Leisure

21 Gorbio

This medieval hilltop village, 10km (6mi) northwest of Menton, provides welcome relief from souvenir shops along the main tourist trail. Strolling around the **central square** is not a bad way to spend an afternoon. There you will find a 300-year-old elm tree, and the grand castle of the Alziari counts, the baroque Église St-Barthélémy and the 15th-century Chapelle des Pénitents Blancs. There are also several other interesting churches and chapels to be seen in or near the village.

BOAT TOURS AND FESTIVALS

- Cities have a completely different charm when you see them from the water. Kids and adults alike will love taking a trip between Monaco and Italy aboard ***Le Brigantin*** for around two hours in the twilight (Vieux Port de Menton; tel: 06 09 60 11 72; July, Aug 8pm; April, May, June, Sep 7pm; March, Oct 6pm; €22; kids aged 3 to 12 years, 15 €). Insider Tip
- The **Jardin des Agrumes** at the Palais Carnolès (3 avenue de la Madone; tel: 04 93 35 49 71; Wed–Mon 10–noon, 2–6; free) is set in the beautiful surroundings of the Monégasque princes' former summer residence. Kids will enjoy discovering the numerous varieties of oranges and lemons on show.
- Many small villages hold **festivals** throughout the year that are repositories for traditional ways of life, such as Peille's **Wheat and Lavender Festival** in August, Coaraze's **Medieval Festival** in August, and **Winter Solstice Fireworks** in September. The festivals are often colourful and great fun for children. Check with local tourist offices for more details

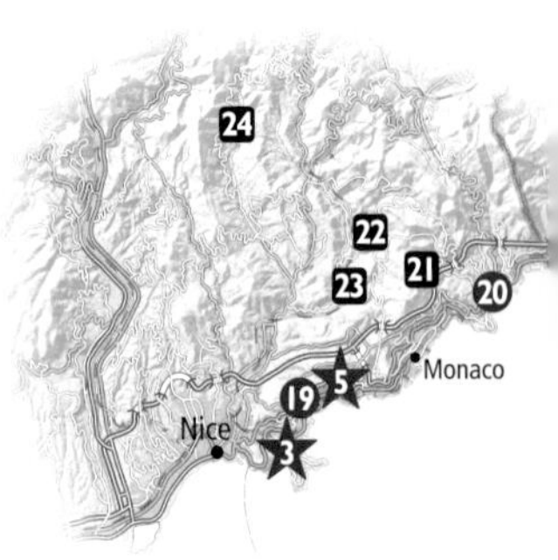

The best time to visit Gorbio is during the Fête Dieu (Corpus Christi) in May and June, when the enchanting **Procession dai Limaça** takes place. This night-time procession takes its name from the snail shells (*limaça* in Provençal) which are filled with olive oil and lit to create little flickering lamps that illuminate the village during the procession. A traditional pagan ritual, the procession gives thanks for the winter's olive harvest and wards off any demons that might damage the next crop. The snail is a pagan symbol of renewal, and the shell-lamps are fixed onto walls, doors and pavements, lighting up the village with a spectacular glow.

187 E3

Tourist Office
Mairie: 30 rue Garibaldi
04 92 10 66 50

22 Peille

Just a short distance inland and set in wild, underpopulated countryside, Peille is a perfect retreat from the touristic frenzy of the coast. It is reached by steep, narrow roads and stands on a ridge 20km (12.5mi) inland from Monaco. Historically, Peille's remote and inaccessible location was not only an excellent defence strategy, but it allowed the village to develop independently, to the point where it had its own Provençal dialect, Pelhasc.

The village also had its own individual ideas on religion. During the Middle Ages, it was excommunicated several times rather than pay the bishop's tithes. The **Chapelle des Pénitents Noirs** was converted into a communal oil press and its splendid domed Chapelle de St-Sébastien into the Hôtel de Ville (Town Hall).

Peille has plenty of character. Along the cobbled alleys and passageways you will find old buildings with fine doorways, and fountains and other Gothic and Renaissance stonework. Inside the **Église Ste-Marie** is a painting of the village in medieval times, showing the now-ruined feudal castle of the Counts of Provence in its former glory (ask at the Mairie for the key). The church also has a 16th-century polyptych of the Rosary by Honoré Bertone of the Nice School.

187 D4

Tourist Office
Mairie: Place Carnot
04 93 91 71 71

23 Peillon

Peille's twin and neighbouring village, Peillon is one of the Riviera's most beautiful hilltop villages, nestled among the lofty, rocky peaks high above the Peillon valley, standing at 1,225ft (373m) and cleverly camouflaged against the landscape. From high up, these medieval *villages perchés* (perched villages) had a distinct advantage over any invaders, as the villagers could watch over the hinterland as well as the coast. Today the village's natural defences keep it from major tourist development, and as a result, although much restored, the village remains remarkably unspoiled and uncommercialised.

The terraced houses of Peille, perched above the Faquin ravine

Pellion's huddle of cobbled alleys, steps and arches lead up to a charming little **church** at the summit. But the main attraction here is the **Chapelle des Pénitents Blancs** just outside the village, with 15th-century frescoes by Giovanni Canavesio depicting the Passion of Christ. Phone the Mairie in advance to arrange a visit. Beyond the chapel, a **footpath walk** to Peille takes about two hours along what was once a Roman road.

187 D3

Tourist Office
Mairie: 672 avenue de l'Hôtel de Ville
04 93 91 98 34

24 Coaraze

This tiny and picturesque village is perched on a peak at 2,100ft (658m), in the hills behind Nice. The village owes its name to a local legend which claims the people of Coaraze captured the devil and, in order to escape, he had to cut off his tail. In the local dialect, *coa* means "cut" and *raza* "tail".

The village is also reputed to be a sunny place, and is sometimes

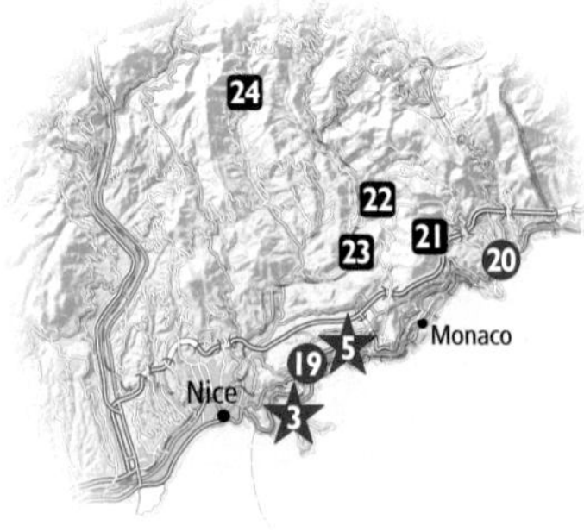

called the **Village du Soleil** (Village of the Sun). This inspired Jean Cocteau and other artists in the 1960s to decorate the town with large, colourful ceramic **sun dials** which can be seen throughout the village. Cocteau's is on the town hall.

A quiet cobbled lane in Coaraze

Like other medieval hilltop villages, Coaraze has a maze of cobbled stairways, lanes, vaulted passageways, fountains and sunny squares. It has also become something of a chic hideaway, with fashionable Niçois purchasing second homes where they can escape the heat of the city.

On the outskirts of the village is the **Chapelle Bleue**, renamed after the artist Ponce de Léon redecorated the interior with bright blue murals and vivid green stained-glass windows in 1965. The chapel was formerly known by the more sombre name, Chapelle Notre-Dame des Sept Douleurs (Our Lady of the Seven Sorrows). The small road beside the Bar Tabac Les Arts leads to the chapel, which can be reached either by car or on foot (20 minutes return).

187 D4

Tourist Office
7 place Sainte-Cathérine
04 93 79 37 47 Tue–Sat 10–12, 3–5

Where to... Stay

Prices
Expect to pay per double room, per night:
€ under €80 **€€** €80–€150 **€€€** over €150

BEAULIEU-SUR-MER

La Réserve €€€
One of the most exclusive seafront hotels of the Riviera, with a two Michelin-starred restaurant. Hôtel La Réserve in Beaulieu-sur-Mer reached the height of its fame in 1887 when millionaire playboy James Gordon Bennett, owner of the *New York Herald*, was cast out from American society following a scandal, and moved here to run the Paris edition of his paper from the hotel.
187 D3 5 boulevard Maréchal-Leclerc
04 93 01 00 01; www.reservebeaulieu.com
Hotel closed 26 Oct–19 Dec

ÈZE

Château Èza €€€
The view from this château is breathtaking, making the climb to reach the top truly worthwhile. The former home of a prince of Sweden, this stunning hotel consists of several medieval houses that have been linked together to form a luxury eyrie. The perched restaurant terrace is incredible (➤ 71).
187 D3 Rue de la Pise
04 93 41 12 24; www.chateaueza.com
Closed Nov to mid-Dec, restaurant closed Mon–Tue in low season

MENTON

Napoléon €€€
One of the best places to stay in this town next to the Italian border. It's worth trying to reserve a room with a terrace and a view of the sea.
187 E3 29 Porte de France
04 93 35 89 59; www.napoleon-menton.com
Closed Nov to 25 Dec

Paris Rome €€–€€€
Small, friendly lodgings by Port Garavan with twenty tastefully furnished rooms. Lying just a few steps away from the Old Town, it's an ideal starting point for walks or a swim in the Mediterranean. The name is appropriate: Menton lies pretty much half way between Paris and Rome.
187 E3 79 Porte de France
04 93 35 70 35; www.paris-rome.com
Closed Nov to late Jan

Prince de Galles €–€€
Facing the sea, this Italian-style three-star hotel is convenient for the town centre and has splendid views across to Italy. There are 64 comfortable, soundproofed rooms – some with sea views – a panoramic terrace and a tropical garden with two majestic palms under which you can dine in the summer
187 E3 4, avenue Général de Gaulle
04 93 28 21 21; www.princedegalles.com

PEILLON

Auberge de la Madone €€–€€€
This typical *auberge* has been lovingly decorated in traditional Provençal style. The rooms are filled with quality antiques, and outside there is a terrace with a wonderful view over the surrounding countryside; the perfect place

to enjoy the establishment's Michelin-starred regional cuisine.
187 E3 **2 place au Village**
04 93 79 91 17; www.auberge-madone-peillon.com
Closed 6 Nov–22 Dec

ROQUEBRUNE

Vista Palace €€€

Don't be put off by the sight of this rather ugly modern building. Perched on a cliff 300m (985ft) above sea level on the Grande Corniche and overlooking Monaco, it has the most spectacular views and inside you will find the ultimate in luxury accommodation
187 E3 **D2564/Grande Corniche**
04 92 10 40 00; www.vistapalace.com

ROQUEBRUNE-CAP-MARTIN

Les Deux Frères €€

This hotel, boasting wonderful views of the Mediterranean and Monaco, has 12 lovely rooms which are themed and stylish. The Marine room features blue-and-white striped bed linen, the Medieval room a wrought-iron bench, and the Moroccan room a leopard skin. Meals are served in the restaurant, on the terrace overlooking the sea, or by the fireplace in winter.
187 E3 **Le Village, place des Deux Frères**
04 93 28 99 00; www.lesdeuxfreres.com

ST-JEAN-CAP-FERRAT

Hôtel Brise Marine €€–€€€

This Italian-style villa built in 1878 is today a welcoming three-star hotel. The villa's ochre façade and blue shutters overlook the sea, and there are excellent views from the garden, terraces and from some of the elegant bedrooms. The hotel doesn't have a restaurant on site, but there are several close by in the town (► 84).
187 D2 **58 avenue Jean Mermoz**
04 93 76 04 36; www.hotel-brisemarine.com
Closed Nov–Jan

Grand Hôtel du Cap Ferrat €€€

The recent refurbishment has done this hotel with 49 rooms and 24 suites a power of good. Opened in 1906, it boasts beautiful grounds, a magnificent pool with sea views and its own gourmet restaurant. It now looks just as fabulous as when it first became a favourite tourist haunt over a century ago.
187 D2
71 boulevard du Général de Gaulle
04 93 76 50 50; www.ghcf.fr
Closed Jan to Easter

Hôtel Royal Riviera €€€

Attractively refurbished, this extravagant hotel has sumptuous rooms, its own helipad, magnificent gardens and popular poolside lunchtime barbecues.
187 D2 **3 avenue Jean Monnet**
04 93 76 31 00; www.royal-riviera.com

LA TURBIE

Hostellerie Jérôme €€€

This old Provençal house has luxurious rooms with views of either the village or the sea. The food at the *hostellerie* is excellent – the two Michelin-starred restaurant serving everything from breakfast (€15) to an exceptional *dégustation* menu (€98–€140).
187 D3 **20 rue du Comte de Cessole**
04 92 41 51 51; www.hostelleriejerome.com
Closed 25 Nov–13 Jan

VILLEFRANCHE-SUR-MER

Hôtel Welcome €€€

Originally a 17th-century convent, this restored ancient building has a distinctly modern feel. All the rooms are bright and have balconies with views over the bay. However, there are artistic and historic associations: Jean Cocteau stayed here when he was working on the frescoes of the Chapelle St-Pierre.
187 D3 **3 quai Amiral Courbet**
04 93 76 27 62; www.welcomehotel.com
Closed 11 Nov–21 Dec

Where to...
Eat and Drink

Prices
Expect to pay per person for a three-course meal, excluding drinks:
€ under €25 **€€** €25–€60 **€€€** over €60

BEAULIEU-SUR-MER

La Raison Gourmande €€
Sunny Provençal décor complements traditional French and Provencal cuisine in this pleasing restaurant under the watchful eye of Jackie Lelu. The emphasis is on fish and seafood such as fresh lobster and sea bass, but carnivores are also well catered for with specialities such as foie gras and duck breast.
187 D3 26 avenue Maréchal Foch 04 93 01 13 12; www.laraisongourmande.com Closed Sun, Mon

ÈZE

La Bergerie €€
Traditional grilled and barbecued dishes with a good choice of Côtes de Provence wines. Dine in winter by the welcoming open fire, and in summer on the shady terrace overlooking the sea.
187 D3 Grand Corniche 04 93 41 03 67 Dinner only Fri–Sun

Le Cactus €
Take a break from sightseeing at this affordable little café, with a lunchtime menu that includes salads, crêpes, ice cream and restorative cups of tea.
187 D3 La Placette, entrée Vieux Village 04 93 41 19 02 Mar–Oct 9–9; Sat–Sun and school hols only in winter

Château Èza €€
For a special meal, this ten-room château has a restaurant that serves superb food as well as having panoramic views looking down onto the sea some 400m (1,300ft) below. The menu is contemporary and gourmet, featuring fresh seafood, quality vegetarian options and enticing desserts. A good selection of wines is available.
187 D3 Rue de la Pise 04 93 41 12 24; www.chateaueza.com Closed 1 Nov–15 Dec

La Chèvre d'Or €€€
A wonderful view of the sea and coastline and a cosmopolitan cuisine including raw bass prepared sushi-style, tagine of chicken with lemon grass, or fillets of bream *à la plancha* can be found in this extravagant and well-renowned two Michelin-starred restaurant in the luxury Château de la Chèvre d'Or hotel.
187 D3 Moyenne Corniche, rue du Barri 04 92 10 66 66 www.chevredor.com Daily noon–2, 7–11

Le Nid d'Aigle €
This "Eagle's Nest" restaurant serves up Provençal classics in an informal setting just across from the Jardin Exotique. A great place to try the local specialities at a good price.
187 D3 1 rue du Château 04 93 41 19 08 Daily in season. Closed 9 Jan–8 Feb

GORBIO

Les Terrasses €
Provençal cuisine and local pasta dishes are on the menu at this friendly café/restaurant in lofty Gorbio.
187 E3 88 place de la République 04 93 35 95 78 Closed dinner Oct–May

MENTON

A Braijdade Meridounale €€
Set in the Old Town, this welcoming, rustic restaurant specialises in Provençal dishes and grilled meats.
187 E3 66 rue Longue
04 93 35 65 65
Closed Wed; 15 Nov–7 Dec

Cro'cantine €
A salad bar for light bites that sits between the pedestrian zone and the beach in Menton.
187 E3 3 rue Trenca 04 93 51 85 62
Closed Mon, Sun dinner only

La Martina €–€€
Antonio Ciambarella serves up cuisine from his homeland just across the border.
187 E3 11 place du Cap
04 93 57 80 22 Closed Jan and Wed

Mirazur €€€€
Talented Argentinian chef Mauro Colagreco took over this restaurant in 2006 and quickly acquired a Michelin star. The pleasing contemporary decor is matched by a 360-degree view of the sea. Increasing popularity and limited tables makes booking essential.
187 E3 Avenue Aristide Briand
04 92 41 86 86 Lunch, dinner. Closed Mon; Tue (except July–Aug), Sat–Sun lunchtime

PEILLON

Auberge de la Madone €€€€
This Michelin-starred family-run restaurant has a menu featuring Niçois classics full of flavour, with lashings of olive oil, truffles, goat's cheese, olives and mountain cheese. There are garden-fresh vegetables, pasta, game birds and veal, all accompanied by an excellent wine list. The food is matched by the wonderful view from the terrace where dinner is served.
187 D3 2 place au Village 04 93 79 91 17; www.chateauxhotels.com/madone
Closed Wed, 6 Nov–22 Dec

ROQUEBRUNE-CAP-MARTIN

Le Grand Inquisiteur €€€
These cave-like, vaulted dining rooms were once used to shelter livestock. Today they are perfect for a candle-lit dinner *à deux*.
187 E3 15 rue du Château
04 93 35 05 37 Tue–Sat dinner only, Sun lunch and dinner

La Grotte €€
"The Cave" is a popular troglodyte restaurant at the entrance to the village, with tables spilling out into the square, and a good *plat du jour* or pizza at a reasonable price.
187 E3 Place des Deux-Frères
04 93 35 00 04 Closed Wed; Oct–March closed Tue dinner

ST-JEAN-CAP-FERRAT

Capitaine Cook €€€
Just outside St-Jean, this seafood restaurant serves a range of quality shellfish. The terrace is perfect for summertime dining.
187 D2 11 avenue Jean Mermoz
04 93 76 02 66 Closed Wed; Thu lunch; 3 Nov–26 Dec

Equinoxe €€€
This restaurant enjoys a fantastic location by the harbour with a terrace right next to the sea. They only use the freshest produce.
187 D2 Bavenue Claude Vignon
04 93 76 01 01 Closed Tue and mid-Jan to mid-Feb

LA TURBIE

Hostellerie Jérôme €€€
The two Michelin-starred restaurant attached to this lovely old 15th-century house serves meals showcasing regional produce. A stylish establishment with delicious food.
181 D3 20 rue du Comte de Cessole
04 92 41 51 51; www.hostelleriejerome.com
Closed Mon–Tue except July–Aug; 6 Nov–10 Feb

VILLEFRANCHE-SUR-MER

L'Aparté €–€€

A little restaurant tucked away in an Old Town alleyway. Its menu bears various influences from all around the Mediterranean coast, sometimes in quite surprising combinations!

187 D3 1 rue Obscure 04 93 01 84 88; www.restaurant-laparte.fr Closed Mon

Les Garçons €–€€

Although it's been decorated and renamed, this eatery in a small, Old Town street with a quiet terrace still serves the same cooking. Exotic culinary combinations and good-value dishes at lunch.

187 D3 18 rue du Poilu 04 93 76 62 40 Closed Tue, Wed

La Mère Germaine €€€

One of the most popular waterfront seafood restaurants in Villefranche-sur-Mer. Menus change daily, depending on the catch.

187 D3 9 quai Amiral Courbet 04 93 01 71 39 Closed 12 Nov to 24 Dec

Where to... Shop

MARKETS

Many of the small villages along the Corniche roads hold daily or weekly markets.

Along the Corniche Inférieure, **Beaulieu-sur-Mer** has a daily fruit and vegetable market (place du Marché). Insider Tip At the same location there are clothes and household goods for sale on Saturdays. An antiques market is also held on the third Sunday of month.

Villefranche-sur-Mer holds a flea market (Jardin François Binon and avenue Amélie Pollonnais) each Sunday, and a Provençal market (Jardin François Binon and promenade de l'Octroi) every Saturday morning.

Of the Grande Corniche villages, **Roquebrune** has a daily Provençal market (place du Marché), and in mid-September holds an annual flea market. **La Turbie** has a general market every Thursday morning.

Menton has a daily food market (les Halles), with fresh meat, fruit, vegetables and cheese; a clothes market every Saturday morning (Vieux Port) and a flea market each Friday (place aux Herbes).

FOOD

Maison Herbin (2 rue Palmero, Menton; tel: 04 93 57 20 29; www.confitures-herbin.com; factory tours available at 10:30am on Mon, Wed & Fri) is one of the best destinations for food lovers in Menton. They sell hundreds of varieties of jams and conserves, preserved vegetables and candied fruits.

SPECIALITY

The 100-year-old **Coutellerie E Garnero** (8 rue St-Michel, Menton; tel: 04 93 57 03 60) specialises in the unlikely combination of knives and umbrellas. It has to be one of the most eccentric shops on the Riviera.

L'Herminette Èzasque (1 rue Principale, Èze; tel: 04 93 41 13 59, summer daily 10–7, winter 10–6), situated within the walls of Èze's old gateway, is bursting with *santons* (traditional clay figurines) and gifts and sculptures made from olive wood.

PROVENÇAL GOODS

Les Images de Provence (21 rue St-Michel, Menton; tel: 04 93 57 09 98, open daily 9–7) designs and prints its own beautiful Provençal fabrics, which it sells by the metre or transformed into finished items, from tablecloths, napkins and bed linens to other soft furnishings.

Where to... Go Out

FESTIVALS AROUND NICE

In **February,** Menton holds the Fête du Citron, a 15-day festival celebrating the area's main crop: lemons (➤ 26). The highlight is a parade of floats decorated with thousands of lemons. There are also static displays in the Jardin Biovès.

In **March**, Villefranche-sur-Mer hosts a *bataille des fleurs* – a battle of the flowers, or, less dramatically, a flower competition; you'll find others throughout the area.

April brings various religious festivals with the coming of Easter, such as the Procession of the Dead Christ (Maundy Thursday/Good Friday) in Roquebrune-Cap Martin.

May Day (Fête du Travail) on **1 May** is a public holiday in France, with festivals taking place throughout the country. Also in May, Menton holds a parade of vintage cars and a festival of Franco-Italian street theatre.

June is an excellent time to visit Gorbio and experience the Procession dai Limaça, where villagers celebrate the previous winter's olive harvest with a magical night-time procession (➤ 78). Check with the tourist office for exact dates, as the procession sometimes takes place in May. June is Gardens Month in Menton, with private and public gardens in the town open to visitors. Throughout France, the Fête de la Musique is celebrated with outdoor concerts.

July and **August** are packed with various festivals. There are numerous arts and music festivals.

In **July**, a series of musical evenings is held at Monastère de l'Annonciade in Menton, and there are music festivals and Latin dance performances in the gardens. In Roquebrune-Cap Martin, a Medieval Festival takes place at the start of the month. The Fête de St-Pierre (second Sunday in July) is celebrated in Cap d'Antibes, Villefranche-sur-Mer and Nice. Throughout the country, Bastille Day celebrations including fireworks, parties and *batailles des fleurs* are held on **14 July**.

During the Menton Music Festival in **August**, there are open-air chamber music concerts (all month), open-air theatrical evenings, and a Karting Grand Prix. Roquebrune has a Passion Procession (**5 August**), and in Peille a Fête des Blès et de la Lavande (wheat and lavender festival) is held.

The **first Sunday of September** is the Festin des Baguettes in Peille, and Menton holds plant and garden shows during the Mediterranean Days of the Garden.

Christmas markets spring up around towns during **December**. Look out for nativity displays with *santons* and the Holy Family.

OTHER ENTERTAINMENT

The **Théâtre Francis Palermo** (Palais de l'Europe, avenue Boyer; tel: 04 92 41 76 50) shows French plays, operettas and recitals.

Formal attire is required to visit the **Casino de Menton**, with its slot machines, games rooms, two bars, restaurant and club Le Brummell (2 avenue Félix Fauré; tel: 04 92 10 16 16; open 10am–3am (Fri–Sat until 4am).

Golf Club de Monte-Carlo (route du Mont Agel, La Turbie; tel: 04 92 41 50 20; open Mon 8–5, Tue–Sun 8–6), has 18 holes and views to the coast and Italian Alps.

Monaco

Little Treats

Atten-shun!

The **changing of the guard at the Palace of Monte-Carlo** takes place daily at 11:55am sharp (➤ 98).

A Zen Oasis

The **Japanese garden** (➤ 101) with its red bridges, tea house and waterfall is dedicated to the memory of Princess Grace.

Refreshments on the Roof

It's worth spending an entire day at the **Musée Océanographique** (➤ 96). Grab a bite to eat up on the sunny roof terrace.

Getting Your Bearings

Rich, chic and exclusive, Monaco is a magnet for the world's jetsetters, attracted by the lack of taxes and the world's highest incomes. Renowned for its princesses and excesses, it also boasts the world's most celebrated casino – a symbol of all that is dazzling, opulent and glamorous in Monte-Carlo.

Monaco's real crowd-puller is the Grand Prix, which takes place annually in May, when thousands of spectators flank the narrow twisting pavements of Monte-Carlo, wild in flag-waving suspense for a day of ear-splitting noise and heart-stopping speed right through the centre of town.

Even though the Grand Prix is over in a day, Monégasques live life in the fast lane all year round in

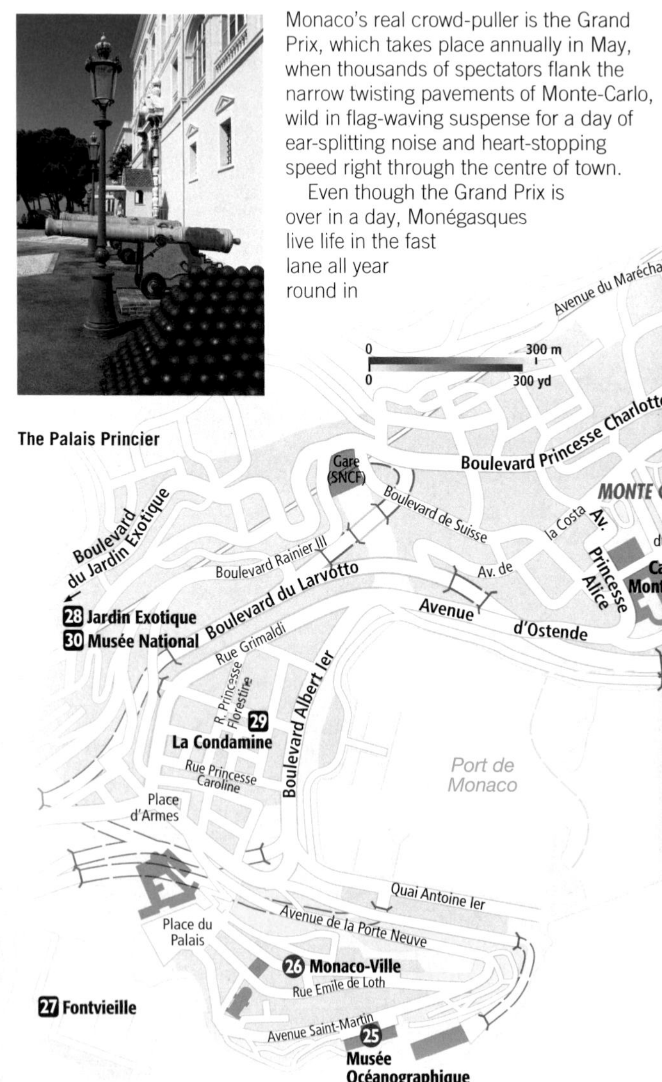

The Palais Princier

TOP 10

Don't Miss

At Your Leisure

their tiny Principality – a spotlessly clean, pint-sized strip of sky-scraper-clad land squeezed between the sea and the mountains.

Monaco is the second smallest sovereign state in the world, after the Vatican. Only 7,500 of its 35,000 residents are actually locals. The remainder are all prepared to pay extortionate real-estate prices just to be part of Monaco's über-rich community of millionaires, gamblers, "offshore" bankers and royalty. Citizenship here is the most sought after in the world and dependent on having two million euros and an apartment in the Principality. Out of countless applications, only 4,000 have been accepted in the last 15 years. These include Karl Lagerfeld, Anthony Burgess, Steffi Graf, Alain Prost and Claudia Schiffer. After all, this is the home of the rich and famous and the world's most sophisticated holiday playground.

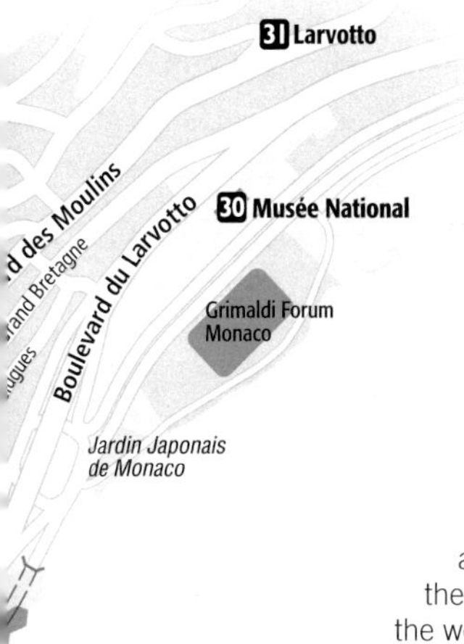

Monte-Carlo's casino

Monaco

The Perfect Day

This walking tour lets you discover the many facets of this tiny Principality, from the Old Town of Monaco-Ville and the chic museum quarter to La Condamine marina. Afterwards, change things up a gear by exploring Monte-Carlo, home to high rises, designer boutiques, restaurants, bars and the famous casino. For more information see the main entries (► 94–101).

Morning

Spend the morning exploring ㉖ **Monaco-Ville** (► 97), with its ancient narrow streets and pastel-coloured houses perched on The Rock, a sheer-sided finger of land extending 800m into the sea. At its heart, the lavish neo-Romanesque **cathedral** (► 99), funded by casino profits, contains precious 16th-century retables by Niçois artist Louis Bréa and the tomb of the much-mourned Princess Grace.

In summer, when Prince Albert II is away, guided tours of the **Palais Princier** (Prince's Palace, above; ► 97) take you through the priceless treasures of the State Apartments and the small Musée Napoléon. When he is in residence, you must content yourselves with the Changing of the Guard (daily at 11:55 am).

The elevated position of Monaco-Ville affords visitors bird's-eye views of the port quarter, ㉙ **La Condamine** (► 101), a busy commercial district wrapped around one of the Riviera's most prestigious moorings. Many of the luxury yachts moor stern-to, and give onlookers a glimpse of the high life.

Lunch

Tuck into some traditional Monégasque cuisine at **Le Castelroc** (► 104), opposite the Prince's Palace.

Afternoon

Allow a couple of hours to visit Monaco's must-see sight, the 25 **Musée Océanographique** (below; ➤ 95), one of Europe's finest aquariums and museum of marine science in the world. Formerly under the direction of ocean explorer Jacques Cousteau, it offers a dazzling collection of marine life, nautical instruments, the world's first submarine and a 20m (65.5ft) whale skeleton. The café on the second floor is a great place to stop for a coffee while taking in the panoramic view from the terrace. Then head to the chic 27 **Fontvieille** district (➤ 100), which contains specialist attractions to please all the family: the late Prince Rainier's private collection of classic cars; the Naval Museum with 180 models of famous ships; the Museum of Stamps and Coins, documenting Monaco's unique postal history; a sculpture trail and the fragrant Princess Grace Rose Garden.

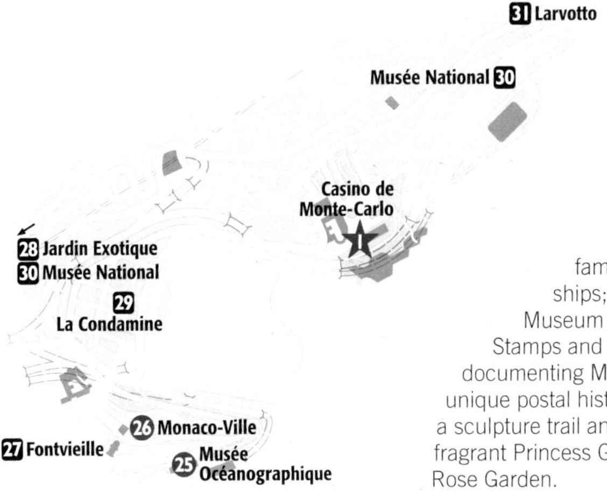

Evening

Fontvieille is considered the "Chelsea of Monaco" and there's nowhere better to celebrity-spot than on the cool terrace of the **Columbus brasserie** (➤ 102), owned by Formula One driver David Coulthard.

Later in the evening, even if you are not a gambler, it is worth visiting the ornate ★1 **Casino de Monte-Carlo** (➤ 92) to play a game or two. Then, if you have any money left, rub shoulders with the rich and famous and listen to live music at **Sass Café** (➤ 107) or **Jimmy'z** (➤ 107), arguably the most exclusive disco on the French Riviera.

Casino de Monte-Carlo

No visit to Monaco would be complete without visiting the world's most famous casino, with a façade so grand it borders on the ridiculous. The casino was for many years the chief source of income for the Principality, and today symbolises the opulence and glamour of Monte-Carlo.

The Grimaldi princes of Monaco once ruled a much larger stretch of coast and used the tax levied on Menton's olives and lemons as their main source of income. The high taxes provoked a revolt in 1848, with Menton and Roquebrune

Monte-Carlo's casino

Relaxing in the Café de Paris after a few games at the casino

claiming their independence from the Principality and causing the Grimaldis to lose 80 per cent of their land. As a result, Prince Charles III was pushed into financial crisis. In 1878 the Prince (after whom Monte-Carlo is named) opened the Casino de Monte-Carlo to save himself from bankruptcy. The scheme put 95 per cent of the casino's takings into the royal coffers, and was so successful that, five years after its opening, the Prince abolished taxation altogether, a situation still enjoyed in Monaco today. Yet gone are the days when the Monégasques could live entirely off the folly of others. Revenue from the casino has declined, so that now it is worth much more as a tourist attraction.

The splendid building was designed by Charles Garnier, architect of the Paris Opéra. Known in its heyday as the "Cathedral of Hell", its lavish *belle-époque* interior is a riot of pink, green and gold, with marble floors, bronze sculptures, onyx columns and highly ornate ceilings, lit by crystal chandeliers. To the left of the casino is the **Café de Paris** and the casino's **Salons Américains** gaming room. You must be 18 to enter this clattering room stuffed with poker and slot machines, but there is no admission charge.

Insider Tip You can stroll around the casino gardens, admire the array of lavish cars parked outside the entrance and view the ostentatious entrance hall of the casino proper without paying, but you will be charged a fee to enter the more serious gaming rooms. This is where bronzed, bejewelled gamblers come from all over the world to try their luck at the gaming tables. Ten euros will gain you entry into the

Salons Européens, a mini-Vegas beneath gilded rococo ceilings where you'll find roulette, craps and blackjack tables. A further 10 euros and suitable attire is required to enter the exclusive **Salons Privés**, where the décor is even more extravagant and inordinate sums are staked on the roulette and *chemin de fer* tables. Few tourists enter this part of the casino; cameras are not allowed and business is serious as the croupiers silently slide chips to poker-faced players. If you enter this far into the casino, don't miss the **Pink Salon Bar**, famed both for its ceiling depicting female nudes smoking cigars, and the fact that in 1891 Charles Deville Wells turned $400 into $40,000 in a three-day gambling spree, inspiring the song *The Man Who Broke the Bank at Monte-Carlo.*

The casino building also houses the ornate **Salle Garnier opera house**, which takes its name from the famed architect. The casino is flanked on either side by the swanky **Café de Paris**, and the **Hôtel de Paris**, home of decadent dining room Louis XV (➤ 104). Around the casino, a golden circle of designer boutiques and jewellers make great shopping should you have winnings to blow.

TAKING A BREAK

Take in the atmosphere with a drink on the terrace of the **Café de Paris** (➤ 107).

---

187 E3

Tourist Offices
2A boulevard des Moulins
377 92 16 61 16
Mon–Sat 9–7, Sun 10–12. Additional tourist information kiosks are set up at the railway station and the main attractions in summer

Casino de Monte-Carlo
Place du Casino
377 92 16 20 00; www.casino-monte-carlo.com
€10

INSIDER INFO

- You must be **18** to enter the casino, and have suitable identification, such as a **passport**.
- The casino follows a **strict dress code,** and if you intend to enter the casino proper, it is a good idea for men to wear a jacket and tie. Shorts and T-shirts are frowned upon, and a jacket and tie are required to enter the private rooms in the evening. Uniforms of any kind are not allowed.
- Monégasque citizens and members of the clergy are **not allowed to gamble**.
- Credit cards are **not** accepted.
- 

Just around the corner, **Sun Casino** has slot machines open from 11am, table games from 5pm, and free entry (Fairmont Monte-Carlo; tel: 377 92 16 21 23; www.casino-monte-carlo.com).

25 Musée Océanographique

Perched on a sheer cliff high above the Mediterranean, this museum of marine science, with its spectacular aquarium, is the finest of its kind, and a highlight of Monaco.

Explore the dazzling underwater world at the Musée Océanographique

The prestigious museum was founded in 1910 by Prince Albert I, who was a keen oceanographer, as an institute for scientific research and to house the many marine specimens he collected on his voyages. Financed by profits from the casino, it took 11 years and 100,000 tonnes of white stone from La Turbie (➤ 74) to build. The resulting structure, with its staggering 85m (279ft) façade that plunges straight into the sea, is a masterpiece of monumental architecture.

The museum is built over several floors, and its main drawcard is the **aquarium** in the basement, which exhibits thousands of rare fish with beautifully lit displays of living corals from all over the world. The largest fish are behind a thick glass panel to the left of the entrance, connected to the part of the reef exposed to the open sea. There are 2,000 specimens of fish belonging to more than 250 species including 11 species of sharks and rays.

Other tanks contain an array of sea life, including delicate jellyfish, Caribbean moray eels and their friend the small cleaning shrimp, sinister black lantern-eye fish (nicknamed "demons of the night") and many cunningly camouflaged marine chameleons, such as the wide-eyed flounder.

The first floor contains some exceptional **collections** of nautical instruments and marine flora and fauna. These include the skeleton of a 20m (65.5ft) whale complete with its baleens for filtering krill, the **laboratory** installed in Prince Albert's last boat, *Hirondelle II*, and the world's first submarine – pedal-powered – was built in 1774 and used against English ships during the American War of Independence. Displays demonstrate the natural phenomena of waves, tides, currents and salinity.

The ground level has **models** of all the magnificent ships built for the sovereign's voyages, and a **cinema** where films made by marine explorer Jacques Cousteau, who directed the research centre here until 1988, are regularly screened.

TAKING A BREAK

The **café, La Terrasse,** on the second floor of the museum is open for most of the year. Close by, in the old quarter, try **Da Sergio** (place de la Mairie; tel: 04 91 16 53 64) for cheap pizzas and an espresso.

187 E3
Avenue St-Martin 377 93 15 36 00; www.oceano.mc
Jul–Aug daily 9:30–7:30; April–June, Sep 9:30–7; Oct–March 10–6. Closed during the Grand Prix
€14, kids aged 4–12: €7; young people aged 13 to 18 and students: €10

A giant octopus watches over the entrance hall of the Musée Océanographique

INSIDER INFO

- An **English-language guide** to the museum is available for €8, but the aquarium also has information panels in several languages, including English. The displays on the first floor are mostly in French.
- Insider Tip On the second floor of the museum is a café and **terrace with panoramic views** stretching over the Principality, mountains and out to sea. An information panel points out landmarks and places of interest in the area.

26 Monaco-Ville

Monaco is today made up of several districts, although it started out, like many other Provençal hilltop villages, on top of a rock. The original town was Monaco-Ville, consisting of the palace and the Old Town. They cling on to The Rock (Le Rocher), which juts 800m out into the Mediterranean with a sheer drop of 300m (984ft) into the sea below.

The Renaissance-style facade of the Prince's Palace, home to the royal Grimaldi family

Palais Princier

The Prince's Palace stands solidly at the western end of The Rock. The current palace was constructed over the bones of an original stronghold, built in the 13th century by the Genoese. Disguised as a Franciscan monk, François Grimaldi penetrated this stronghold and took control of Monaco in 1297. The current prince, Albert II, is his direct descendent, continuing the dynasty of the oldest ruling family in Europe.

FRANÇOIS GRIMALDI

Monaco was founded in 1215 as a colony of Genoa. The Genoese built a fortress atop the strategically important Rock, but it was seized in 1297 by François Grimaldi who, disguised as a monk in need of shelter, was admitted into the fortress together with his men, also in disguise. Once inside, they killed the guards and took control of the garrison. Despite seizing power in 1297, there was a 300-year struggle for The Rock, during which time Monaco was captured and recaptured by several parties, before the Grimaldis gained permanent possession and established themselves as princes of Monaco in the 17th century. Above the entrance to the palace is the Grimaldi family crest with its two sword-bearing monks. A statue of François Grimaldi, dressed as a monk with a sword hidden beneath his cloak, also stands in front of the palace.

The elegant palace seen today dates from the 17th century. Standing guard in front of the palace is the immaculately preened Prince's Guard, armed with rifles and flanked by gun carriages set to protect the princely seat from anyone with any more smart monk-disguise ideas. The ten minute

Insider Tip **Changing of the Guard** takes place every morning at 11:55am. When Prince Albert is in residence, the royal colours are flown from the tower.

From June to October visitors can take **audio-guided tours** through the palace. The tour covers the Court of Honour, the Hercules Gallery (decorated with 17th-century frescoes), the Throne Room, and the plush State Apartments filled with priceless treasures. The small **Musée Napoléon** in the south wing of the palace contains a collection of Napoléon Bonaparte's personal items, including some of his socks and one of his hats.

Old Quarter

A large proportion of Monaco-Ville is taken up by the palace and its surrounding gardens and plaza. The rest of The Rock is covered by the Old Town, which often draws toy-town comparisons. It's an immaculately kept labyrinth of cool,

A labyrinth of narrow streets: the Old Town of Monaco-Ville

The formidable fortifications of the palace

cobbled streets, with lovely fountain-filled squares and fine Italianate façades, although, inevitably, the shops around the royal palace sell the usual tacky souvenirs.

In rue Colonel Bellando de Castro, at the heart of the Old Town, is Monaco's neo-Romanesque **Cathédrale St-Nicholas**, where Rainer III is buried next to the much-loved Princess Grace (1929–82), whose grave is often covered in flowers. The stone used to construct the cathedral was taken from La Turbie. It's not an especially attractive cathedral, but along with the tombs of Princess Grace and Rainer III, it houses a Louis Bréa altarpiece and the tombs of the other Grimaldi princes. Other things to see in the Old Town include the often-overlooked **Musée de la Chapelle de la Visitation**, housing religious art by Ribera, Rubens and other Italian baroque artists; **St-Martin Gardens**, offering stunning sea views; and the outstanding **Musée Océanographique** (➤ 85).

---

187 E3

Tourist Office
2a boulevard des Moulins 377 92 16 61 66; www.monaco-tourisme.com
Mon–Sat 9–7, Sun 10–12

Palais Princier
Place du Palais 377 93 25 18 31; www.palais.mc
April to late Oct daily 10–6 1, 2 Entry by guided tour only, €8

Musée Napoléon
April to late Oct daily 10–6 €4

INSIDER INFO

- Monaco-Ville is closed to visitors' vehicles, but can be reached by a long, steep **walkway** from place d'Armes, or by **elevator** from parking des Pêcheurs on the seafront at the bottom of The Rock. There are several **free** public lifts and escalators in Monaco, all of which are marked on a free map available at the tourist office.
- If you're in town in summer, look out for the **open-air cinema** showing original-language films every night on Europe's largest screen at the Terraces du Parking-des-Pecheurs (end June to early September; tel: 377 95 25 86 60).
- Unless you are into motor racing, don't come to Monaco during the **Grand Prix** in May, when thousands of visitors cram into the Principality and many roads are closed.

At Your Leisure

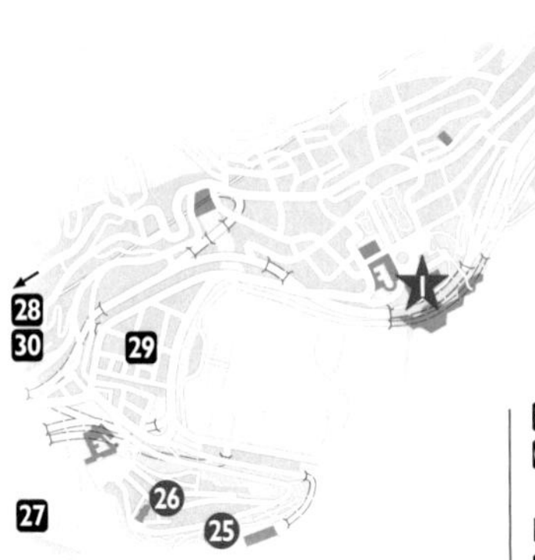

27 Fontvieille

This zone of modern residential and commercial development, built on reclaimed land below The Rock of Monaco-Ville, has a yacht harbour, sports stadium, shops, numerous museums, and a **zoo (Jardin Animalier)** where tropical animals are acclimatised to the European environment.

Stroll along the **sculpture trail**, a path lined with modern sculptures that winds its way up from the place du Campanile St-Nicholas towards the **Roseraie Princesse Grace**. This garden is dedicated to the former Hollywood actress and wife of Princc Rainer III, who died in a car accident on the Moyenne Corniche in 1982. The garden, in avenue des Papalins, is a peaceful oasis, fragrant with the scent of 4,000 rose bushes.

The museums in Fontvieille include the **Musée des Timbres et des Monnaies**, a stamp and coin gallery; the **Musée Naval,** with hundreds of models of famous ships; and the **Collection des Voitures Anciennes**, a collection of gleaming, historic motor vehicles.

187 E3

Jardin Animalier
Terrasses de Fontvieille
377 93 25 18 31
Jun–Sep daily 9–noon, 2–7; March–May 10–noon, 2–6; Oct–Feb 10–noon, 2–5
€5; children: €3

Musée des Timbres et des Monnaies
Terrasses de Fontvieille 377 93 15 41 50
Daily Jul–Sep 10–6; Oct–June 10–5 €3

Musée Naval
Terrasses de Fontvieille
377 92 05 28 48; www.musee-naval.mc
Daily 10–6 5, 6 €4

Collection des Voitures
Terrasses de Fontvieille
377 92 05 28 56; www.palais.mc
Daily 10–6. Closed 25 Dec 5, 6 €6

28 Jardin Exotique

In a lofty location above Fontvieille, just off the Moyenne Corniche (N7), lies the Jardin Exotique (below). It contains several thousand cacti and succulents of vivid colours and amazing shapes, some nearly 10m (30ft) high.

The ticket price includes a tour of the **Grottes de l'Observatoire**, caves which were inhabited in the Palaeolithic era. Entrance to the **Musée d'Anthropologie Préhistorique** is also included. It

Jardin Exotique, Monaco

FUN FOR KIDS: A CIRCUS, A ZOO AND FAMOUS FOOTBALLERS' FOOTPRINTS

- Fontvieille has several attractions for kids, including a **zoo** and various hobby museums along the Terrasses de Fontvieille (➤ 100).
- **The footprints of such famous footballers as Zidane, Drogba** and **Ibrahimović** line the Promenade Grace Kelly from the Grimaldi Forum to Larvotto beach.
- The aquarium in the **Musée Océanographique** (➤ 95) is fascinating for kids
- The **Monte-Carlo International Circus Festival** is held annually at the end of January (➤ 108).
- There is a **diving pool** on quai Albert 1er at Port Hercule, a great place to cool off in summer; in winter, it is converted into an **ice-skating rink**.

has a display of prehistoric mammoth bones and some early human artefacts.

187 E3 62 boulevard du Jardin-Exotique 377 93 15 29 80 Mid-May to mid-Sep daily 9–7; mid-Sep to mid-May 9–6 or nightfall 2 €7

29 La Condamine

In medieval times La Condamine referred to cultivable land at the foot of a village or a castle. Today this area, at the foot of the royal palace, is a busy shopping area around the port of Monaco, and the starting point of the Formula 1 Grand Prix. **Rue Grimaldi** is the main shopping street, where there are everyday food stores. Monaco's food market has been taking place in **place d'Armes** daily since 1880. This area also has the **railway station**, some reasonably priced hotels and bars where the old locals still speak Monégasque. Strolling along the harbour you'll find some casual restaurants, and views of the extravagant yachts moored in Monaco port.

187 E3 1, 2, 4, 5, 6

Daily excursions around The Rock June to mid-Sep at 11, 2:30 and 4, from quai des États-Unis, Port d'Hercule; tel: 377 92 16 15 15

30 Musée National

Monaco's National Museum is housed in two villas dating from the early 19th century. They're home to the Principality's various collections and are frequently used to stage thematic exhibitions.

187 E3

Villa Sauber

17 avenue Princesse-Grace

377 93 30 91 26

Daily 10–6; June–Sep 11–7 €6

Villa Paloma

56 boulevard du Jardin Exotique

377 98 98 48 60

Daily 10–6; June–Sep 11–7 €6

31 Larvotto

What Monaco lacks naturally, it creates artificially. Rainer III was responsible for extending Monaco by a fifth of its size, reclaiming land to create Fontvieille, and constructing man-made beaches and swimming facilities here at Larvotto on the other side of the French border. Larvotto is also home to **Le Sporting Club**, an exclusive 6ha (15-acre) seafront area with casinos where lavish concerts are held in the summer.

Near Larvotto beach, in stark contrast to the glitz of Monte-Carlo, is the peaceful **Jardin Japonais**, an authentic Shinto garden with bubbling ponds, waterfalls and a wooden tea house. Insider Tip

The **Grimaldi Forum** is a large convention centre where temporary exhibitions are held. On the top floor of the forum is the sophisticated restaurant, Zelo's (➤ 107).

187 E3

Le Sporting Club

Avenue Princesse Grace

377 92 16 20 20

Where to... Stay

Prices
Expect to pay per double room, per night:
€ under €80 **€€** €80–€150 **€€€** over €150

Hôtel Ambassador €€–€€€
This small hotel not far from the station is one of the cheaper places to stay in the Principality. There's a Pop Art pizzeria on the ground floor.
187 E3 10 avenue Prince Pierre 377 97 97 96 96; www.ambassadormonaco.com

Columbus €€€€
While the rest of Monaco is trying to capture the glory of its *belle-époque* heyday, this chic designer hotel steps away from the old razzmatazz and into the 21st century, offering all the luxury and none of the fuss. Neutral tones and contemporary design give this hotel a simple and relaxed feel. It also has a stylish modern brasserie.
187 E3 123 avenue des Papalins, Fontvieille 377 92 05 90 00; www.columbushotels.com

Hôtel de France €€
Hôtel de France is one of the few affordable hotels in the Principality. Near the train station in La Condamine, this bright little hotel is cheerful and welcoming, with comfortable rooms, some of which have balconies.
187 E3 6 rue de La Turbie, Monte-Carlo 377 93 30 24 64; www.monte-carlo.mc/france

Fairmont €€€
A modern hotel with around 600 rooms and suites right next to the sea. Boasts several restaurants and every creature comfort.
187 E3 12 avenue des Spélugues 377 93 50 65 00; www.fairmont.de/monte-carlo

Hôtel Hermitage €€€€
You need a princely sum to stay at this luxury *belle-époque* palace in the heart of Monte-Carlo, overlooking the Mediterranean. It features a spectacular Winter Garden where you can breakfast under a stained-glass dome designed by Gustav Eiffel. Its lavish pink and gold restaurant, Le Vistamar, has panoramic views and serves fabulous seafood. There is direct access to Les Thèrmes Marins de Monaco Spa and Health Resort, and a helicopter shuttle service between Monaco and Nice airports.
187 E3 Square Beaumarchais, Monte-Carlo 377 98 06 25 25; www.hotelhermitagemontecarlo.com

Hôtel Metropole €€€
The timeless elegance and luxury of this 19th-century palace has had a designer make-over. Outside you'll find an Italianate courtyard and a pretty pool. The magnificent spa and the rooms inside combine to form a temple to luxury and gracious living. Joël Robuchon's two Michelin-starred restaurant is also here (► 104).
187 E3 7 avenue J F Kennedy 377 97 97 90 00; www.portpalace.com

Miramar €€€
Most of the eleven rooms at this small hotel by Port Hercule boast beautiful views of the marina right in the middle of the Principality.
187 E3
1 avenue John Fitzgerald Kennedy
377 93 30 86 48; www.miramarmonaco.com

Hôtel Olympia €€–€€€

On the border of Monaco and Beausoleil, but only minutes from the casino, this attractive and very reasonable little hotel has 31 rooms. They are well maintained and tastefully decorated and the staff are both friendly and helpful. No restaurant.

187 E3 ✉ 17 bis Général Leclerc, Beausoleil ☎ 04 93 78 12 70; www.olympiahotel.fr

Hôtel de Paris €€€

Monte-Carlo's first and most famous hotel, full of showy *belle époque* features, marble colonnades and crystal chandeliers. The Hôtel de Paris opened in 1865 to provide the kind of accommodation fit for visiting tsars, royalty and aristocrats, and today guests staying at Monte-Carlo's most prestigious address still enjoy an extreme level of luxury and exclusivity. It houses three restaurants, including the gastronomically élite Louis XV (► 104), and offers direct access to the fashionable Thèrmes Marins spa resort, as well as every other possible luxury.

187 E3 ✉ Place du Casino, Monte-Carlo ☎ 377 98 06 30 00; www.hoteldeparismontecarlo.com

Hôtel Le Versailles €€

Conveniently situated between the station and The Rock, and just a few minutes' walk away from Monte-Carlo, this two-star hotel has reasonably priced rooms with all the basics, as well as a decent restaurant.

187 E3 ✉ 4–6 avenue Prince-Pierre, La Condamine ☎ 377 93 50 79 34; www.monte-carlo.mc/versailles

Where to...
Eat and Drink

Prices
Expect to pay per person for a three-course meal, excluding drinks:
€ under €25 **€€** €25–€60 **€€€** over €60

Dining in Monaco can be a truly glamorous affair, as it boasts no fewer than eight Michelin stars, but eating economically is not out of the question. Being so close to the Italian border, pasta and pizza are good, inexpensive options.

Le Bambi €

Give your wallet a rest at this friendly eatery in La Condamine, one of several in the area that serves good-value Italian food. The dish of the day is particularly economical.

187 E3 ✉ 11 rue Princesse-Antoinette, La Condamine ☎ 377 93 30 35 06 ⏲ Sun–Fri 11–3, 6–11

Café Llorca €–€€

As well as his gourmet restaurant in La Colle-sur-Loup near Nice, famous Michelin-starred Chef Alain Llorca has opened a bistro on the first floor of the Grimaldi Forum with beautiful views of the sea. Serves simple lunches at relatively low prices (for Monaco!)

187 E3 ✉ avenue Princesse-Grace ☎ 377 99 99 29 29; www.cafellorca.mc ⏲ July–Sep 10–6; Mon–Fri 9–5 rest of year

Le Castelroc €€

A crowded and popular lunch spot opposite the royal palace that has been run by the same family for more than 50 years. Serving

exceptional Monégasque cuisine, the menu includes some wonderful seafood, such as *stocafi* (stockfish) cooked with garlic, wine, tomatoes and olives.
187 E3 Place du Palais, Monaco-Ville
377 93 30 36 68 Closed Sat and Jan

U Cavagnetu €€
A friendly restaurant that's one of the few value-for-money eateries serving typical Monégasque cooking in the Principality. Diners can choose to sit inside or out on the terrace.
187 E3 14 rue Comte Felix Gastaldi
377 93 30 35 80 Daily 12:15–2, 7:30–9:30 (Nov–Murch lunch only)

Joël Robuchon Monte-Carlo €€€
Big-name chef Joël Robuchon's simple food philosophy, that food should taste like what it is, is quite refreshing in this land of excess, and his restaurant here presents dishes with no more than three flavours on one plate, allowing you to fully enjoy the taste of every ingredient. This seemingly simple theory works well within the restaurant's elegant, but not overly excessive, surroundings.
187 E3 Hôtel Métropole, 4 avenue de la Madone, Monte-Carlo
377 93 15 15 15 Closed Wed

Loga €–€€
Mediterranean cuisine with simple, reasonably priced lunches and fancy set menus in the evening.
187 E3 25 boulevard des Moulins
377 93 30 87 72
Closed Sun and Wed dinner

Le Louis XV €€€
A gastronomic shrine run by celebrated chef Alain Ducasse with a very highly regarded three Michelin stars. Set within the majestic Hôtel de Paris, dining here is the height of hedonistic luxury. The (hugely expensive) Mediterranean-inspired menu changes seasonally, with food served in a dining room that transports you to 17th-century Versailles. Book well ahead.
187 E3 Hôtel de Paris, place du Casino, Monte-Carlo
377 98 06 88 64; www.alain-ducasse.com
Thu–Mon noon–2, 7:30–9:30 (also Wed dinner July–Aug). Closed Dec, 2 Feb–11 March

La Maison du Caviar €€
This simple yet smart restaurant serves copious quantities of caviar, blinis, salmon and vodka – redolent of the days of the Tsar.
187 E3
1 avenue St-Charles, Monte-Carlo
377 93 30 80 06
Closed Sat lunch, Sun and July

Maya Bay €€–€€€
A Buddha statue keeps a watchful eye in this stylish Asian/Japanese modern restaurant, adorned with oriental wood, kimonos and bonsai trees. Service is good and attentive and the cuisine is fusion style.
187 E3 Avenue Princesse Grace
377 97 70 74 67 Closed Sun, Mon; Nov

Pasta Roca €–€€
A small Italian eatery complete with a terrace in Monaco's Old Town. Serves a selection of simple meals, decent pizzas and salads at relatively low prices.
187 E3 23 rue Comte Félix Gastaldi
377 93 30 44 22 Closed Wed

Polpetta €€
Hidden away from the clamour of central Monte-Carlo, this Italian restaurant nonetheless attracts jetsetters and celebrities for a taste of *la dolce vita*. A rustic *trattoria* serving up wonderful antipasto, homemade pasta, seafood risotto and veal. Extensive Italian wine list.
187 E3 2 rue Paradis
377 93 50 67 84
Closed Tue; 10–30 June

Quai des Artistes €€–€€€
A contemporary Parisian-style brasserie down by the port with a reasonably priced menu that

includes dishes such as a splendid *assiettes de fruits de mer*. For *al fresco* dining there is a good-sized terrace where you can sit out in the sunshine and enjoy your meal.
187 E3 4 quai Antoine 1er, La Condamine
377 97 97 97 77; www.quaidesartistes.com
Closed 24 Dec, 31 Dec

Le Saint Benoit €€

The panoramic views from the main terrace over the marina are quite stunning and perfectly complemented by an airy and spacious dining room. The very modern décor makes a refreshing change from the ubiquitous rustic style. The menu specialises in fish and seafood.
187 E3 10 ter av. Costa
377 93 25 02 34
Closed Sun dinner; 21 Dec–7 Jan

Stars'N'Bars €

For families looking for somewhere less formal to take the kids, this popular, American-style bar-restaurant serves burgers, wedges and Tex-Mex food, has games to keep kids occupied and is open for most of the day. Sporting memorabilia lines the walls, and there's an excellent view over the port from the terrace. If you need to go online there's also an internet café, and a disco in the evenings.
187 E3 6 quai Antoine Ier, La Condamine
377 97 97 95 95; www.starsnbars.com
Daily; closed Mon in winter.
Food served 11:30am–midnight

Where to... Shop

For a full guide to the shops and restaurants in Monaco, pick up the Monaco Shopping Guide available at the tourist office (2a boulevard des Moulins; tel: 377 92 16 61 16; www.monaco-tourisme.com).

FASHION & JEWELLERY

Monaco has a reputation for high fashion, jewellery and boutique shopping, and if this is what you are looking for, you won't be disappointed by the strip of designer shops known as the "golden circle" around the Casino and Hôtel de Paris.

Along **avenue de Monte-Carlo**, big names Gucci, Valentino, Hermès, Lalique and Prada strut their stuff. On the other side of the Hôtel de Paris, **avenue des Beaux-Arts** sparkles with Cartier, Céline, Bulgari, Louis Vuitton, Yves Saint Laurent, Piaget and Dior.

Inside the **Hôtel Hermitage** on place Beaumarchais is an array of elegant shops, including the exclusive Italian label Prada, and Salvatore Ferragamo, a label made famous by its trademark Italian shoes, but also encompassing a full range of couture for men and women.

After debuting her first haute couture store in London, **Isabell Kristensen**, the Danish fashion designer, opened a second boutique in Monaco (18 rue Princesse Marie de Lorraine; tel: 377 97 70 41 94). She's mainly lived in the Principality since 2000, and enjoys excellent relationships with the royal family.

Swedish fashionista **Helen Rimsberg** has three boutiques (one for casual wear at 2 rue des Orangers, and two in the rue Princesse Florentine – one for evening dresses and one for shoes and bags; tel: 377 93 25 82 26). They all sell second-hand wares from such top brands as Chanel, Hermès, Gucci, Prada and Dior. Check them out for some fabulous deals.

Boutiques also stretch along the **avenue Princesse-Grace**, and on the boulevard des Moulins towards Larvotto.

For designer labels at discounted prices, look in **Stock Griffe** (5 bis, avenue St-Michel; tel: 377 93 50 86 06).

The **Galeries du Métropole** in the heart of Monte-Carlo (below the Métropole hotel, avenue de la Madone, Mon–Sat 10–7:30) has it all under one roof, keeping shoppers in an extravagant mood by flaunting *belle-époque* décor such as marble alleys and glass chandeliers. You can find just about anything here – it has three levels of shopping with 80 boutiques specialising in fashion, beauty, household goods and leisure equipment.

SPECIALITY

Also within the Centre Commercial le Métropole is the big French store **FNAC**, selling books (some in English), CDs and electronic goodies. You can order tickets for theatre, opera and concert performances here (Centre Commercial le Métropole; tel: 377 93 10 81 81).

Manufacture de Monaco (Centre Commercial le Métropole, 4 rue de la Madon; tel: 377 93 50 64 63) is a small, exclusive shop which supplies Monaco's royal family with traditional Monégasque porcelain, silverware, crystal and table linen.

In **La Condamine** you'll find shops at the more affordable end of the scale. **Marie Dentelle** (10 rue Princesse-Caroline; tel: 377 93 30 43 40) is an Aladdin's cave of feminine gift ideas, brightly coloured local pottery, and beautiful bed linen, including quilts made in traditional Provençal material.

The more affordable **rue Grimaldi** in La Condamine is the shopping street for real Monégasques and Formula 1 fans. A plethora of sporting paraphernalia from Porsche and Ferrari can be found at the **AS Monaco Football Store** (16 rue Grimaldi; tel: 377 97 77 74 74), a boutique dedicated to the local team that spent €170 million on international talent after being promoted to France's top league in 2013 in the hope of recapturing their winning form of the past.

As ever, **stamps from the Principality** make popular souvenirs. You'll find them at the museum in the district of Fontvieille (► 100) or at the local post offices.

FOOD & DRINK

Les Caves du Grand Échanson (7 rue de la Colle; tel: 377 92 05 61 01) supply exclusive wines and spirits to the royal family.

L'Oenothèque (Sporting Club d'Hiver, 2 avenue Princesse Alice; tel: 377 93 25 82 66) is an old wood-panelled oenothèque, the largest in Europe, which stocks over 100,000 bottles of fine cognacs, armagnacs and French wines.

For more ordinary shopping, the bakeries and flower shops along **rue Princesse Caroline** in La Condamine are refreshingly modest. The **Fontvieille Centre Commercial** is a large mall and supermarket where Monégasques make their everyday purchases.

MARKETS

For a real taste of Monaco, the daily vegetable, flower and fruit market takes place at the **place des Armes**, in La Condamine, with both indoor and outdoor markets from 9–12. The place des Armes is an attractive spot, with cafés and an old fountain. At Port de Fontvieille there is a flea market at Espace Fontvieille, from 9 to 5 on Saturdays.

There is also a daily fruit and vegetable market in nearby **rue du Marché**, Beausoleil, just minutes' walk from the casino. In the same street, the bakery **Moulin de Païou** (tel: 04 93 78 48) sells wonderful fresh croissants and pastries.

Where to... Go Out

Visit the tourist office to pick up an in-depth guide to the nightlife and entertainment in Monaco, with up-to-date listings for what's on and when.

NIGHTLIFE

The **Café de Paris** (place du Casino; tel: 377 98 06 76 23; www.montecarlosbm.com/restaurants-in-monaco/brasseries/, from 8am), famed brasserie of the Hôtel de Paris, has an outdoor terrace in a prime position for people-watching. It's popular with those looking to experience the high life, and its glamorous reputation seems enough to compensate for the expense. English king Edward VII was a frequent visitor here, and the delicious flambéed dessert *crêpe suzette* was created here, named after one of his companions. As well as serving food, the café has a gaming room with slot-machines to rival those in the casino.

A night out in Monaco would not be complete without a visit to **Casino de Monte-Carlo** (place du Casino; tel: 377 92 16 20 00; www.casino-monte-carlo.com, open noon–dawn). This fabulous *belle époque* casino is a famous haunt of the rich and famous. Dress to impress – and men are required to wear jacket and tie to enter the private rooms in the evening. You must be over 18, and bring your passport to enter (➤ 92).

In order to party with the jet set, head to **Jimmy'z** (Le Sporting Club, avenue Princesse Grace; tel: 377 92 16 22 77, May–Oct 11pm–5am; Nov–April Wed–Sun 11:30pm–5am). You'll have to pass the highly selective entry process, so dress as if you're famous, look beautiful and be prepared to pay an extortionate amount of money for your drinks. It's a half-indoors, half-outdoors affair, with a Cuban cigar room, a glass-tiled dance floor, and a Japanese garden.

The **Living Room** (7 avenue des Spélugues; tel: 377 93 50 80 31, open Mon–Sat 11 pm–6 am) is a hip club in the centre of Monte-Carlo, with a mix of dance music and live music. Beware the fashion police on the doors, and expect the drinks to be pricey.

Sass Café is a small but fabulous address that's popular with celebs (11 avenue Princesse Grace; tel: 377 93 25 52 10; www.sasscafé.com). It boasts a restaurant and live music every evening from 11.

The terrace of **Zelo's** (10 avenue Princesse Grace; tel: 377 99 99 25 50) on the top floor of the Grimaldi forum, with panoramic views over the yacht-filled harbour, is one of the best places in Monaco to enjoy an evening cocktail. This hip restaurant-bar serves good food, but is also perfect for a glamorous pre-dinner drink or a tipple in the small hours. The low lighting, relaxed lounge atmosphere and terrace with a view make it a good night spot.

CINEMA

Le Sporting (Galerie du Sporting d'Hiver, place du Casino; tel: 377 93 25 36 81; www.cinema2monaco.com, open daily 2–9) in the centre of Monte-Carlo is Monaco's main cinema complex. Set inside an arcade of smart shops, they show some films in their original languages. They also have open-air screenings on the Terrasses du Parking des Pêcheurs in summer.

MUSIC

Salle Garnier, Monaco's opera house (Opéra de Monte-Carlo, place du Casino; tel: 377 92 16 22 99; www.opera.mc) has played host to many great artists over the years, and stages new productions annually, with orchestral music performed by the Philharmonic Orchestra of Monte-Carlo. The seating capacity is only 524 and seats are regularly sold out so advance booking is necessary. Details of coming events can be found on the website (in French).

La Salle des Étoiles (Le Sporting, avenue Princesse Grace; tel: 377 98 06 36 36; www.sportingmontecarlo.com, end June–early Sep only from 8pm) is a concert hall in a majestic setting that welcomes big international stars to its stage. Enjoy cocktails on the terrace before a show, and bear in mind that the dress code is evening wear and requires men to wear a dinner jacket.

HEALTH & BEAUTY

While many of the beaches in Monaco charge a fee, a swim at **Plage du Larvotto** (avenue Princesse Grace) is free. There are paying sections, and it's patrolled by lifeguards during the high season.

The **Country Club de Monte-Carlo** (155 avenue Princesse Grace, Roquebrune; tel: 04 93 41 72 00; www.mccc.mc, daily 8am–8:30pm) is the site of the ATP Masters Tennis Championship, with 23 clay courts and two hard courts, all of which are open year-round and have wonderful views over the Mediterranean. There's also a pool, a fitness centre with physiotherapists, a sauna and a Jacuzzi. Day passes can be purchased by non-members.

Float away at the **Thermes Marins de Monte-Carlo** (2 avenue Monte-Carlo; tel: 377 98 06 69 00; www.thermesmarinsmontecarlo.com, daily 8–8). This blissful spa overlooking the sea is renowned for thalassotherapy. It has a complex of pools, heated sea-baths and *hammams* (Turkish baths), as well classic spa treatments, solariums, massages with essential oils, and the latest in marine therapy.

FESTIVALS & SPORTING EVENTS

Ste Dévote, patron saint of Monaco, was martyred in Corsica, and her body was placed in a boat bound for Africa. Legend has it that a dove that flew out of her mouth led the boat towards Monaco. On the site where the boat ran aground, the Église Ste-Devote stands today. Her feast day is celebrated on **27 January** with a national holiday. Mass is celebrated in Monégasque, and in the evening there is a procession and symbolic boat-burning in front of the church.

Also held in the last week of **January** is the Monte-Carlo Rally: a three-day event testing the driving skills of competitors as they race along the icy roads outside Monaco. For information, contact the Automobile Club de Monaco (23 boulevard Albert Ier; tel: 377 93 15 26 00; www.acm.mc).

The circus comes to town end **January/early February** each year for the Festival International du Cirque (espace Fontvieille, avenue des Ligures; tel: 377 92 05 23 45; www.montecarlofestivals.com). Circus performers from around the world strut their stuff, with the best acts invited to perform again on the closing night.

In **April** you'll find some of the world's top tennis players in Monaco for the ATP masters tennis championship (Country Club de Monte-Carlo, 155 avenue Princesse Grace, Roquebrune; tel: 04 93 41 30 15; www.mccc.mc).

Monte-Carlo's most famous event is in **May**, when the Grand Prix transforms the Principality into a race track (Automobile Club de Monaco, 23 boulevard Albert Ier; tel: 377 93 15 26 00; www.acmmc).

Throughout **August,** an International Fireworks Festival takes place in Monaco.

In and Around Cannes

Handprints

Look for the handprints from the likes of Brad Pitt and Catherine Deneuve on the **Allée des Stars in Cannes** (➤ 117).

Wine from the Abbey

Have a taste (or three!) of the wines and liqueurs made by the Cistercian monks at the **Abbaye des Lérins** (➤ 119).

Red Rocks

Drive from Saint-Raphaël to Théoule-sur-Mer to admire the red porphyry rocks of the **Corniche de l'Esterel** (➤ 122).

Getting Your Bearings

There's no denying Cannes is one of the world's most sophisticated resorts – the "Queen of the Coast" and "Pearl of the Riviera" – with its grand *belle époque* hotels, designer boutiques and palm-lined promenade framing a voluptuous sandy bay. Little wonder this elegant town is twinned with Beverly Hills. Best known for the glitz and glamour of its annual International Film Festival, behind its glamorous façade the Old Town, Le Suquet, oozes character, with its maze of medieval buildings and ancient fishing harbour.

The Corniche de l'Esterel near Cannes

Cannes takes centre stage amid several chic, somewhat over-developed resorts and millionaires' yacht-havens, including Antibes and Juan-les-Pins. They provide a stark contrast to the wild, deserted Corniche de l'Esterel, with its ragged shoreline of startlingly red cliffs and craggy inlets, and the tiny, unspoiled Îles de Lérins, with their scenic walks and lovely coves for bathing.

Just inland from this dramatic and varied coastline lies the authentic soul of the region: market towns and ancient honey-coloured villages hidden in a wild, beautiful landscape of lavender fields, vineyards and olive groves, fragrant with the perfumes of Provence and illuminated by a crisp and brilliant light which has drawn artists to the south coast for centuries.

The area has long attracted a rich assortment of artists, actors, chefs, writers and royalty to its shores. As the cradle of Impressionism, it boasts a remarkable legacy of art collections, including those of Musée Picasso, Fondation Maeght and Musée Renoir. It is also a popular area for traditional Provençal crafts – notably hand-blown glass in Biot and perfume-making in Grasse.

TOP 10

- 6 Musée Picasso ➤ 114
- 7 Cannes ➤ 116
- 9 Îles de Lérins ➤ 119
- 10 Fondation Maeght ➤ 121

Don't Miss

- 32 Corniche de l'Esterel ➤ 122

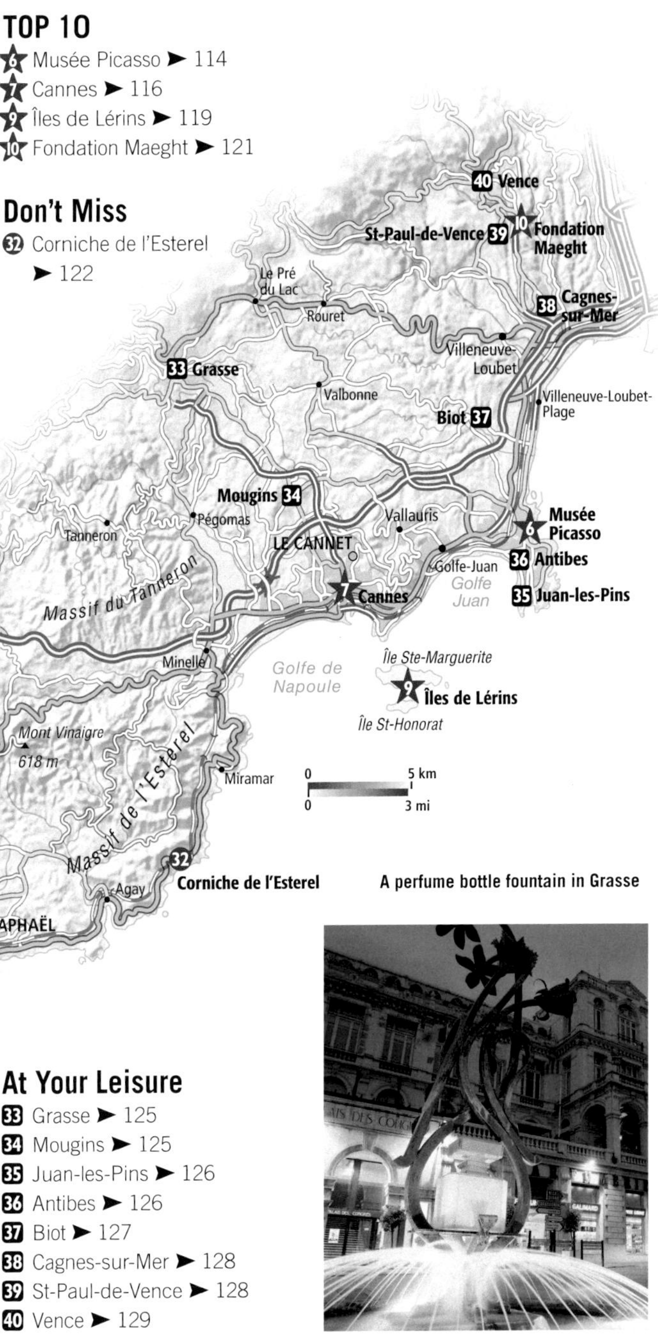

A perfume bottle fountain in Grasse

At Your Leisure

- 33 Grasse ➤ 125
- 34 Mougins ➤ 125
- 35 Juan-les-Pins ➤ 126
- 36 Antibes ➤ 126
- 37 Biot ➤ 127
- 38 Cagnes-sur-Mer ➤ 128
- 39 St-Paul-de-Vence ➤ 128
- 40 Vence ➤ 129

In and Around Cannes

Two Perfect Days

If you're not sure where to begin your travels, this itinerary recommends two practical and enjoyable days out in and around Cannes taking in some of the best places to see. For more information about the places of interest see the main entries (➤ 114–129).

Day One

Morning

Potter round **Cannes** (above; ➤ 116). Admire the luxury hotels and private beaches of the Croisette and the Palais des Festivals (venue of the Film Festival) and search out your favourite celebrity's handprint in the paving stones of the allée des Stars. Then explore the old Roman hilltop town to the west, known as **Le Suquet** (➤ 118), with its castle containing the **Musée de la Castre** (➤ 118). There are plenty of tempting bars and cafés for refreshments, too.

Lunch

Enjoy a classic set menu at **Aux Bons Enfants** (➤ 133), or treat yourself to a lavish picnic from Cannes' **Marché de Forville** (➤ 135) to eat on the unspoiled Îles de Lerins. And be sure to visit **Ceneri** (➤ 135) to pick up some cheeses!

Afternoon

It is a short boat-ride to the **Îles de Lérins** (➤ 119) from Cannes harbour. Visit the austere fort on Île

Vence 40
Fondat Maegh 10
St-Paul-de-Vence 39
38 Cagnes-sur-Mer
33 Grasse
Biot 37
Mougins 34
Musée Picass 6
Antibes 36
Cannes 7
35 Juan-les-Pir
Îles de Lérins 9
Corniche de l'Esterel 32

Ste-Marguerite, where the Man in the Iron Mask was imprisoned, and the monastery-fortress on Île St-Honorat. Both islands offer fantastic walks and bathing opportunities.

Evening

Return to Cannes for a once-in-a-lifetime meal at the exemplary two-Michelin-starred **La Palme d'Or** (➤ 133).

Day Two

Morning

Visit the modern art collection at ★10 **Fondation Maeght** (below; ➤ 121), on the outskirts of St-Paul-de-Vence, then explore this delightful hilltop village, with its steep, cobbled alleys, art galleries and chic boutiques.

Lunch

Café de la Place in St-Paul-de-Vence (➤ 128) makes an ideal lunch venue. Enjoy some hearty regional cuisine on the terrace overlooking locals playing pétanque.

Afternoon

Nature lovers should head to the 32 **Corniche d'Esterel** (➤ 122) to swim in the secret coves and tiny deserted bays, and to walk amid the blood-red porphyry mountains of the Massif de l'Esterel – while art aficionados should visit the ★6 **Musée Picasso** (➤ 114) in the fashionable resort of Antibes. Here the celebrated Spanish artist once had his studio in a seaside fortress. He left his entire output of that period on permanent loan to the castle museum, and today it forms one of the finest collections of his work in the world.

Evening

Head into the *arrière pays* (hinterland) for dinner in one of the villages. 34 **Mougins** (➤ 125), known as a culinary centre *par excellence*, boasts some of the region's finest restaurants, including **Le Mas Candille** (boulevard Rebuffel; tel: 04 92 28 43 43; www.lesmascandille.com; closed Sun–Tue in winter) and **Moulin de Mougins** (➤ 133). L'Amandier (place du vieux village; tel: 04 93 90 91; www.amandier.fr) is a little cheaper and offers cooking lessons.

6 Musée Picasso

The striking fortress of Château Grimaldi in Antibes, used by Picasso as a studio in 1946, today houses one of the world's finest collections of his works.

Art fans can't leave without paying a visit to the Picasso Museum

The Grimaldi family ruled for centuries from this beautiful 13th- to 16th-century castle, constructed following the design of an ancient Roman fort. In 1928, the city of Antibes bought the castle to house its Museum of Art, History and Archaeology. When Pablo Picasso (1881–1973) returned to his beloved Mediterranean in 1946, after spending the war years in Paris, he had nowhere suitable to work, so the Mayor of Antibes lent him a room in Château Grimaldi.

The museum isn't just home to nearly 250 works by Picasso himself, but also contains a beautiful room dedicated to Nicolas de Staël, who committed suicide in Antibes in 1955. It's also worth checking out the collection of pieces by Hans Hartung and the terrace of sculptures by Germaine Richier, Joan Miró, Anne and Patrick Poirier, and Arman. Despite everything else the museum has to

INSIDER INFO

If you are staying in Antibes for a few days, a combined ticket covers entrance to several museums in town: the **Archaeological Museum** in the 17th-century Bastion St-André; the **Peynet Museum**, housing the work of Raymond Peynet and also holding exhibitions of humorous cartoons and illustrations; the **Napoleonic Museum**; **Tower Museum**; and **Fort Carré**. It's valid for seven consecutive days and costs €7.5. Ask about it at the tourist office, or in the museums.

offer, however, the works Picasso created here in 1946 are definitely the stars of the show.

Much of the artist's work from this period reflects his joyous post-war mood. His work here took on a new dimension, reflecting the *joie de vivre* of the Mediterranean, bathed in sunny colours and incandescent light. A combination of his bold new techniques and the mythological themes that had begun to fascinate him led Picasso to create such masterpieces as *Ulysée et les Sirènes* (1947), *Nu Couché au Lit Bleu* (1946) and his famous *La Joie de Vivre* (1946).

Although Picasso spent only three months working here, it was one of his most prolific phases. In gratitude, he donated the complete works of this period to the castle museum, together with a lively collection of tapestries, sculptures and more than 150 ceramics designed at nearby Vallauris.

Musée Picasso, housed in the Château Grimaldi, Antibes

TAKING A BREAK

Nearby are cafés around the port and a **food market** at cours Masséna (➤ 135).

185 E4

Tourist Office
11 place Genéral de Gaulle, Antibes ☎ 04 92 90 53 00; www.antibesjuanlespins.com
Jul–Aug daily 9–7; Sep–June Mon–Fri 9–noon, 1:30–5:30, Sat 9–noon, 2–6

Musée Picasso Antibes
Château Grimaldi, place Mariéjol
☎ 04 92 90 54 20; www.antibesjuanlespins.com
15 June to 15 Sep Tue–Sun 10–6; 10–noon, 2–6 rest of year; closed holidays
€6; under 18 free

7 Cannes

Classy Cannes brings to mind movies and film stars, expensive boutiques, palatial hotels and paparazzi. After all, it is one of the world's most chic resorts and, within France, second only to Paris for shopping and major international cultural and business events. This is largely thanks to the world-famous Cannes International Film Festival, which is held here every May, turning the town into Hollywood-on-Sea.

With so much glitz and glamour, it is easy to forget Cannes' humble origins as a simple fishing village. Named after the canes and reeds of the surrounding marshes, these have since been transformed into luxury yacht havens. Cannes was first put on the map in 1834 by retired British Chancellor Lord Brougham, who was forced to stop in Cannes *en route* to Nice because of an outbreak of cholera. Enchanted by its warm climate and quaint setting, he abandoned his former plans, built a villa here and stayed for 34 winters, singing the praises of Cannes to his most distinguished compatriots. Soon gentry and royalty followed his example by the hundreds. Grand hotels sprang up along the waterfront and by the end of the century Cannes had become the "aristocracy's winter lounge".

According to a popular rhyme from 1920s, Menton was tasteless, Monte-Carlo was pretentious, and Nice was merely 'loud'. Only Cannes was praised as 'stylish'. Nevertheless, it didn't take off as a summer resort until the 1930s. Mass tourism arrived in the 1950s, and the town has been benefiting from it ever since.

You won't find any famous museums, galleries or buildings here, but Cannes' casinos and markets, sandy beaches, luxury boutiques (on the shore and in the **rue d'Antibes**) and boat trips to the Îles de Lérins (► 119) mean you'll never be bored.

Boulevard de la Croisette

Visitors flock to Cannes' sandy beaches in summer

Modern Cannes is built round the fabulous boulevard de la Croisette, which competes with the Promenade des Anglais in Nice (► 48) as the region's most elegant seaside promenade. Like the Promenade des Anglais, La Croisette is lined with palms and grand *belle-époque* hotels on one side and a sparkling bay on the other. The hotels at the eastern end of the promenade are attractions in their own right. The famous twin cupolas of the **Hôtel Carlton**, opened in 1912, were modelled on the prized assets of the courtesan and *femme fatale* La Belle Otero, who was associated with such powerful men as the British King Edward VII and Russian tsars Peter and Nicholas. Otero was reputedly such a heartbreaker that six men committed suicide after their affairs with her ended.

Other glamorous hotels along La Croisette include the **Majestic Barriere**, the **Noga-Hilton** and the white art deco masterpiece, the **Martinez** (► 131). The main hotels have their own beaches, each with bars, restaurants and immaculate rows of coloured parasols and plush mattresses. The private beaches aren't always reserved exclusively for hotel guests, but if you're tempted to sit on a deckchair, keep in mind you'll be charged about €35 for the pleasure. There's a public beach at the western end of La Croisette, and also along Cannes' other seafront boulevard, **du Midi**. La Croisette has been a focus for the *paparazzi* since Brigitte Bardot graced the beaches here in 1953, and those same beaches are packed in summer with sunbathers making the most of the soft sand.

The famous film festival is centred around the unsightly **Palais des Festivals,** on the waterfront at the western end of the boulevard de la Croisette, near the flower market. Along the **allée des Stars,** in front of the Palais des Festivals, you can see where film stars have had their handprints immortalized in the paving stones. Today the most likely places to spot celebrities at festival time are the Hôtel Carlton or Hôtel Martinez.

Le Suquet

The boulevard de la Croisette comes to an end at the Palais des Festivals, where the Old Town begins. Originally the Roman hilltop town of Canois Castrum, this area, situated on a small hill to the west of modern Cannes, is today known as **Le Suquet**. This was Cannes' original fishing village and, appropriately, shares its name with the Provençal word for a kind of fish soup. Unlike much of Cannes, **Le Suquet** has managed to preserve the air of warmth and intimacy of bygone days. Its lively lanes of fishermen's cottages have been transformed into cosy restaurants, and the district is crowned by an imposing **castle** and watch tower affording sweeping coastal views.

Cannes' castle was constructed by the monks of Lérins in the 11th and 12th centuries, together with a small chapel, and today houses the **Musée de la Castre**, containing archaeological and ethnographical collections from all over the world. The austere church in the centre of the Old Town, **Notre-Dame d'Espérance**, was built in 1648 when the chapel became too small.

At the foot of the hill, in the Vieux Port (Old Port), bobbing fishing craft are juxtaposed with millionaires' yachts. Stroll along the spacious waterside esplanade, **La Pantiéro**, or head over to the tree-shaded **square Lord Brougham**, where you'll often see the locals playing a game of pétanque. The **allée de la Liberté**, shaded by palm trees, has a vibrant morning flower market. From here, narrow shopping streets lead down to the daily covered market, **Marché Forville**, where you'll find mouthwatering displays of regional produce.

TAKING A BREAK

La Piazza, close to the port, serves good Italian food (► 133).

185 E4

Cannes Tourist Offices
Palais des Festivals et des Congrès, 1 boulevard de la Croisette
04 92 99 84 22; www.cannes-destination.fr
Jul–Aug daily 9–8; Sep–June 9–7
Gare SNCF, rue Jean-Jaurès
04 93 99 19 77 Mon–Sat 9–7

Musée de la Castre
place de la Castre
04 93 38 55 26
Jul–Aug daily 10–7; 6 April–June, Sep Tue–Sun 10–1, 2–5; closed Oct–June Mon
€6 for temporary exhibitions

The Old Town (Le Suquet) and harbour

INSIDER INFO

- Book a long way ahead for any kind of **accommodation** in Cannes at any time of year.
- During the **film festival** in May, hotel prices skyrocket and the town is packed. Unless you want to star-gaze, this is not the best time to come.

9 Îles de Lérins

The charming Lérins islands, a short ferry ride from Cannes, are a perfect refuge from the crowded Riviera resorts, where you can enjoy a quiet stroll along the shore, a picnic and a swim in the unspoiled coves and bays.

The fort on Île Ste-Marguerite, where the Man in the Iron Mask was imprisoned

The tiny, car-free Îles de Lérins lie just 20 minutes by ferry from Cannes. They are named after two saints – St Honorat, who founded a monastery on the smaller of the two islands at the end of the fourth century, and his sister St Marguerite, who set up a nunnery on the other island – and were once the most powerful ecclesiastical centres in the south of France.

Ferries frequently run to **Île Ste-Marguerite**, the largest of the islands. There are peaceful paths and picnic areas under pine trees, coves and bays in which to swim, and simple fish restaurants by the quay. The island's main attraction is the **Fort Royal**, which contains the **Musée de la Mer** (Maritime Museum), made up of old prison cells. The fort was used as a prison from 1685 until the early 20th century, its most illustrious occupant being the shadowy Man in the Iron Mask. You can see the stark cell in which he was incarcerated from 1687 to 1698, as well as murals painted by the imprisoned artist Jean Le Gac. The first floor holds Ligurian, Greek and Roman artefacts excavated on the island, alongside objects recovered from ships sunk off its shores.

The smaller, farther **Île St-Honorat** is owned by Cistercian monks who arrived here in the fifth century, building the **Ancienne Monastère Fortifiée,** which dominates the island's south. The ruins of this abbey are open to visitors daily. The monks have since built a new home for themselves, and today an active group of 25 Cistercians maintain a simple and austere life in the 19th-century Abbaye Notre Dame de Lérins. The monks produce wine, lavender, oranges, honey and a sweet liqueur, made from aromatic Provençal plants that can be purchased in the souvenir shop.

Insider Tip

Both islands offer pleasant **walking trails**. One of the most enjoyable is a shaded route round Île St-Honorat and past the **seven chapels** scattered across the island, of which both **Chapelle de la Trinité** and **Chapelle Ste-Croix** are particularly interesting.

TAKING A BREAK

There are several **cafés and restaurants** on Ste-Marguerite at the port where the ferry arrives. There are also designated **picnic areas** on the island.

---

185 E3

Tourist Office
Palais des Festivals et des Congrès, 1 boulevard de la Croisette, Cannes
04 92 99 84 22; www.cannes-destination.fr
Jul–Aug daily 9–8; Sep–June daily 9–7

Île Ste-Marguerite

Musée de la Mer
Fort de l'Île Ste-Marguerite 04 93 43 18 17
Oct-March Tue–Sun 10:30 –4:45; April–Sep Tue–Sun 10:30–5:45
€6, free on 1st Sun of month

Île St-Honorat

Abbaye Notre Dame de Lérin
04 92 99 54 00; www.abbayedelerins.com Church open all year

Ancienne Monastère Fortifiée
04 92 99 54 00 10:30–4. Guided visits July to mid-Sep Mon–Fri 10:30–12:30, 2:30–4:45, Sun 2:30–4:45 Guided tour: €2; mid-Sep to June entry free

Chapelle de la Trinité
Guided visits July–Sep Mon–Fri 10:30–12:30, 2:30–4:45, Sun 2:30–4:45
Free

INSIDER INFO

- **Mass** is said at the Abbaye Notre Dame de Lérins, Île St-Honorat, on weekdays at 11:25 am, and on Sundays at 9:50 am.
- It is **forbidden to ride bicycles** on the islands. Dogs are welcome but must be kept on a leash.

Getting there: Île Ste-Marguerite: Compagnie Maritime departs from quai Laubeuf, Cannes (tel: 04 92 98 71 30; www.trans-cote-azur.com, April–Oct on the hour 9–12, 2–4; Nov–March on the hour 10–12, 2–3; €12.50). Journey takes 15 minutes. Service also departs for Ste-Marguerite from quai Lunel, Port de Nice (tel: 04 92 00 42 30).

Île St-Honorat: Société Planaria departs from quai des Îles (next to quai Laubeuf), Cannes (tel: 04 92 98 71 38, May–Sep on the hour 8–noon, 2–3, and 4:30, 5:30; Oct–April on the hour 8–noon, 2–3, and 4:30; €14). Journey takes 20 minutes.

10 Fondation Maeght

Hidden in a woodland above St-Paul-de-Vence, this is one of the most important collections of modern art in Europe.

Fondation Maeght, St-Paul-de-Vence

The Maeght Foundation was established by Marguerite and Aimé Maeght, successful art dealers and close friends of many artists, including Matisse, Miró, Braque, Bonnard and Chagall. Their private collection formed the basis of the museum. Intended to function as a living creative space, the foundation provided accommodation for artists and aimed to be the ideal environment in which to display contemporary art.

The building blends artfully into the wooded surroundings. It respects the curves of the landscape and is full of natural light.

The permanent collection contains works by nearly every major artist of the past 50 years, focusing on Bonnard, Chagall, Giacometti, Léger, Kandinsky and Miró. Behind the museum, Miró's **Labyrinthe** is a multi-level maze of mosaics, sculptures, fountains, trees and ceramics by the Spanish Surrealist. Also in the grounds are **cour Giacometti**, a courtyard peopled with Giacometti figures; and a tiny, sombre **chapel** housing Braque's stained-glass window, *White Bird on a Mauve Background* (1962), created in memory of the Maeghts' son, who died in childhood.

TAKING A BREAK

There is a **café** at the foundation (open April to November) and several others in St-Paul-de-Vence (► 128).

---

185 E5

Montée des Trions ☎ 04 93 32 81 63; www.fondation-maeght.com

Jul–Sep daily 10–7; Oct–June 10–6

€15; under 10 free

32 Corniche de l'Esterel

Edging a wild massif of blood-red porphyry mountains, the picturesque Esterel coast road from St-Raphaël to Théoule-sur-Mer passes some of the Riviera's most spectacular scenery.

The Corniche de l'Esterel, also known as the Corniche d'Or (Golden Coast Road) or N98, was carved into the impressive seafront cliffs over a century ago. The Touring Club de France was involved in its development, and the route is perennially popular with cyclists. Just as dramatic by car, bus or train, the tortuous road offers stunning views of wild red mountains and a sparkling blue sea,

and is punctuated by viewpoints overlooking inviting beaches, sheltered yacht harbours, jagged inlets and deserted coves. The Massif de l'Esterel provides a perfect backdrop, with its harsh, rugged mountains of brilliant red volcanic rock jutting out into the sea.

Travelling from east to west, start at **Théoule-sur-Mer**, a small seaside resort at the edge of the Parc Forestier de la Pointe de l'Aiguille, an extensive coastal park offering a variety of scenic walking trails. Once owned by American sculptor Henry Clews, the castle in **Mandelieu-La Napoule** (avenue Henry Clews; tel: 04 93 49 95 31; www.chateau-lanapoule.com, Feb–Nov 10–6; Nov–Feb 2–5 (weekends 10–5); €3) is also well worth a visit.

Le Trayas is at the highest point of the corniche. Just beyond, a strenuous inland trail climbs the Pic du Cap Roux. The road continues to twist and turn westwards via **Anthéor, Agay** and **Le Dramont** to **St-Raphaël**, the Esterel's main resort, beautifully situated around a deep horseshoe bay that is considered one of the best anchorages on this stretch of coast. Napoleon put St-Raphaël on the map when he landed here on his return from Egypt in 1799. It developed into a fashionable seaside resort in the 19th century. Sadly, many of the *belle-époque* hotels were destroyed during World War II, but it still remains popular with families, mainly because of its large sandy beach. **Insider Tip**

The red rocks of the Pic du Cap Roux provide spectacular scenery along the corniche

To avoid the crowds in summer when the Corniche de l'Esterel can be packed, take the N7 from **Fréjus** to **Cannes**, which follows the path of the Roman Via Aurelia through extensive cork forests past Mont Vinaigre (614m/2,015ft), the highest peak in the Esterel. A short path leads to its summit, from where there is an overview of the wilderness that for centuries was a popular haunt of brigands and a refuge for hermits and escaped galley slaves from Toulon. **Insider Tip**

TAKING A BREAK

Kick off (or finish) your coastal trip at **Jilali B** (► 134), right on the beach at Théoule-sur-Mer.

---

185 C2–D3

Tourist Office: Théoule-sur-Mer
1 Corniche d'Or 04 93 49 28 28; www.theoule-sur-mer.org

St-Raphaël
Rue Waldeck Rousseau 0494 19 52 52; www.saint-raphael.com

The wild, rocky coastline of the Corniche de l'Esterel

INSIDER INFO

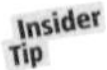

There are various places along the Corniche de l'Esterel to pull over and enjoy the view. Look out for **Calanque du Petit Caneiret**, where there is a wonderful view of the rocky red pinnacles.

Getting there: Local **trains** run hourly from Cannes to St-Raphaël, stopping at Agay and Théoule-sur-Mer. Check timetables for details.

The **Rafaël bus** (tel: 04 94 83 87 63) No 8 runs hourly from St-Raphaël to Le Trayas, with eight services a day meeting a connecting bus from Le Trayas to Cannes. See the Cannes or St-Raphaël tourist office for more details.

At Your Leisure

The bell tower of the Cathédrale Notre-Dame-du-Puy towers over the red rooftops of the Old Town, Grasse

33 Grasse

Lavender fields are one of the most memorable sights of Provence, and the flowers they produce are a key ingredient in the modern perfume industry. **Molinard, Galimard** and **Fragonard** are the great perfumeries located in Grasse (All three offer factory tours), the perfume capital of the world, which supplies perfumes to all the biggest names, including Chanel and Dior. Roses and jasmine, flowers essential to the industry, are celebrated with their own **festivals** in May and August.

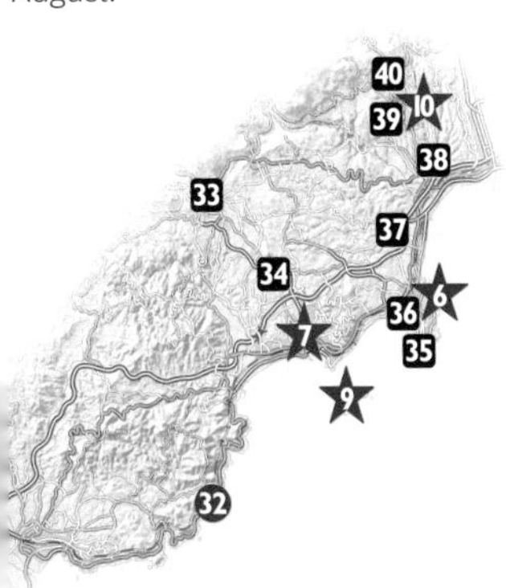

The **Musée International de la Parfumerie** (3 rue du Jeu de Ballon; tel: 04 97 05 58 11; www.museesdegrasse.com; 10–7 in summer; Wed–Mon 11–6 during the rest of the year; €4) is dedicated to the cultural history of perfume.

185 D5

Tourist Office

Palais des Congrès, 22 cours Honoré Cresp

04 93 36 66 66; www.grasse.fr

Jul–Sep Mon–Sat 9–7, Sun 9–1, 2–6; Oct–June Mon–Sat 9–12:30, 2–6

34 Mougins

Outwardly, Mougins seems a typical Provençal hilltop village, but inside its medieval ramparts you will find one of the French Riviera's smartest villages, whose past residents have included Jacques Brel, Yves St Laurent, Catherine Deneuve and Picasso – who spent the last 12 years of his life here. Numerous celluloid portraits of him can be seen in the **Musée de la Photographie**.

Mougin's main attraction, however, is the sheer number of renowned restaurants. People come from all around to dine at

Catching the sun, Antibes

Amandier, **Le Mas Candille** or, for a real treat, **Le Moulin de Mougins** (► 133).
185 D4

Tourist Office
39 place des Patriotes
04 98 92 14 00; www.mougins.fr

Musée de la Photographie
67, rue de l'Eglise, Porte Sarrazine
04 93 75 85 67
Jul–Aug daily 10–8; Sep–Oct, Dec–June Wed–Sun pm. Closed Nov
Free

35 Juan-les-Pins

Juan-les-Pins and Antibes merge together at the head of the Cap d'Antibes peninsula. Known for the annual **jazz festival** held here every July since the 1960s, the resort has a lively nightlife throughout the year.

Named for the pine forest that stood behind the coastline, Queen Victoria's son, the Duke of Albany, established a resort here in the 1880s, but it remained obscure until the 1920s, when Nice restaurateur Monsieur Baudoin went into partnership with American tycoon Frank Jay Gould to launch the Riviera's first summer resort, at a time when beach holidays were quite a novelty. Success followed, aided by the scandalous wearing of modern style swimsuits in public, and Juan gained its racy, hedonistic air.
185 E4

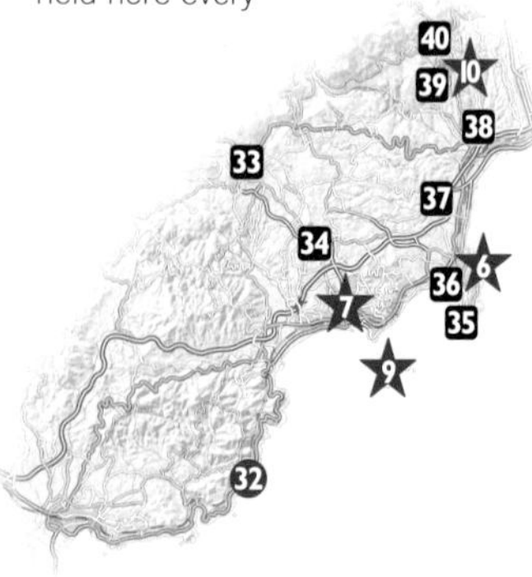

Tourist Office
51 boulevard Guillaumont
04 97 23 11 10; www.antibesjuanlespins.com
Jul–Aug Mon–Fri 9–noon, 2–6, Sat 9–noon; Sep–June Mon–Fri 9–12:30, 1:30–6

36 Antibes

Antibes is the biggest city in the area, but is less showy than either Nice or neighbouring Cannes. Nonetheless, it still manages to attract its share of luxury yachts. The most appealing parts of the town are in the old quarter, where Italianate buildings are crowded into the remains of a 17th-century defensive wall designed by the military engineer Vauban.

Antibes' main attraction is the **Musée Picasso** (► 114), where artworks, mostly dating from the time Picasso spent here in 1946, are housed in a fortress that was once owned by the Grimaldis of Monaco.
185 E4

Tourist Office
11 place du Géneral de Gaulle
04 92 90 53 00; www.antibesjuanlespins.com
Jul–Aug daily 9–7; Sep–June Mon–Fri 9–12:30, 1:30–6, Sat 9–noon, 2–6

37 Biot

This pretty hilltop village is set in a typical Provençal landscape of cypresses, olives and pines. It encompasses a mass of steep, cobbled lanes fanning out from the arcaded main square, which is lined by quaint sand-coloured houses and dotted with cafés and antiques shops.

Some of the streets are decorated with huge earthenware jars, ablaze with geraniums and tropical plants; for centuries, Biot has been a prosperous pottery centre. It's also known for its gold and silverwork, ceramics, olive-wood carvings and thriving glassworks. You can see pieces created by local artisans in the **Musée d'Histoire Locale et de Céramique Biotoise**. Visitors can watch glass-blowers demonstrating the manufacture of their unique *verre bullé* (bubble glass) at the **Verrerie de Biot** (► 135). Insider Tip

Twenty minutes' stroll from the village is the **Musée National Fernand Léger**, with a brilliantly coloured mosaic façade and huge stained-glass windows. The Cubist painter Léger bought a villa here in 1955, intending to make Biot his home, but sadly died 15 days later. His widow founded the museum in 1959. It contains some 348 of his works, and was the first major museum in France to be dedicated entirely to one artist.
185 E4

Tourist Office
46 rue St Sébastien
04 93 65 78 00; www.biot-tourisme.com

Musée d'Histoire Locale et de Céramique Biotoise
6 rue Saint Sébastien
04 93 65 54 54
15 June to 15 Sep Tue–Sun 10–6; Wed–Sun 2–6 rest of year
€4

Musée National Fernand Léger
Chemin du Val de Pôme
04 92 91 50 30; www.musee-fernandleger.fr
May–Oct Wed–Mon 10–6; Nov–May Wed–Mon 10–5
€5.50; free under 26; free 1st Sun of month

Biot is a centre of glassblowing

38 Cagnes-sur-Mer

Cagnes is divided into three: the main beach area and old fishing quarter of **Cros-de-Cagnes,** with its traditional boats called *pointus* and a glut of excellent fish restaurants; **Cagnes-Ville,** a busy commercial centre with a smart racecourse (France's second largest) right beside the sea; and **Haut-de-Cagnes**. This inviting hilltop village, with its brightly coloured houses smothered in bougainvillaea, mimosa and geraniums, is encircled by medieval ramparts and crowned by a 14th-century castle, built as a pirate lookout by Admiral Rainier Grimaldi. The castle contains the **Château-Musée**, which houses several permanent exhibitions, including the Olive Tree Museum and the Museum of Modern Mediterranean Art, with works by Chagall, Matisse and Pierre Auguste Renoir (1841–1919), Cagnes' most famous artist.

Renoir spent his last 12 years just outside Cagnes at Domaine des Collettes, as arthritis forced him to leave Paris for a warmer climate. His villa is now the **Musée Renoir**, where his palette and wheelchair have been preserved, along with paintings, drawings, sculptures and bronzes.

185 E5

Tourist Office
6 boulevard Maréchal Juin
04 93 20 61 64; www.cagnes-tourisme.com

Château-Musée de Cagnes
Place Grimaldi, Haut-de-Cagnes
04 92 02 47 30
Wed–Mon 10–noon, 2–5 (6pm May–Sep). Closed mid-end Nov €4

Musée Renoir
19 chemin des Collettes 04 93 20 61 07
May–Sep Wed–Mon 10–noon, 2–6; Oct, Dec–April 10–noon, 2–5. Closed Nov
€6

39 St-Paul-de-Vence

This large picture-postcard hilltop village, draped gently over a hill close to Cagnes, was appointed a "Royal Town" by King François in the 16th century, and the wealth of the village is still apparent.

In the 1920s, St-Paul-de-Vence was discovered by a group of young, impoverished artists – Signac, Bonnard, Modigliani and Soutine – who stayed at the modest Auberge de la Colombe d'Or, paying for their lodgings with their paintings. Word of the *auberge* spread and soon other artists and young intellectuals arrived. Today the exclusive **Hôtel La Colombe d'Or** boasts an impressive past guest list including Braque, Camus, Derain, Maeterlinck, Matisse, Kipling, Picasso and Utrillo and, as a result, one of the finest private collections of modern art in France.

The village is still an artists' colony, although perhaps more apparent and better described as a tourist honeypot, with coach-loads flocking to the **Fondation Maeght** (► 121) and to the smart shops and galleries which line its steep, cobbled streets. Despite the crowds, it remains one of Provence's most exquisite villages, especially at

A narrow lane in St-Paul-de-Vence

THRILLS AND SPILLS

- **Mougins:** At Buggy Cross, three tracks offer racing on quad bikes, karts or mini-motorcycles, and there are even vehicles for over-4s (by Eco-Park at Parc départemental de la Valmasque; tel: 04 93 69 02 74; www.buggycross.fr).
- **Eco Parc Mougins:** This park in the grounds of the former automobile museum by the motorway boasts some exhibits that will interest kids and adults alike. It's also home to a giant playground with balance courses, slides, play cabins and swings for kids aged twelve months to 14 years (772 chemin de Font-de-Curranlt; tel: 04 93 46 00 03; www.ecoparc-mougins.fr; Tue–Sun 10–7).
- **Antibes:** Antibes Land is an amusement park with a jungle area, big wheel, and even bungee-jumping (N7; tel: 04 93 33 68 03; www.azurpark.com, open April–Oct daily).
- **Marineland:** Performing sea lions, killer whales, dolphins and close underwater encounters with sharks (safely, from within a transparent tunnel). Children love the Jungle des Papillons with exotic butterflies, huge hairy spiders and other creepy-crawlies. Younger children enjoy the pony rides, face-painting and stroking the animals at La Petite Ferme Provençale. Water slides and crazy golf are also on site (avenue Mozart; tel: 04 93 33 49 49, open Feb–Dec daily 10–6, Wed and Sat–Sun until 8, July–Aug 10am–midnight) www.marineland.fr.

night when the narrow alleys are lit with tiny lanterns and the atmosphere is wonderfully romantic.

185 E5

Tourist Office
2 rue Grande 04 93 32 86 95; www.saint-pauldevence.com

40 Vence

Once the Roman forum of Vintium, this delightful village became a strategic bishopric in the Middle Ages. Its 10th-century **cathedral** is the smallest in the whole of France, and has an interior rich in treasures, and with Roman tombstones. A 20th-century addition is a remarkable Chagall mosaic. Artists and writers – including D H Lawrence, Gide, Valéry, and Dufy – have long been attracted to the town, just 10km (6mi) from the crowded coast. In 1941, Henri Matisse moved here, but soon fell seriously ill. Dominican sisters nursed him back to health, and in gratitude he built and decorated the beautiful **Chapelle du Rosaire** for them. The interior is compelling in its simplicity, with powerful black line-drawings of the Stations of the Cross on white *faïence*, coloured only by pools of yellow, blue and green light from the enormous stained-glass windows. Matisse worked on this masterpiece well into his 80s, considering it his "ultimate goal".

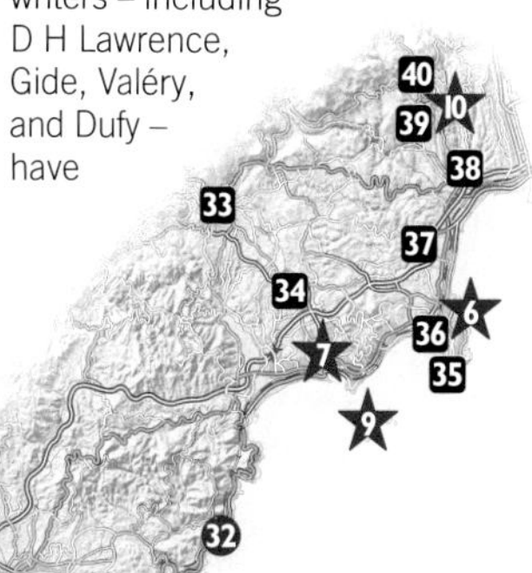

If you're travelling to or through Vence by car, there's free parking available near the swimming pool (*piscine*).

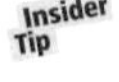

185 E5

Tourist Office
Place du Grand-Jardin
04 93 58 06 38; www.ville-vence.fr
Mon–Sat 9–6; also Sun 10–6, July–Aug

Chapelle du Rosaire
468 Avenue Henri Matisse 04 93 58 03 26
Mon, Wed, Sat 2–5:30; Tue, Thu 10–11:30, 2–5:30; Sun service at 10, Fri 2–5:30 school hols only. Closed mid-Nov to late Dec €5

Where to... Stay

Prices
Expect to pay per double room, per night:
€ under €80 **€€** €80–€150 **€€€** over €150

ANTIBES

Hotel du Cap Eden Roc €€€

This swanky and incredibly expensive hotel (a room here will set you back anywhere from €460 to €1,600) on the Cap Antibes is the height of luxury, generally patronised by celebrities. Non-guests can use the bar and, for a fee, ride the cable car from the hotel to the private beach.
185 E4 Boulevard J F Kennedy 04 93 61 39 01; www.hotel-du-cap-eden-roc.com

La Jabotte €–€€

Small is beautiful in this charming, family-run hotel set in a side road off the Plage Salis. The service is excellent and the blue shuttered rooms are exquisitely decorated. Set around a courtyard, some have their own little terraces.
185 E4 Avenue Max Maurey 04 93 61 45 89; www.jabotte.com

Le Relais du Postillon €€

This comfortable old coaching inn in the heart of Old Antibes has 16 peaceful rooms, and is within walking distance of the Musée Picasso. The restaurant serves gourmet meals. Sit out on the garden patio in summer, or by the cosy fireplace in winter. A public car park is nearby.
185 E4 8 rue Championnet
04 93 34 20 77; www.relaisdupostillon.com

BIOT

Galerie des Arcades €–€€

A 15th-century hotel in a splendid arcaded square, with a restaurant covered in artworks and specialising in local Provençal cuisine.
185 E4 16 place des Arcades
04 93 65 01 04 Closed November

CANNES

Carlton Intercontinental Hotel €€€

Legendary hotel with 338 rooms, including 36 über-luxurious suites. Stay in the Sean Connery suite for class and luxury befitting James Bond. The Carlton has everything from restaurants and bars to fitness centres and ballrooms, and is surrounded by some of Cannes' most upmarket boutiques.
185 E4 58 La Croisette
04 93 06 40 06;
www.hotel-restaurant-les-arcades.com

Cézanne €€–€€€

This modern boutique hotel has attractive bedrooms decorated in stylish muted tones highlighted by bright, sunny colours. There is a hammam and a fitness centre. Breakfast served al fresco under the palm trees is a delight. It also has a private beach
185 E4 40 boulevard d'Alsace
04 92 59 41 00; www.hotel-cezanne.com

Chalet de l'Isère €

Just 10 minutes' walk from the Palais des Festivals, this two-star hotel is good value. Bedrooms are simple, clean and comfortable. Breakfast can be served in the pretty garden.
185 E4 42 avenue de Grasse
04 93 38 50 80; www.hotelchaletisere.com

Hôtel l'Esterel €
This modern hotel is just across from the train station. The simple rooms lacks character, but are affordable, comfortable and clean, and there are wonderful views over Cannes from the breakfast room on the top floor.

185 E4 ✉ 15 rue du 24 Août
☎ 04 93 38 82 82; www.hotellesterel.com

Martinez €€€
The deluxe Martinez contains Cannes' top restaurant, La Palme d'Or (► 133), and is an excellent place for star-spotting during the film festival. Features include a stylish art deco interior, luxurious Givenchy spa and a private beach.

185 E4 ✉ 73 La Croisette
☎ 04 93 90 12 34;
www.cannesmartinez.grand.hyatt.com

Hôtel Molière €€
A centrally located hotel with a grand façade, immaculately kept gardens and comfortable rooms decorated in Provençal colours, most with balconies. It's close to boulevard de la Croissette and the beaches. Book well in advance, especially if you're planning to be here at festival time.

185 E4 ✉ 5–7 rue Molière
☎ 04 93 38 16 16; www.hotel-moliere.com

GRASSE

Auberge du Vieux Château €€
Four small but beautifully furnished rooms boasting canopy beds and panoramic views. The Auberge sits near the church in the medieval hilltop village of Cabris, 5km (3mi) to the west of Grasse. There's also an outstanding restaurant.

185 C5 ✉ place Panorama, Cabris
☎ 04 93 60 50 12;
http://aubergeduvieuxchateau.com

Bastide St-Antoine €€€
This luxurious hotel, set in the grounds of an olive grove, is a truly special place to stay. It has 11 spacious rooms, and a well-renowned two Michelin-starred restaurant, where the creations by chef Jacques Chibois are sublime.

185 D5 ✉ 48 avenue Henri-Dunant
☎ 04 93 70 94 94; www.jacques-chibois.com

MOUGINS

Le Manoir de l'Étang €€€
An intimate, 19th-century manor house, set in 5ha (12 acres) of parkland, with pool and solarium, a classy restaurant and a choice of five golf courses nearby. In the summer you can dine on the restaurant's quality local cuisine charmingly seated by the pool.

185 D4 ✉ 66 allée du Manoir, route d'Antibes
☎ 04 92 28 36 00; www.manoir-de-letang.com
Closed Nov to mid-March

Le Mas Candille €€€
A superb 18th-century country house in vast grounds with a spa and pool. Its restaurant has been regarded as the very best in Mougins for a number of years.

185 D4 ✉ 18 boulevard Rebuffel
☎ 04 92 28 43 43; www.lemascandille.com
Closed Jan

ST-PAUL-DE-VENCE

La Colombe d'Or €€€
Once a modest 1920s café where Braque, Matisse, Picasso and Léger used to pay for their drinks with canvasses. Now a popular deluxe hotel.

185 E5 ✉ Place du Général de Gaulle
☎ 04 93 32 80 02; www.la-colombe-dor.com
Closed 22 Oct–20 Dec, 10–20 Jan

La Grande Bastide €€–€€€
An 18th-century country house with 14 charming Provençal-style rooms and views of St-Paul. Offering excellent value for accommodation, it doesn't have a restaurant.

185 E5 ✉ 1350 Route de la Colle
☎ 04 93 32 5030; www.la-grande-bastide.com
Closed 26 Nov–20 Dec, 15 Jan–15 Feb

Hostellerie Les Ramparts €

One of the best-value places to stay in the village. Nine charming rooms and a restaurant.
185 E5 72 rue Grande
04 93 24 10 47; www.hostellerielesremparts.com

Le St-Paul €€€

This romantic old hotel offers four-star accommodation at the heart of the village and a Michelin-starred restaurant as an added bonus. The views over the valley and the village are spectacular.
185 E5 86 rue Grande
04 93 32 65 25; www.lesaintpaul.com

ST-RAPHAËL

Le 21 €€

This hotel with 28 rooms sits right in the middle of the town. Nevertheless, it's just 200m (650ft) from the beach. It's housed in a restored 19th-century building located on a small square.
184 C2 21 place Maréchal Galliéni
04 94 19 21 21; www.le21-hotel.com
Closed Jan

VENCE

Château du Domaine St-Martin €€€

Attractive villas built around a ruined Templar fortress with a swimming pool and facilities for riding, fishing and tennis.
185 E4 Avenue des Templiers
04 93 58 02 02; www.chateau-st-martin.com
8 March–14 Nov

Le Relais Cantemerle €€

A tranquil oasis in the heart of the Vençoise hills, with elegant, spacious rooms, a pool and an excellent restaurant.
185 E4 258 Chemin Cantemerle
04 93 58 08 18; www.relais-cantemerle.com

Where to... Eat and Drink

Prices
Expect to pay per person for a three-course meal, excluding drinks:
€ under €25 **€€** €25–€60 **€€€** over €60

ANTIBES

Le Figuier de St-Esprit €€€

This very beautiful little restaurant not far from the Musée Picasso was built around a fig tree by the town walls. Christian Morisset – the famously moustachioed former Michelin-star chef from *Juana* in Juan-les-Pins – serves up such innovative culinary delights as cannelloni with squid and mussels, and rabbit saddle with zucchini flowers.
185 E4 14 rue St Esprit, Antibes
04 93 34 50 12; www.christianmorisset.fr
Closed Wed, Tue dinner; 15 June to 31 Aug; 23 Nov to 21 Dec

Le Brûlot €

An unpretentious and cosy Provençal restaurant with a rustic interior and an antique wood oven, of which it makes good use. Traditional cuisine includes *socca*, grilled steak in Provençal herbs and scampi flambéed with *pastis*.
185 E4 3 rue Frédéric Isnard
04 93 34 17 76; www.brulot.com
Mon–Sat. Closed Aug

BIOT

Le Jarrier €€

This restaurant located in an old jar factory serves up imaginative renditions of traditional local dishes. It also boasts a terrace with pleasant views and a number of tables to sit outside.

185 E4 30 passage de la Bourgade
04 93 65 11 68; www.lejarrier.com
Closed Mon, Sat lunch; Sun dinner

CANNES

Astoux et Brun €€

A popular bistro with large shellfish platters, fresh oysters and a wide range of *fruits de mer*.

185 E4 27 rue Félix Faure
04 93 39 21 87; www.astouxbrun.com
Daily 8am–midnight

Aux Bons Enfants €€

A real local institution in the pedestrian zone, just a few steps away from the Forville Market Hall. Serves authentic, honest Provençal cuisine. They don't own a telephone and you have to pay in cash.

185 E4 80 rue Meynadier Daily

Caffe Roma €

A lively Italian bar-restaurant near the Palais des Festivals with a dining room and sunny terrace. Specialities include ravioli stuffed with cheese and spinach, and veal with lemon sauce and pine nuts. Leave room for their homemade tiramisu.

185 E4 1 square Mérimée
04 93 38 05 04; www.cafferoma.fr
Daily 7am–1 am

La Palme d'Or €€€

Join the stars at Cannes' most prestigious, two Michelin-starred restaurant to experience the latest culinary creations of prize-winning chef Christian Willer.

185 E4 Hôtel Martinez, 73 La Croisette
04 92 98 74 14
Closed Sun–Mon 2 Jan–28 Feb

La Piazza €

Home-made pasta, pizzas and robust meat and fish dishes in a big, buzzing restaurant near the Old Port. Not to be confused with La Pizza (similar name, inferior pizzas) on the *quai*.

185 E4 9 place Cornut-Gentille
04 92 98 60 80; www.restaurant-lapiazza.com
Daily noon–2:30, 7–11:30

La Tarterie €

Delicious sweet and savoury tarts to eat in or take away – perfect for a picnic on the Corniche de l'Esterel.

185 E4 33 rue Bivouac Napoléon
04 93 39 67 43 Daily

GRASSE

La Bastide St-Antoine €€€

Jacques Chibois, one of the Riviera's top chefs, serves up delectable Provençal cuisine in this two Michelin-starred restaurant surrounded by olive groves. Book well ahead.

185 D5 48 avenue Henri-Dunant
04 93 70 94 94; www.jacques-chibois.com
Daily noon–1:30, 8–9:30

Le Café des Musées €–€€

This little café with a miniature terrace right next to the Musée International de la Parfumerie serves reasonably-priced Provençal specialities, fresh salads and vegetable quiches at lunchtime.

185 D5 1 rue Jean Ossole 04 92 60 99 00 Lunchtime only; Closed Sun

MOUGINS

L'Amandier €€

Insider Tip

This restaurant on the approach to the medieval village enjoys stunning views of the surrounding landscape that stretch right down to the sea. Check out their traditional Provençal cooking and their creatively composed set menus.

185 D4 48 avenue Jean-Charles Mallet
04 93 90 00 91; www.amandier.fr
Closed Wed except during the high season

Le Moulin de Mougins €€€

In the late 1960s, Roger Vergé made this old, 16th-century oil mill famous thanks to his light, stylish "nouvelle cuisine" creations which featured fresh produce, a great deal of vegetables and a lack of heavy sauces. Chef Sébastien Chambru has adopted both the luxurious décor and the culinary philosophy of his predecessor, Alain Llorca.

185 D4 Quartier Notre-Dame-de-Vie
04 93 75 78 24; www.moulindemougins.com
Closed Mon, Nov–April

ST-PAUL-DE-VENCE

Café de la Place €–€€

Simple bistro fare in this modest eatery at the entrance to the village. It overlooks a lively pétanque pitch in the leafy square, which provides great entertainment when match is in play.

185 E5 Place Général de Gaulle
04 93 32 80 03 Open 7am–midnight, 8pm winter; Closed Nov–23 Dec

Chez Andreas €€

A cheerful café-bar perched on the village ramparts with views over the valley, ideal for a light lunch or a glass of wine as the sun goes down.

185 E5 Rempart Ouest 04 93 32 98 32
Daily noon–midnight

Le Mas d'Artigny €€–€€€

Set in beautiful parkland and part of an exquisite Relais et Château hotel, this gourmet restaurant serves exceptional fish dishes.

185 E5 Route des Hauts de St. Paul
04 93 32 84 54; www.mas-artigny.com
Daily

Le Saint-Paul €€€

Stylish dining in the restaurant, part of this lovely hideaway hotel. Seafood and fishy delights with the freshest seasonal produce feature in the elegant dining room.

185 E5 86 rue Grand
04 93 32 65 25; www.lesaintpaul.com
Closed Wed lunch; Tue March–Nov

THÉOULE-SUR-MER

Jilali B €€

This restaurant right next to the sea specialises in fresh fish dishes and boasts a large terrace.

185 D3 16 avenue du Trayas
04 93 75 19 03; www.jilalib.com
Closed mid-Nov to early Feb, Mon, Tue

Where to... Shop

FASHION & SCENT

Cannes is well known for its boutique shopping. A shopping festival takes place here each January, with fashion shows in the Palais des Festivals. The main shopping streets are **rue de Antibes** and **boulevard de la Croisette**, where – between the Majestic and Carlton hotels – you'll find the likes of Chanel, Gucci, Bulgari, Louis Vuitton, Dior, Dolce and Gabbana and Cartier, to name but a few.

This region is well known for its sweet scents. One of the two major perfume factories in Grasse, **Parfumerie Fragonard** (20 boulevard Fragonard; tel: 04 93 36 44 65) has some of the finest perfumes from Provence for sale.

Professional perfumers need at least two years to create a new scent. Nevertheless, the **Studio des Fragrances** (5 route de Pégomas, Grasse; tel: 04 93 09 20 00) lets visitors invent their own perfume in less than two hours. You can even order your new fragrance for a couple of years after the workshop. Kids will enjoy it, too.

L'Occitane (54 rue d'Antibes, Cannes; tel: 04 93 39 99 23) has all-natural fragrances, soaps and skincare products embracing the scents, colours and traditions of

Provence. **L'Herbier en Provence** (7 Descente de la Castre, St-Paul-de-Vence; tel: 04 93 32 91 51) has locally made soaps, herbs, perfumes and bath products.

FOOD & DRINK

Ceneri (22 rue Meynadier, Cannes; tel: 04 93 39 63 68) confirms the fact that no one does cheese quite like the French. They sell over 300 varieties, from huge rounds of runny Brie to tiny *boutons de culotte* (trouser-button) goat's cheese.

Pick up some wine to go with your cheese at **La Petite Cave de Saint-Paul** (7 rue de l'Étoile; tel: 04 93 32 59 54), an authentic 14th-century cellar in St-Paul-de-Vence with a huge selection of Provençal wines.

Staying in St-Paul, **A Casta** (57 rue Grande; tel: 04 93 32 70 60) sells such regional specialities as truffle oil, absinthe, herbs and spices.

La Cave Gourmande (203 rue Grande; tel: 04 93 32 16 96) is a candy shop with pick-and-mix marshmallows, caramels and lollipops.

Nougat is the local sweet speciality. Stock up at St-Raphaël's **Nougat Cochet** (98 boulevard Félix Martin; tel: 04 94 95 01 67).

ARTS & CRAFTS

All kinds of art of varying quality are on sale in the region. **Eger.M** in Biot (2 place des Arcades; tel: 0622 65 66 06) has works by a selection of local artists and designers.

St-Paul-de-Vence is stuffed to the gills with galleries. One of the oldest art houses is the **Galerie Art Seiller** by Pauline Seiller (28 rue Grande; tel: 04 93 32 10 93; www.artseiller.com). They're constantly discovering and exhibiting new artistic talent.

Biot is famed for its pottery and glassware. A good dozen ceramicists and glassblowers still work in the village today. The traditional bubble-flecked glassware from **Verrerie de Biot** (Chemin des Combes; tel: 04 93 65 03 00; www.verreriebiot.com) makes an unusual souvenir or gift.

MARKETS

Antibes has a market in the cours Masséna selling fruit, vegetables and flowers (June–Aug daily, Sep–May Tue–Sun). A flea market takes place every Thursday and Saturday at place Jacques Audiberti. There are also clothes markets in place Barnaud (open Tue and Sat) and parking de la Poste (open Thu am). **Biot** has a fruit and vegetable market on Tuesday and Friday mornings.

Cagnes-sur-Mer has an attractive market in the Cité Marchande with a good range of fresh fruit, vegetables, meat, dairy produce and flowers (Tue–Sun am). There's an additional food market in boulevard Kennedy (Fri am), and a general market with clothes and bric-à-brac on Wednesday morning, opposite the bus station.

Cannes' Marché de Forville (rue du Marché de Forville, open Tue–Sun 7am–1pm) is a busy market, with bright displays of fruit, vegetables, flowers and cheeses. An antiques market takes place here on Monday. Cannes also has a daily flower market at les Allées de la Liberté, and a Marché Brocante (flea market) at place de l'Étang on Friday 3–7pm.

Grasse has a general market in the place aux Aires (open Tue–Sun am), and an antiques market (1st and 3rd Fri of month) in cours H Cresp.

Vence's place du Grand Jardin is the town's main market place, where you'll find fresh fruit and vegetables, as well as clothes and general items for sale daily. There's also a flea market held here on Wednesdays.

Where to... Go Out

NIGHTLIFE

Le Baoli (Port Canto, boulevard de la Croisette; tel: 04 93 43 03 43; lebaoli.com) with its restaurant and lounge-bar is one of the more popular clubs in Cannes.

Morrison's Irish Pub (10 rue Teisseire; tel: 04 92 98 16 17, daily 7pm–2am) is just what you'd expect in an Irish pub. There is live music on Wednesday and Thursday.

La Siesta (route du Bord-de-la-Mer, between Antibes and Biot; tel: 04 93 33 31 31, mid-June to mid-Sep daily, rest of year Fri–Sat 11pm–5am) is one of the Riviera's most exotic nightclubs, with open-air dance floors, fountains, a pool, restaurant and casino.

If you fancy a flutter in Cannes, head to the town's casinos. Try the **Palm Beach Casino** (Pointe Croisette; tel: 04 97 06 36 90; www.casinolepalmbeach.com) with its slot machines, restaurant and disco, or check out the **Casino Croisette** (1 Jetée Albert Edouard; www.lucienbarriere.com; entry fee charged for games rooms) which has bars and restaurants where you can chill out between games.

If you forgot your jacket, you can still play the slot machines, poker and blackjack in casual attire at **Casino de Cagnes-sur-Mer** (116 boulevard de la Plage; tel: 04 92 27 14 40; www.cagnes.groupe tranchant.com; open 10am–4am; hosts regular theatre and cabaret shows).

CINEMA

Cannes has very few film screenings in English. **Cinema Les Arcades** (77 rue Félix-Fauré; tel: 04 93 39 10 00) regularly screens films in their original language.

THEATRE & MUSIC

Anthéa (260 avenue Jules Grec; tel: 0483 76 13 00; www.anthea-antibes.fr), a new venue that opened in Antibes in 2013, boasts spaces for opera, theatre and concerts that can seat up to 1,200 people. Its ambitious programme of events is intended to rival the likes of Nice, Cannes and Monaco.

Théatre Alexandre III (19 boulevard Alexandre, Cannes; tel: 04 93 94 33 44) stages a variety of plays, from the classics to modern works.

The 19th-century church, **Église Réformée de France** (9 rue Croix, Cannes; tel: 04 93 39 35 55) hosts choral, classical and chamber music concerts, and organ recitals.

During the Cannes Film Festival, the **Palais des Festivals et des Congrès** (1 boulevard La Croisette; tel: 04 93 39 01 01; www.cannes.fr) is abuzz with cinephiles. At other times it hosts exhibitions, plays, ballet and concerts.

HEALTH & BEAUTY

Thalazur Antibes (770 chemin Moyennes Bréguières, Antibes; tel: 04 92 91 82 00) offers thalassotherapy and swimming pools, a gym, *hammam*, sauna, Jacuzzi, solarium and nursery.

Spa Shiseido au Mas Candille (boulevard Clément-Rebuffel, Mougins; tel: 04 92 28 43 43, 10–7) uses a combination of Eastern techniques such as shiatsu and qi (or chi), as well as Shiseido products in all its treatments.

Les Thermes Marins in Cannes (47 rue Georges Clémenceau; tel: 04 92 99 50 10; www.les thermesmarins-cannes.com) is an ultramodern thalassotherapy (sea water treatment) centre at the 1835 Hotel by the old harbour.

In and Around St-Tropez

Little Treats

A Cemetery by the Sea
Look for the grave of music producer Eddie Barclay at the **Cimetière Marin de St-Tropez** (➤ 145) – it's decorated with records.

Winter Blooms
Spring begins in late January/early February in **Bormes-les-Mimosas** (➤ 153) when the hills come alive with yellow flowers.

Cork Oaks
Drive from **La Garde-Freinet** (➤ 155) to the Tortoise Village near Gonfaron to see the largest cork oak forests in France.

Getting Your Bearings

The former fishing village of St-Tropez is undoubtedly one of the smartest resorts on the French Riviera – it's the capital of "see-and-be-seen" and a veritable tourist honeypot. Despite the summer crowds, St-Tropez remains one of the most seductive resorts of southern France, exuding a carefree *joie de vivre*, with its picturesque pastel-shaded houses, tiny bistros and chic boutiques, all basking in the scorching Mediterranean sunshine, while millionaires' ostentatious yachts line the port. For decades this hedonistic image has drawn artists, writers and celebrities. Its star-studded list of residents today includes Jean-Paul Belmondo, Jean-Michel Jarre and the most famous Tropezienne of all – Brigitte Bardot.

The razzmatazz of heady St-Tropez is juxtaposed by the tranquillity and beauty of the *arrière pays* (hinterland). The St-Tropez peninsula has retained all the charm of the Provençal countryside beside the sea, splashed with wild flowers and swathed in vineyards. In their midst, the beautiful hilltop villages of Ramatuelle and Gassin afford magnificent views of the Gulf of St-Tropez and the distant Îles d'Hyéres from their sloping streets. Farther inland is a region of wild, unexplored landscapes and slumbering villages where the pace of life is slow and locals play pétanque in the shade of plane trees or laze in cafés, offering visitors a chance to sample the true *douceur de vivre* of rural Provence.

TOP 10

Don't Miss

At Your Leisure

Reminiscent of Venice: Port Grimaud

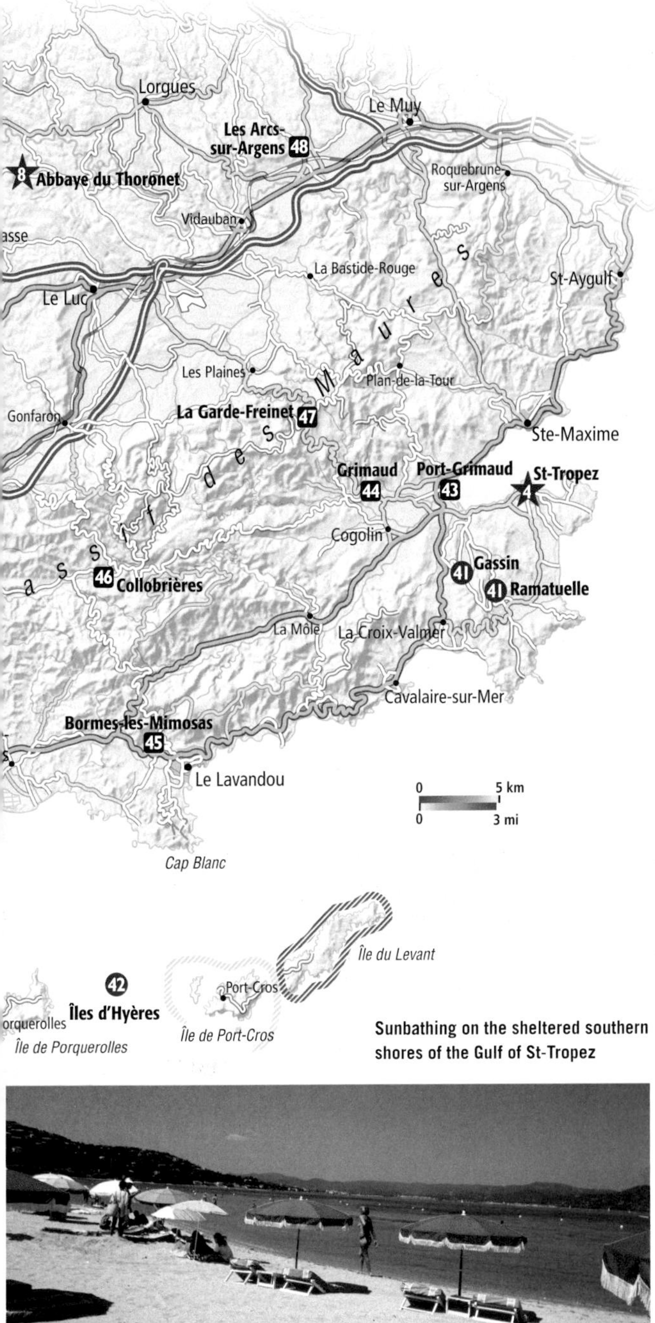

Sunbathing on the sheltered southern shores of the Gulf of St-Tropez

In and Around St-Tropez

Three Perfect Days

If you're not sure where to begin your travels, this itinerary recommends practical and enjoyable days out in St-Tropez taking in some of the best places to see using the Getting Your Bearings map on the previous page. For more information see the main entries (➤ 142–156).

Day One

Morning

Start your tour of 4 **St-Tropez** (➤ 142) at the photogenic harbour (above), which remains remarkably unchanged despite the razzmatazz of this trend-setting resort. **Sénéquier** (➤ 160) is the perfect place for breakfast and people-watching. Wander the maze of cobblestoned back streets at leisure, working up to **La Citadelle** (➤ 144) for its sweeping coastal views, then taste some culinary delights in the morning **Marché Provençal** (➤ 161, Tue and Sat) in place des Lices.

Lunch

Having whet your appetite, **Le Café** (➤ 160) serves a light but satisfying lunch inside or out on the terrace.

Afternoon

Visit the **Musée de l'Annonciade** (➤ 145) with its magnificent post-Impressionist canvases, painted by the first artistic visitors to St-Tropez – Signac, Matisse, Bonnard, Utrillo and Dufy. Spend the rest of the afternoon lazing (and celebrity-spotting) on St- Tropez's fabled beaches in the **Baie de Pampelonne** (➤ 143).

Evening

Return to St-Tropez for dinner at **Le Girélier** (➤ 160) or, for that special occasion, at legendary chef Alain Ducasse's **Rivea** (➤ 160). Then party till dawn with the famous and fabulous at Les Caves du Roy or **La Bodega de Papagayo** (➤ 162).

Day Two

Morning

Explore the St-Tropez peninsula, its beautiful coastline and ancient villages. 41 **Ramatuelle and Gassin** (► 148) are especially attractive, with their steep streets, narrow alleyways and ice-cream-coloured houses tumbling down the hillsides.

Lunch

Le Micocoulier (place dei Barri; tel: 04 94 56 14 01) and Le Bello Visto (place dei Barri; tel: 04 94 56 17 30) in Gassin both offer appealing Provençal menus and breathtaking views.

Afternoon

Catch the ferry from Le Lavandou to visit the 42 **Île de Port-Cros** (► 150), the wildest of the Îles d'Hyères. The island has palm-fringed shores, extensive nature trails and offshore snorkelling tours.

Evening

Return for a classic Provençal dinner at **Lou Portaou** (► 159) in the floral village of Bormes-les-Mimosas.

Day Three

Morning

Start the day at the 8 **Abbaye du Thoronet** (► 146), a beautiful 12th-century abbey in the heart of the unspoiled Vallée d'Argens.

Lunch

Head south along picturesque winding country lanes to 46 **Collobrières** (► 154), at the heart of the surprisingly unfrequented Massif des Maures.

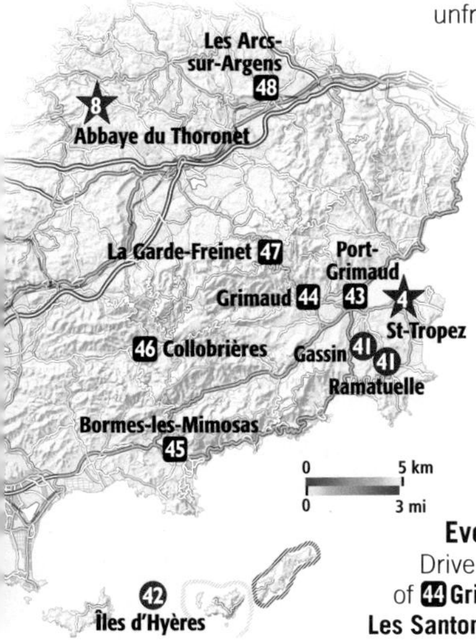

Afternoon

The Massif des Maures is a fantastic place for rambling; its low hills are covered in dense forests of cork oaks, conifers and chestnut trees. Take time to explore and you will find the seemingly endless woodland is interrupted by the occasional sunny meadow or a splash of mimosa.

Evening

Drive to the ancient hilltop village of 44 **Grimaud** (► 152), for dinner at **Les Santons** (► 159).

4 St-Tropez

With such a big and glamorous reputation, you might be surprised to find that St-Tropez is only a small town of about 5,500 people. Having reached the height of international fame in the 1950s and '60s with the rise of bikini-clad resident Brigitte Bardot, it continues to attract glitterati, millionaires and holidaymakers, all seduced by the luxury, relaxed atmosphere and natural beauty of this coastal village.

There's no doubt that life in St-Tropez can be extravagant, decadent and excessive. The French endearingly call it St-Trop, pronouncing the "p", but nonetheless evoking the *double entendre*: *trop* with a silent "p" is French for "too much". In summer, St-Tropez may well be too much for some, but if it's glamour you seek, it's the perfect place to rub shoulders with celebrities in the waterfront cafés, or get a close-up view of the yachts moored before the distinctive backdrop of pink and yellow pastel-coloured houses (reconstructed after being destroyed in World War II). But take time to discover another side of St-Tropez: explore the maze of narrow streets and peaceful squares of the Vieille Ville, or Old Town, where there is a village-like atmosphere and friendly markets and bistros.

Don't attempt to drive to St-Tropez in the high season. The traffic is terrible, with long waits on the roads into town, and no parking once you get there. **Insider Tip** Instead, use the large public parking areas at Port Grimaud and take the passenger ferry across the bay.

Vieux Port

Despite large numbers of visitors and the huge luxury yachts moored here, the picturesque Old Port, lined with pastel-painted houses and cosy cafés, manages to maintain a village-like charm. However, the **waterfront** is still very much the place to pose, especially during summer.

A game of *boules* in the place des Lices

St-Tropez's Old Port, overlooked by pastel-coloured buildings

Try to arrive in style, preferably aboard an enormous yacht. But if you lack the finances for such a venture, there's no shame in wandering along the quayside, ogling the yachts and trying to catch a glimpse of their millionaire owners tucking into langoustines on deck, waited on by a white-frocked crew.

The quay curves along a sapphire-blue bay, punctuated at one end by the ruins of the town's old fortifications, **Tour Vieille, Tour Suffren** and **Tour de Portalet**, and the harbour breakwater, **Môle Jean-Réveille** – a good place to snap a photo of the whole port. Sitting behind Môle Jean-Réveille is the old fishermen's district, **La Ponche**, with **Tour Jarlier**, another fragment of the old fortifications, nearby. At the other end of the quay is the **Musée de l'Annonciade** (➤ 145).

Vieille Ville

Closed to traffic in summer, the Old Town is a cluster of narrow streets lined with small old houses and a handful of chic boutiques. The streets here are generally uncrowded, despite the large numbers of people sauntering along the nearby quay.

At the edge of the Old Town is the **place des Lices**, the town's main square and the real heart of St-Tropez, lined with ancient plane trees and Bohemian cafés such as **Le Café** (➤ 160). Visit on Tuesday or Saturday for the market, or at any time for a game of pétanque and a glass of *pastis* with the locals.

Beaches

The best beaches in St-Tropez are situated on the **Baie de Pampelonne**, a peninsula with over 6km (4mi) of enticing golden sand, neatly divided into individual beaches. It was along these sandy beaches that girls first dared to bathe topless in the nude.

La Citadelle

La Citadelle overlooks the town

The ruins of St-Tropez's 16th- and 17th-century defences sit on an oleander-covered hilltop to the east of town. The citadel is worth visiting for the view alone, which embraces the orange curved-tile roofs of the Old Town, the dark and distant Maures and Esterel hills, and the shimmering blue of the bay, flecked with sails. Keep an eye out for peacocks, those supermodels of the avian world; a number of them have decided to take up residence in the citadel grounds.

In the citadel keep is the **Musée Naval**, a maritime museum linked to the Musée de la Marine in the Palais de Chaillot in Paris. It displays models of ships, and focuses on the maritime history of St-Tropez. There is also an interesting display about the 1944 Allied invasion that destroyed much of the town.

ST TORPES

St-Tropez is named after Tropez, or Torpes, a Roman centurion martyred under Nero in AD 68. His head was buried in Pisa, while his decapitated body was put in a boat and cast out to sea with a dog and cockerel, who were expected to consume his remains. St Torpes' link with St-Tropez was established when the boat washed up on the shore here, his body miraculously untouched. The town's most important festival – the Bravade de St-Torpes (16–18 May) – has been celebrated in his honour for more than 400 years. A gilt bust of St Torpes and a model of his boat can be seen in the 19th-century baroque church, Église de St-Tropez, with its distinctive pink-and-yellow bell tower.

Musée de l'Annonciade

In the late 19th and early 20th centuries, St-Tropez was an active centre for the artistic avant-garde, and this museum in a former 16th-century chapel showcases artworks from the period, with a particular focus on scenes of the local area. There are a hundred or so canvases here, encompassing movements such as Pointillism and Fauvism. Be sure to seek out Paul Signac's *L'Orage* (1895), Camoin's *La Place des Lices* (1939), and works by Dufy, Dérain and Vuillard. There is also a painting by Matisse (*La Femme a la Fenêtre*, 1920), but enthusiasts of his work will be much more satisfied by visiting the Musée Matisse in Nice (➤ 44).

La Tarte Tropezienne, the pastry and coffee shop famous for its sweet custard brioche

184 B1

Tourist Office
Quai Jean-Jaurès
0892 68 48 28; www.ot-saint-tropez.com
Jul–Aug daily 9:30–8; April–June, Sep 9:30–12:30, 2–7; Oct–March 9:30–12:30, 2–6. Closed Sun in Nov and Jan

La Citadelle
Montée de la Citadelle
04 94 97 59 43
Apr–Sep 10–12:30, 1:30–6:30; Oct–March 10–12:30, 1:30–5:30. Closed 1 Jan and selected hols
€3, under 8 free

Musée de l'Annonciade
Place Georges-Grammont
04 94 17 84 10
Jun–Sep Wed–Mon 10–noon, 2–6; Oct, Dec–May Wed–Mon 10–noon, 2–6. Closed Nov and selected hols
€6, under 12 free

INSIDER INFO

- Pick up a **plan de la ville (town map)** at the tourist office. It has a detailed street plan of St-Tropez and a map of the surrounding areas, including a breakdown of the various beaches.
- Visit in mid-May or mid-June to catch one of the two colourful **bravades** festivals: the Bravade de St-Torpes in May, or the Bravade des Espagnols in June, which commemorates the involvement of the men of St-Tropez in the defeat of Spanish raiders farther along the coast in 1637. Insider Tip
- To gain a good overview of St-Tropez take the **walk** (➤ 166). Insider Tip

8 Abbaye du Thoronet

It's worth wandering away from the coast to explore this abbey. Nestled deep in woodland in the Var region, Abbaye du Thoronet is one of the great sights of the Provençal interior.

Situated just off the D79 country road from Brignoles to Draguignan, Le Thoronet is the oldest of three 12th-century abbeys built in Provence by Cistercian monks – an order dedicated to a life of simplicity, austerity and manual labour. Their philosophy is reflected by the unadorned architecture of this lovely Romanesque abbey, and the woodland setting, which conveys a sense of serenity and peace.

Rebelling against the corrupt riches of the Church, the Cistercians expressed their religious devotion through a rigorous, harshly simple and self-sufficient lifestyle. Based at Cîteaux in Burgundy, as their movement grew, the Cistercians founded three great abbeys in Provence: Le Thoronet, Silvacane and Sénanque. The monks shunned society, and chose to build their abbeys in isolated settings.

Building started on the Abbaye du Thoronet in 1160 and was completed in 1190, maintaining a Provençal Romanesque style despite the movement towards Gothic architecture at the time. Although the monks here strived

The abbey church of Thoronet

The upper level of the cloisters

towards a simple lifestyle of self-sufficiency and contemplation, the monastery soon became extremely wealthy with the benefit of large donations. However, over the years, poor harvests, a series of raids in the 14th century, and attacks during the Wars of Religion resulted in the gradual desertion of the abbey. During the French Revolution the building was seized by the State and subsequently sold, although in 1854 the government repurchased and restored this extraordinary building.

On entering the gatehouse, the beautifully proportioned **church**, with its square bell tower and rather low red-tile roof, is directly ahead. The church's interior is a sober and unembellished affair, but beside the church are the attractive **cloisters**, built over three levels to accommodate the uneven ground. In the middle of the cloisters is the **fountain house**, containing a fountain where the monks used to wash their hands before meals. Also nearby is the less austere **chapter house**, where early Gothic influences can be seen in the architecture. A **dormitory,** where the monks slept, is on the top floor of the chapter house.

TAKING A BREAK

In nearby Le Thoronet are the **Hostellerie de l'Abbaye** (Chemin du Château tel: 04 94 73 88 81); and **Le Tournesol** (rue des Trois Ormeaux tel: 04 94 73 89 91, lunchtimes only).

Abbaye du Thoronet
182 C5 Le Thoronet 04 94 60 43 90; www.le-thoronet.fr
Apr–Sep Mon–Sat 10–6:30, Sun 10–noon, 2–6:30; Oct–March Mon–Sat 10–1, 2–5, Sun 10–noon, 2–5. Closed 1 Jan and selected hols
€7.50, under 18 free; free to all 1st Sun of month

INSIDER INFO

- **Mass** is sung here by the sisters of Bethlehem every Sunday at noon.
- **Medieval music** concerts are held in the abbey. Contact the Centre des Monuments Nationaux (tel: 04 94 60 43 90; www.le-thoronet.fr) for more information.

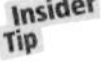

41 Ramatuelle & Gassin

Just a short distance inland from St-Tropez lies a surprisingly uncrowded peninsula, scattered with wild flowers, home to the charming villages of Ramatuelle and Gassin, and surrounded by some of the region's best vineyards.

Photogenic Ramatuelle on the St-Tropez peninsula is a typical Provençal hilltop village

The hilltop village of **Ramatuelle** began as a stronghold of the Saracens, who called the village Rahmatu'llah, Arabic for "God's Gift". This impossibly pretty village is today, along with neighbouring Gassin, one of the most fashionable places in the region in which to own a *résidence secondaire*. Despite the influx of affluent second-home owners, Ramatuelle maintains its Provençal identity, and is a lovely place to visit, particularly during the two-week **Festival de Ramatuelle** held in August each year, when jazz musicians and thespians take to the stage. At other times of the year, the village is worth a visit just to delight in wandering along its old streets lined with houses that climb steadily up the hill; to explore its little artisan shops and art galleries; and admire its Romanesque church. Situated across from the tourist office, the church has a 17th-century doorway carved from green serpentine stone. The town is laid out concentrically and the **centre of the village** is through an arch to the left of the church.

From Ramatuelle, take the Moulins de Paillas road (D89) to Gassin. In between the two villages are what remains of five ancient windmills, the **Moulins de Paillas** (one of which has been restored). There are fantastic views from here out to sea towards the Îles d'Hyères, and across the surrounding countryside. The twin peaks of la Sauvette (779m/2,556ft) and Notre-Dame-des-Anges (780m/ 2,560ft), the highest points in the **Massif des Maures**, are clearly visible.

The medieval village of **Gassin** also has spectacular panoramas of the area, having been established as a lookout point during the time of the Saracen invasions. This colourful Provençal village is blessed with more than its fair share of smart boutiques and restaurants, thanks to its proximity to St-Tropez.

A cobbled lane in Ramatuelle

TAKING A BREAK

In Gassin, most of the restaurants are located in the **place dei Barri**, a paved square at the top of the village, where you can dine alfresco, enjoying the views that encompass everything from the mountains and vineyards, to nearby villages and the coast. Try **Le Microcoulier** or **Le Bello Visto** (► 141).

If you're just looking for a snack to keep you going, check out the bakeries (*boulangerie*) in the village instead. Most serve a selection of sandwiches and little salads around lunch-time.

---

183 F3

Tourist Office
Place de l'Ormeau, Ramatuelle
04 98 12 64 00; www.ramatuelle-tourisme.com
Jul–Aug daily 9–1, 3–7:30; mid-season Mon–Sat 9–1, 3–7; low season Mon–Fri 9–12:30, 2–6

INSIDER INFO

- This area is renowned for the excellent **Côtes du Provence wines** that are produced here. On the D61 between St-Tropez and Ramatuelle there are various châteaux where the wines can be tasted. Visit the Ramatuelle tourist office for more information about wineries to visit in the area.
- Try not to arrive **hungry** at a small village in search of a late lunch. Many restaurants, cafés and **pâtisseries** close at 1 or 2pm and don't open again until the evening. This is particularly true during winter, when they may also be closed for months at a time. Insider Tip

42 Îles d'Hyères

The town of Hyères was a favourite holiday spot for the English aristocracy who wintered here in the 19th century. However, when summer became a more popular time to holiday than winter, the Îles d'Hyères, off the coast, came into their own, blessed as they are with beautiful beaches, azure seas and dense natural woodland. These quiet, car-free islands make an ideal day trip away from the busy resorts.

Overlooking the old quarter of Hyères

Île de Porquerolles

The largest of the Îles d'Hyères, Porquerolles covers around 18km² (7mi²). A perfect day trip for walkers, cyclists and nature lovers, much of the island is a nature reserve, covered with woodland and peaceful walking paths. On the north coast of the island are beautiful sandy **beaches**, while on the south coast, some 40 minutes' walk away, jagged cliffs offer spectacular views over the sparkling sea. The island also has an impressive botanical garden bursting with olive, fig and peach trees. The **main village** is on the north side of the island. In the **place d'Armes** you'll find hotels and restaurants, as well as a large pétanque pitch. To the south of the village is **Fort Ste-Agathe**, which dates back to the 16th century and today functions as an exhibition space.

Île de Port-Cros

The wildest, most southerly of the islands is a protected national park, 10km² (4mi²) in area and covered with dense, unspoiled woodland. Marked **walking trails** pick through the woodland and its impressive flora. The *sentier botanique* (botanical path) is one of the shorter paths, but there are also more challenging trails of up to 10km (6mi).

The paths also extend into the sea; **snorkellers** can follow an underwater trail full of colourful marine life (free guided snorkelling

GETTING THERE

The Îles d'Hyères, can be accessed by ferry from Port St-Pierre in Hyères, or the harbour on the Giens peninsula.

- In the high season, ferries from Giens continue from Porquerolles to Port-Cros island.
- Ferries from Port St-Pierre go to Port-Cros in one hour, and Le Levant in 90 minutes.
- All three islands can also be reached by a ferry from Le Lavandou, farther east.

The Île de Port-Cros – a National Park that's a popular daytrip destination

tours leave from plage la Palud). Without a snorkel, you can still view the marine life from the glass-bottomed **Aquascope** boat, which makes half-hour excursions.

Île du Levant

This tiny 8km² (3mi²) of rocky land is the most easterly of the three islands. The majority of the island is owned by the army and is strictly off limits to tourists, while the rest is a nudist colony known as Heliopolis. Large numbers of visitors come to the beaches here to work on their all-over tans in the summer, but there are also about 100 permanent residents, whose little chalets sit on the hills behind the harbour.

Tourist Office
182 B2 Rotonde du Park Hotel, avenue de Belgique, Hyères
04 94 01 84 50; www.hyeres-tourisme.com

Île de Porquerolles
182 C1 Daily from Giens, more frequent departures July–Aug
04 94 58 21 81; www.tlv-tvm.com €18.50

Île de Port-Cros & Île du Levant
183 E/F1 Daily from Port d'Hyères, reduced services in winter
04 94 57 44 07; www.tlv-tvm.com; www.portcrosparcnational.fr;
www.iledulevant.com.fr €26.80

INSIDER INFO

- Check the time for the **last ferry** back before going to the islands.
- One of the **best beaches** on the islands is plage de la Palud, at Port-Cros.
- You can't use your car on the islands, so **park** at the ferry terminal at Giens or near Hyères harbour. Ferry crossing times from Hyeres are one hour to Port-Cros and one hour 30 mins to Île du Levant.

- **Nudity** is compulsory on Levant's main nudist beach, plage Les Grottes.
- **You must not** drive a car, cycle (on Port-Cros), camp, smoke, make a campfire, go fishing, drop litter or collect plants. Dogs are to be kept on a lead.

At Your Leisure

43 Port-Grimaud

Port-Grimaud is a modern mini-Venice of pastel-coloured villas on a series of islets, divided by canals and linked by shaded squares and neat bridges. Designed by architect François Spoerry in the 1960s, the village is today one of France's major tourist attractions and the ultimate property development; prices for the 2,500 canalside houses (all with private moorings) are absurdly high and many of the residents simply jet in for their summer holidays.

Port-Grimaud is an appealing place, with lively waterside cafés and scenic waterways, but it's enclosed by high fences, has over-priced facilities, and drivers must leave their cars in an expensive parking area outside the resort. The port is best explored by water-taxi (*coche d'eau*), with boat tours leaving from the main square (**place du Marché**) every ten minutes. At the centre of the village, on its own islet, the pseudo-Romanesque church of **St-François-d'Assise** contains stained glass by Hungarian-born Victor Vasarély, and provides a sweeping view of the harbour from the top of its tower.

183 F3

Tourist Office
Annexe Port Grimaud, Chemin Communal
04 94 55 43 83
Jul–Aug Mon–Sat 9–12:30, 3–7;
June, Sep Mon–Sat 9–12:30, 2:30–6:15

Pleasure boats moored in front of the pastel-coloured villas of Port-Grimaud

44 Grimaud

Medieval Grimaud is one of Provence's most photogenic hilltop villages, and is well worth a visit. It is crowned by the ruins of a romantic 11th-century **château** which belonged to the Grimaldi family, after whom the village is named. From the château there are impressive vistas over Port-Grimaud and down to the gulf of St-Tropez.

Insider Tip

Hidden amid flower-filled streets and shaded squares, you will find

a beautiful Romanesque church (**Église St-Michel**) on the atmospheric rue des Templiers, a restored 12th-century mill and the **Hospice of the Knights Templars**.
183 E3

Tourist Office
1 boulevard des Aliziers 04 94 55 43 83; www.grimaud-provence.com
Jul–Aug Mon–Sat 9–12:30, 3–7; April–June, Sep Mon–Sat 9–12:30, 2:30–6:15; Oct–March Mon–Sat 9–12:30, 2:15–5:30

45 Bormes-les-Mimosas

Perched on a hilltop on the Massif des Maures, just inland from the coast, Bormes-les-Mimosas is a steep medieval village with ice-cream coloured houses, evocative lanes and passageways climbing up towards the ruins of a château on the hilltop.

During February, when the mimosa is in full bloom, the village celebrates with a sensational *Corso Fleuri* – an extravaganza of floral floats made from thousands of tiny yellow mimosa flowers. The village is perennially pretty and in summer bright bougainvillaea and geraniums replace the mimosa blooms.

Seek out the **circuit touristique** that starts at the Maisons des Associations on boulevard de la Republique. If you can't find the signs for the *circuit* (they are often stolen), pick up a map and information in English at the tourist office. The *circuit* explores Bormes' steep medieval stairways and alleys. Watch out for the charmingly named Venelle des Amoureux (Lovers' Lane), Draille des Bredouilles (Gossipers' Way) and, steepest of all, rue Roumpi-Cuou (Bone-Breaker road).

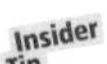

Along the route are the town's main sights, which include a fine 16th-century **chapel** dedicated to Bormes' patron saint, St François de Paule (who rescued the village from the plague in 1481); **Église St-Trophyme**, an 18th-century church built in Romanesque style and where the French president attends Mass in summer; and the ruined 13th- to 14th-century castle at the top of the hill, the **Château des Seigners de Fos**. The château

A colourful, flower-filled path in the village of Bormes-les-Mimosas

is privately owned, but an area next to it is open to the public, with dazzling views across the bay of Le Lavandou and the Massif des Maures.

Gardening enthusiasts should keep an eye out for information plaques about many of the plants along the *circuit touristique*.

The **Musée d'Art et d'Histoire**, at 103 rue Carnot (tel: 04 94 71 56 60, Oct–April Tue–Fri 10–noon, 2–5:30, Sat 10–noon; May, June, Sep Tue–Sat 10–12:30, 2–6, Sun 10–12:30; July, Aug 10–12:30, 3–7; free), holds temporary art exhibitions throughout the year, and also has an exhibition tracing the history of the village.

179 C2

Tourist Office
1 place Gambetta 04 94 01 38 38;
www.bormeslesmimosas.com
Summer daily 9–12:30, 2:30–6:30; winter Mon–Sat 9–12:30, 2–6

46 Collobrières

In the centre of the Massif des Maures, this traditional little village is well known for its produce, particularly the sweet *marrons glacés* (candied chestnuts). Collobrières holds an annual **festival** celebrating the humble chestnut at the end of October. Chestnuts proliferate at the **local market**, held every Sunday, and also on Thursdays in summer. Collobrières is also known for its cork, which grows in the forests nearby.

The village has a 12th-century **bridge** and a curiously arcaded street, **place Rouget de l'Isle**, that is worth exploring. Off the D14 is the beautiful **Chartreuse de la Verne**. This 12th-century Carthusian monastery stands isolated among the dense Maures forest, 12km (7mi) from Collobrières. Founded in 1170, it has been rebuilt many times. The complex encompasses cloisters, chapels and cells in a rambling formation, built from the local red stone, with doorways decorated in green serpentine. Originally inhabited by Carthusian monks, it has been home to a group of Sisters of Bethlehem nuns since the 1980s.

183 D3

Tourist Office

Boulevard Charles Caminat

04 94 48 08 00;

www.collobrieres-tourisme.com

Sep–June Tue–Sat 10–noon, 2–6; July–Aug Mon–Sat Mon–Sat 10–noon, 2–6

Chartreuse de la Verne

Mid-May to mid-Oct Wed–Mon 11–6; mid-Oct to mid-May Wed–Mon 11–5

Free

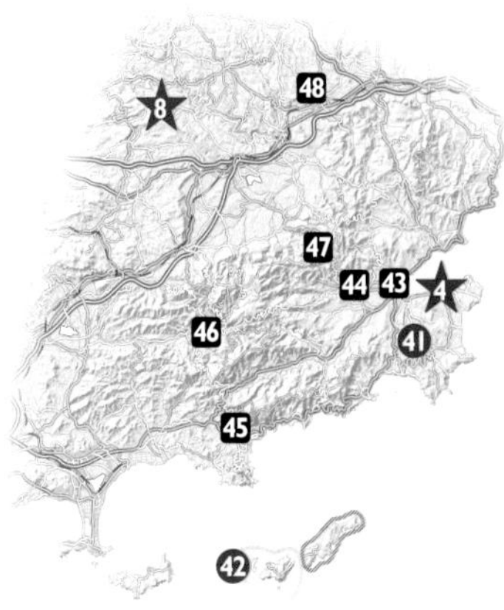

47 La Garde-Freinet

Encircled by groves of cork oaks, eucalyptus and chestnut, this village was France's major producer of cork in the 19th century. Much further back, lofty **La Garde**, perched 360m (1,180ft) above sea level, was one of the last Saracen strongholds in Provence in the 10th century. Today it is known as the "capital" of the Massif des Maures. Alleys, fountains and courtyards make it a wonderful place to wander through.

Insider Tip: A 20-minute walk to **Fort Freinet** to the west will reward you with fantastic views of Le Luc plain and beyond to the foothills of the Alps.

183 E4

Tourist Office

Place de la Republic

04 94 08 99 78;

www.lagardefreinet-tourisme.com

Mon–Fri 9–12:30, 2.30–6; Sun 9–12:30

48 Les Arcs-sur-Argens

This attractive medieval village in the Argens valley, south of Draguignan, has a well-restored old quarter called **Le Parage**, which rises to the ruins of a 13th-century castle.

Collobrières earns its living from processing the bark of cork oaks

From here, there are superb views of the Massif des Maures and the surrounding countryside of vineyards producing Côtes de Provence wines.

The **Maison des Vins Côtes de Provence** (tel: 04 94 99 50 20 www.caveaucp.fr), on the N7 south of the village, is an ideal place to taste and learn about some of the region's wines. Having tasted, you can also buy wine here for very reasonable prices. The **Église St-Jean-Baptiste** (daily 10–noon, 2–5) has a large Provençal-style *crèche tableau* depicting Le Parage as it once was, and a 15th-century polyptych by Jean de Troyes.

Just a few kilometres outside Les Arcs-sur-Argens is the **Château Ste-Roseline**. The property dates back to the 10th century, and produces some of the most prestigious wine in the area. The château began as an abbey and Roseline, the daughter of the Marquis of Villeneuve, was born here. She became a Carthusian nun, and was the mother superior for many years until her death in 1329. Her body lies in a glass case in the vineyard's chapel.

It is an important pilgrimage site with strong artistic significance that attracts many art lovers. In 1978, the **Chapelle de Ste-Rosaline** was decorated by Marc Chagall with a beautiful mosaic representing the Angel's Meal. The chapel also has a magnificent stained-glass window designed by Jean Bazaine and Raoul Ubac, sculptures by Giacometti, and an altarpiece depicting St Roseline in a nativity scene with her parents.

In addition to the chapel and cloister, the historic estate of Château Ste-Roseline has plenty to see and experience, an excellent old vineyard with cellar door wine sales, a restaurant and well-established gardens. Musical and cultural events are held here regularly.

183 E5

Tourist Office
Rue de la Motte 04 94 73 37 30; www.tourisme-dracenie.com
Mon–Fri 9–noon, 2–5

Château Ste-Roseline
Les Arcs-sur-Argens
04 94 99 50 30; www.sainte-roseline.com
Daily

THE TORTOISE VILLAGE

Le Village des Tortues, the Tortoise Village at Gonfaron, is a conservation centre for Hermann's tortoises, a rare species found only on the Massif and in Corsica. You can observe tortoises in their natural environment, visit the clinic for injured tortoises, the nursery for young tortoises and the laboratory where nests and eggs are monitored. There is also a walking trail with information points in English to help you learn more about this endangered species. Insider Tip: The best time of the year to visit is spring, when the tortoises are more active. They hatch from May to June and hibernate from November to March (Les Plaines; tel: 04 94 78 26 41; www.villagetortues.com; March–Nov daily 9–7; €12, €8).

Where to...
Stay

Prices
Expect to pay per double room, per night:
€ under €80 **€€** €80–€150 **€€€** over €150

LES ARCS-SUR-ARGENS

Logis du Guetteur €€–€€€
The comfortable bedrooms in this beautifully restored 11th-century castle have panoramic views over the village and mountains. In the summer months meals are served on a terrace overlooking the outdoor pool, and when the weather is cooler or simply less clement there is a very cosy basement dining room.
183 E5 **Place du Château**
04 94 99 51 10; www.logisduguetteur. com
Closed Feb

BORMES-LES-MIMOSAS

Le Bellevue €
This simple, good-value, family-run hotel boasts spectacular views across the red roofs down to the sea. Its friendly restaurant serves fresh seafood and local Provençal dishes.
183 D2 **14 place Gambetta**
04 94 71 15 15; www.bellevuebormes.com
Closed mid-Nov to mid-Jan

COGOLIN

Bliss Hôtel €€
A comfortable, modern hotel located in the middle of Cogolin.
183 E3 **Place de la République**
04 94 54 15 17; www.bliss-hotel.com

GASSIN

Le Mas de Chastelas €€–€€€
Situated just outside St-Tropez and surrounded by vineyards, this traditional shuttered farmhouse is decorated with bright Provençal fabrics. The restaurant serves exceptional regional cuisine.
179 E2
Quartier Bertaud
04 94 56 71 71; www.chastelas.com
Open weekends only Jan–March, Oct–Dec

GRIMAUD

Le Verger Maelvi €€–€€€
Generously-sized luxury rooms in a Provençal country house with a pool and a large garden.
183 E3
Route de Collobrières
04 94 55 57 80; www.hotel-grimaud.com

RAMATUELLE

Camping Kon Tiki €–€€
A popular camping ground on the edge of Pampelonne beach, with mobile homes available to let You can also bring your own caravan (trailer) or mobile home, or pitch your own tent. Grocery store, restaurant, bar, tennis court and a kid's club.
183 F3 **Route des Plages**
04 94 55 96 96; www.riviera-villages.com
Closed Nov–March

La Ferme d'Augustin €€–€€€
This three-star hotel, close to the beach, has comfortable rooms in a charmingly rustic setting. Terraces look out over the garden and heated outdoor pool (with hydro-massaging jets). Inside there are beamed ceilings and a cosy fireplace in the lounge.

183 F3 Route de Tahiti
04 94 55 97 00; www.fermeaugustin.com
Closed mid-Oct to mid-March

La Vigne de Ramatuelle €€€
Chic yet characterful, this vineyard villa is close enough to St-Tropez's beaches and nightspots while still enjoying a peaceful setting. With 14 rooms and an outdoor pool, it's a good alternative to the town centre.
183 F3 Route des Plages
04 94 79 12 50; www.hotel-vignederamatuelle.com
Closed mid-Oct to March

Villa Marie €€€
Overlooking Pampelonne, this chic boutique hotel and spa is a place of pure indulgence. Enjoy the pool and open-air bar on a balmy evening. The rooms are stylishly decorated and meals can be taken in the restaurant or outside.
183 F3 Chemin Val de Rian, Ramatuelle
04 94 97 40 22; www.villamarie.fr
Closed 6 Oct–24 April

ST-TROPEZ

Benkirai €€€
The handiwork of designer Patrick Jouin has made this new contemporary-style hotel a great success. Most rooms have a balcony or terrace overlooking the lovely swimming pool and bar. Stylish, sleek metal and leather and flamboyant Moroccan reds contrast with cool blues.
183 F3 11 chemin du Pinet
04 94 97 04 37; www.hotel-benkirai.com
Closed mid-Nov to mid-Dec

Hôtel Byblos €€€
Byblos is the jet set's hotel of choice in the summer. Doormen keep out the riff-raff, reserving the sophisticated interior for the privileged guests. Inside, small villas, flower gardens and neat patios are clustered around a pool, fitness centre and boutiques. Byblos is the venue for the chic nightclub, Les Caves du Roy, and Alain Ducasse's restaurant, *Rivea* (► 160).
179 E3 Avenue Paul Signac
04 94 56 68 00; www.byblos.com
Closed 6 Oct–16 April

Château de la Messardière €€€
This luxurious hotel, set on a private hillside with views over the sea, is truly palatial: a 19th-century castle, 2km (1mi) from St-Tropez and a stone's throw from the beach. Facilities include a large swimming pool, fitness and beauty centre, tennis courts and a well-renowned restaurant.
183 F3 Route de Tahiti
04 94 56 76 00; www.messardiere.com
Closed 3 Nov–21 March

Hôtel Les Lauriers €
A two-star hotel set a little away from the action, on a street behind the place des Lices. The rooms are pleasant and cool, and there's a shady garden in which to escape the heat.
183 F3 Rue du Temple
04 94 97 04 88
Closed Nov–March

Hôtel Lou Cagnard €–€€
This comfortable budget hotel is an excellent option, with rooms that are airy, clean and simple. Enjoy breakfast in the lovely, leafy garden on a sunny morning. Private parking available.
183 F3 18 avenue Paul Roussel
04 94 97 04 24; www.hotel-lou-cagnard.com
Closed 1 Nov–27 Dec

White 1921 €€€
This former Town Hall is furnished in an elegant, minimalist style that features a lot of white. It's located on the place des Lices, not far from the harbour.
183 F3 15 place des Lices
04 94 45 50 50; www.white1921.com

Where to...
Eat and Drink

Prices
Expect to pay per person for a three-course meal, excluding drinks:
€ under €25 **€€** €25–€60 **€€€** over €60

BORMES-LES-MIMOSAS

Lou Portaou €€
Market-fresh Provençal cuisine in a pretty medieval building, hidden in a corner of the village.
178 C2
1 rue Cubert des Poètes
04 94 64 86 37
Closed Mon pm, and Tue mid–Sep to mid-June

La Rastègue €€
This Michelin-starred eatery lies a little way below the medieval village. Diners can enjoy watching Jérôme Masson conjuring up his delicious culinary creations with the freshest produce behind a pane of glass in the restaurant itself.
183 D2
48 boulevard du Levant
04 94 15 19 41; www.larastegue.com
Tue–Sat dinner only, Sun lunch and dinner; closed Jan

COLLOBRIÈRES

Auberge-Restaurant des Maures €
Dine on the charming terrace overlooking the Réal Collobrier river in this welcoming family-run rustic restaurant with rooms. Wild boar, features on the menu and nut lovers will be in paradise – the chestnut ice cream is especially delectable.
183 D3
19 boulevard Lazare Carnot
04 94 48 07 10; www.hoteldesmaures.fr
Closed mid-Nov to March

LES ARCS-SUR-ARGENS

Café de la Tour €
A typical village bistro serving simple, tasty dishes at lunchtime made from a selection of fresh ingredients.
183 E5 **35 boulevard Gambetta**
04 94 73 30 56 **Lunch only; closed Wed**

Le Relais des Moines €€–€€€
Sébastien Sanjou is the new culinary star in the village of Les Arcs. He whips up dishes from fresh, regional ingredients in an old, 16th-century sheep farm on the road to the Sainte-Roseline winery. The restaurant boasts a magnificent summer terrace.
183 E5 **Route de Sainte-Roseline**
04 94 47 40 93; www.lerelaisdesmoines.com
Closed Mon and Sep–June Mon, Tue

GRIMAUD

Les Santons €€€
This popular, Michelin-starred restaurant is one of the region's best, so book well ahead. The freshest local ingredients are used to make classic French and Mediterranean dishes.
183 E3 **N558**
04 94 43 21 02; www.restaurant-les-santons.fr
Mon, Thu–Sun 12–2:30, 7–10; Tue–Wed 7–10

RAMATUELLE

Chez Camille €€–€€€
A family business since 1913, this eatery has become famous for its

lobster, grilled fish and bouillabaisse. Set in a fisherman's shack on the beach, the fish is sublimely fresh and it's the preferred spot for an authentic *pieds dans l'eau* experience. Make sure to book at weekends and in the high season.

Insider Tip

183 F3 Quartier de Bonne Terrasse
04 98 12 68 98; www.chezcamille.fr
Closed Tue, Fri lunch, mid-Oct to mid-April

ST-TROPEZ

Le Café €€

Formerly known as Le Café des Arts, this cosy bar/stylish restaurant has a long history as the place for intellectual and artistic debate. An archetypal French bar with brown leather, wooden fittings and pétanque trophies on display. Have a meal or a coffee on the terrace while watching a game. It was also the reception venue for Rolling Stone Mick Jagger's 1971 wedding.

183 F3 5 place des Lices
04 94 97 44 69; www.lecafé.fr
Food daily 12–2:30, 7:30–11; café 8am–midnight

Le Girelier €€

This seafood restaurant right next to the harbour is a traditional Saint-Tropez institution. Some of the fresh fish is grilled simply *à la plancha*.

183 F3 Quai Jean Jaurès
04 94 97 03 87; www.legirelier.fr
Closed Nov to mid-March

La Ponche €€

This legendary luxury hotel in the fishermen's quarter boasts views of the bay and a restaurant serving traditional Provençal cuisine.

183 F3 3 rue des Remparts
04 94 97 09 29; www.laponche.com
Closed Nov to mid-Feb

Rivea €€€

Rivea at the exclusive Hôtel Byblos has undergone a number of changes in recent times: it has a new name, a new menu, and now serves Provençal cuisine with a number of Italian influences (instead of the old eatery's international fare).

183 F3
Avenue du Maréchal Foch
04 94 56 68 20; www.byblos.com
Mid-April to 5 Oct daily 8am–11pm/midnight; Closed Tue and Wed in low season

Sénéquier €€

You can't miss the distinctive red awnings on the waterfront, for this is one of the best-known bars in town and a must for breakfast. There's no denying the coffees are on the pricey side, but it's a St-Tropez experience and really is the place to be on a sunny morning.

Insider Tip

183 F3 Quai Jean-Jaurès
04 94 97 00 90
Daily, summer 8am–2am; winter 8–8

La Table du Marché €–€€

An elegant yet informal bistro-cum-deli, with star chef Christophe Leroy at the helm, serving Provençal dishes created from fresh market produce. The set menu offers good value for dinner, or call in for afternoon tea and the tempting array of pastries and cakes. You can also stock up on quality olive oil, wine and other regional specialities while you're here.

183 F3 11 rue des Commerçants
04 94 97 01 25; www.christophe-leroy.com
Daily 7.30am–midnight

Villa Belrose €€€

Chef Thierry Thiercelin has retained his Michelin star at this hotel restaurant since the end of the 1990s. Located on a hill in Gassin with fantastic views out over the Bay of Saint-Tropez, it serves typical Mediterranean cuisine that hasn't forgotten its Provençal roots.

183 F3 Boulevard des Crètes
04 94 55 97 97, www.villa-belrose.com
Closed mid-Oct to mid-April

Where to... Shop

FOOD & DRINK

A trip to St-Tropez is not complete without sampling the creations from **La Tarte Tropézienne** (36 rue Clemenceau; tel: 04 94 97 71 42; www.tarte-tropezienne.com). The shop takes its name from the tart – a rich cake sandwich filled with custard and topped with sugar – that was popular with Brigitte Bardot during the filming of *Et Dieu Creá la Femme* (*And God Created Woman*) in 1956.

Nestled between vineyards in Gassin, **La Maison des Confitures** (chemin Bourrian; tel: 04 94 43 41 58; www.maisondesconfitures.com), has more than 500 varieties of jam, including some typically regional (thyme, lavender, fig and nut) and savoury (such as onion).

At the **Petit Village** in Gassin (Carrefour de la Foux; tel: 04 94 56 32 04; www.mavigne.com), you can buy the wines of the *Mâitres Vignerons*, which are considered among the best Côtes de Provence wines.

Head to the **Maison des Vins Côtes de Provence** (► 156; RDN 7; tel: 04 94 99 50 20, www.maison-des-vins.fr; summer 10–7, Sun till 6, winter 10–6, Sun till 5) to admire a selection of 800 different wines from the Côtes de Provence, a wine-producing region that stretches from the Montagne Sainte-Victoire to Roquebrune-sur-Argens.

MARKETS

St Tropez's **Marché aux Poissons** (place aux Herbes, open daily 7am–1pm) is a small fish market which provides a different view of life in the town. Try Mediterranean fish such as red mullet, scorpion fish and rainbow wrasse. Cash only.

The **Marché Provençal** (place des Lices, St-Tropez, open Tue, Sat 8–1) has typical Provençal food, as well as an antiques corner and some local crafts. Cash only.

Marché Collobrièrois (place de la Libération, Collobrières, Thu, Sun 8–1) is a lively farmers' market with a good range of chestnut products, from *marrons glacés* and chestnut jam to chestnut-wood wickerwork. Cork products and other regional specialities such as olives and honey are also sold. Credit cards are not accepted.

PROVENÇAL GOODS

Tropézienne fashion history was made with the invention of the Tropézienne sandal in 1927, a Roman-gladiator-style sandal favoured by the likes of Picasso. At **Rondini's** (16 rue Georges Clemenceau; tel: 04 94 97 19 55 www.rondini.fr), the family who originally brought this sandal to the town continue to do so today. The sandals come in a variety of styles from €120 and are a popular souvenir of St-Tropez.

Pépinières Cavatore (26 chemin des Orchidées; tel: 04 94 00 40 23; www.mimosa-cavatore.com) in Bormes-les-Mimosas is a nursery specialising in mimosa – visit in February to see the trees in full bloom. It's worth a visit, even if you aren't planning on buying anything. Credit cards are not accepted.

At **Pipes Courrieu** (58–60 avenue Georges Clemenceau, Cogolin; tel: 04 94 54 63 82; www.courrieupipes.fr, open Mon–Sat 9–12, 2–6), pipes for smoking have been made by the same family since 1802, using the traditional methods. They are made out of briar from Maures' mountains and marked with a silver cockerel, the emblem of Cogolin village.

Where to... Go Out

NIGHTLIFE

There is no shortage of exclusive clubs in St-Tropez. One of the best known is **Les Caves du Roy** below Hôtel Byblos (avenue Paul Signac/ avenue Foch; tel: 04 94 56 68 00; www.lescavesduroy.com; July–Aug daily 11pm–5am, April–June, Sep–Oct Fri–Sat 11pm– 5am). This well-established haunt of the rich and famous can prove difficult to get into, so try to arrive early and look beautiful. Admission is free, but drink prices are extortionate.

La Bodega de Papagayo (résidence du Nouveau Port, rue Gambetta; tel: 04 94 79 95 95; www.papagayo-st-tropez.com) is a restaurant-nightclub near the Old Port. It has a terrace with great views, and is a good place for a bit of celebrity spotting. Clubby music pumping into the small hours makes it popular with the young crowd. Bands perform almost every night during the high season.

The VIP Room (résidences du Nouveau Port; tel: 04 94 97 14 70, open May–Sep daily 9pm–5am; mid-Oct to April 9pm–3am) is all class, and to get inside you must be a VIP, or at least look as if you might be. The crowd here loves to dance, and the music will keep everyone up on their feet all night.

On the first floor of classy Hôtel Sube, **Bar Anglais** (Hôtel Sube, 15 quai Suffren; tel: 04 94 97 30 04, daily 7:30am–1am or 3am May–Oct) has a good range of beers on tap, and some great cocktails, best enjoyed on the tiny balcony, which has views over the port.

If you're not a fan of big clubs, head to the **Bar du Port** (9 quai Suffren; tel: 04 94 97 00 54; daily). A restaurant filled with mirrors and white furnishings by day, it's transformed into a music venue at night.

FESTIVALS

The area is packed with festivals and events. Check with local tourist offices for further information.

In **February**, Bormes-les-Mimosas' famous festival, the Corso Fleuri, celebrates the coming of spring and thus the yellow, vanilla-scented flower after which the village is named.

April brings the Fête de la Transhumance to Collobrières, a celebration of the traditional moving of flocks of sheep.

In **mid-May**, St-Tropez's tribute to its headless patron, St Torpes (or Tropez), takes place at the *Bravade*.

St-Tropez's second festival, Bravade des Espagnols, takes place on **15 June**.

Across France, **14 July** is Bastille Day, commemorating the start of the French Revolution with the storming of the Bastille prison.

August is a great month for local celebrations everywhere. Among them are Collobrières' Grande Fête des Fontaines with rosé wine spurting from the town's fountain. The Festival de Ramatuelle, with theatre and music, also takes place in August (► 142).

The French Riviera's very finest yacht and sailing regatta takes place off the coast of Saint-Tropez from the **end of September** to the **beginning of October**. "La Nioulargue" (now named "Les Voiles de Saint-Tropez"), an event created in a drunken moment by two sailors in 1981, has been an unmissable date in the sailing calendar since 1997.

Collobrières celebrates the Fête de la Chataigne in **October**, in conjunction with the chestnut harvest. There's lively street entertainment and more chestnuts and chestnut products than you could ever consume.

Walks & Tours

1 CAP MARTIN COAST

Walk

DISTANCE 6km (4mi) **TIME** 1.5 hours (longer if you continue to Monte-Carlo) **START/END POINT** Cap Martin/ Cabbé or Monte-Carlo. Note, the journey back to the start point involves a train ride, so check timetables ahead 187 E3

East of Monaco and close to the Italian border, Cap Martin is a rich suburb of Menton, with mansions set among sweet-smelling mimosa and olive trees. This long, linear walk (you return by train) along the Cap Martin coast takes in some of the most attractive scenery on the French Riviera. The sapphire sea sparkles on your left; sweet honeysuckle, mimosa and rhododendrons bloom on your right; and coastal towns lie ahead towards the Principality of Monaco.

1–2

If you are driving to Cap Martin, there is a **parking area** at the seaward end of avenue Winston Churchill on the Cap. From here, walk farther towards the end of the Cap, past **Le Roc Martin** restaurant (on the left) and come to a wide path at the edge of the sea. The path is called **Promenade Le Corbusier**, after the influential 1920s architect. Le Corbusier was connected with this area through his association with designer Eileen Gray, whose house is nearby. The start of the path is marked by a sign for **Ville de Roquebrune-Cap Martin**.

TAKING A BREAK
Cap Martin has expensive, high-quality restaurants. Less expensive places can be found at the other end of the walk in Cabbé.

A magnificent view over Cap Martin

CAP MARTIN WATCHTOWER
The headland at Cap Martin is perfectly positioned to provide good views of the area, and has long been used as a lookout point. The ruins of a fortified medieval watchtower can be found at the centre of the headland today. Also here are the remains of an 11th-century priory, where it is said an arrangement was made between the monks who lived here and the local people, whereby if the tower's bell rang, the people would come to the aid of the monks. One night, the prior rang the bell to test the people's response, and they came running to help, only to find nothing the matter. A few nights later, when the priory was raided by pirates, the townspeople left the ringing bell unanswered and the monks of the priory were all killed.

2–3
Follow the Promenade Le Courbusier as it hugs the coastline, skirting the edges of private gardens and smart hotels. The path heads west along the edge of Cap Martin, providing spectacular views of Monaco. **Eileen Gray's house**, designated a historic monument in 1998, is hidden from view, below the path that continues up the western side of the Cap.

3–4
There are several places along the path where steps lead up to the Cap, but a good option is to continue on to **Cabbé**, where there is a rail connection back to **Carnolès**. From Carnolès station you can return to the **parking area** by heading towards the sea, and then following the coastal path back to where you started.

Rhododendrons bloom along the path in early summer

4–5
To extend the walk beyond Cabbé, carry on to **Monte-Carlo**. Note that the route between Cabbé and Monte-Carlo sometimes strays onto the road. There are train connections from Monaco back to Carnolès.

INSIDER INFO

- Consult a **train timetable** before you set out, and time your walk so that you can meet a train at Cabbé to take you back to Carnolès.
- Bring a **raincoat** if it is a windy day or the sea is rough, as the promenade can be splashed by waves.
- It is best to take this walk in the **afternoon**, when the hottest part of the day has passed and the sun is at a good angle for the views. Insider Tip

2 ST-TROPEZ

Walk

DISTANCE 2km (1.2mi)
TIME 2 hours, plus time for visits
START/END POINT Place des Lices (park at parking des Lices) 183 F3

Stroll around St-Tropez's glamorous high-class shops and marina, taking a detour to an art gallery, continue on towards the old heart of the town and climb La Citadelle, where you have a wonderful vista across the whole town and bay.

TAKING A BREAK
Tarte Tropézienne (➤ 161)
Sénéquier (➤ 160)
La Table du Marché (➤ 160)
Le Café (➤ 160)

1–2

Start at **place des Lices**, a large open area where serious games of pétanque take place under the shade of plane trees, and markets are held on Tuesdays and Saturdays.

2–3

Take the **rue Georges Clemenceau** (with Café Clemenceau on the corner) away from the place des Lices towards the port. Stop off at **La Tarte Tropézienne** (➤ 161) to experience the eponymous sponge cake filled with custard cream that was invented here in the 1950s and has enjoyed enormous popularity ever since. Upmarket boutiques proliferate along this pedestrianised street, and all the way down to the harbour.

Cross the main street and turn left at **quai Gabriel Péri**. The **Musée de l'Annonciade** (➤ 145, closed Tuesday) sits on the corner ahead, where the quay bears right. The permanent collection here includes many pointillist and Fauvist works dating from the end of the 19th century, when St-Tropez was at the centre of the artistic avant-garde.

3–4

Walk back along the quay, so that the water is on your left. You should get a wonderful view of the luxury boats in the harbour from here. Take a couple of minutes to look at the founding father of St-Tropez, Pierre-André de Suffien, an 18th-century admiral whose **statue** will be on your right. Farther along the quay, pick up a town map from the **tourist office** on the right. The famous red-terraced **Café Sénéquier** (➤ 160) is here too. Stop by for a coffee, looking out over the harbour, the yachts and passers-by.

4–5

Follow the waterfront until you come to **Môle Jean-Reveille**, the jetty enclosing the port. Climb up some steps to the paved jetty to enjoy a sweeping view of the town on one side and the Bay of St-Tropez on the other. From the *môle*, head down to the **Tour du Portalet** and enter a little street at the base of the tower, rue Portalet. Turn left into rue St-Ésprit and then the first-right into rue du Puits. Turn left into **place de l'Hôtel de Ville** and take the third right into rue St-Jean to reach the **Église de**

St-Tropez (➤ 144). Turn right down rue du Clocher, and right again at rue Commandant Guichard, where you'll find the church's entrance. The church's bright pink bell tower houses the bust of St Torpes (or Tropez), the town's patron saint, who is celebrated in an annual procession at the Bravade de St-Torpes in May (➤ 144).

5–6
Return to the **place de l'Hôtel de Ville** and turn right to walk through the Porte du Revelen (an arch at the end of the street). On the other side of the arch is the small **Port des Pêcheurs**, the fishermen's port that originally made up St-Tropez. Turning around, walk up the rue des Ramparts, left across the small place des Remparts, and take rue des Quatre-vents until you come to some steps at the end of the street. Turn right down rue de l'Aïoli, take a left between two anchors (across from Baron Lodge), and climb up the steps leading towards **La Citadelle** (➤ 144). Dating back to the 16th century, the citadel houses the **Musée Naval** (➤ 144).

6–7
From the citadel, retrace your path down the steps and cross the road to enter the pedestrian-only rue de la Citadelle. Continue down this street as far as a minor crossroad, where you should turn right into rue des Commerçants. On the right is Christophe Leroy's **La Table du Marché** (➤ 160)

7–8
Outside Chez Fuchs, take the first left down a small alley, rue de Marché, which leads towards **place aux Herbes**, a tiny but lovely square where a daily market is held, there is an arch on the left which leads into the lively **fish market**, where the daily catch of fish is sold by local fishmongers.

8–9
Continue on through the fish market to come out at the **tourist office**. Cross the road into the boutique-lined rue François Sibilli, past place de la Garonne, and continue on along rue François Sibilli to return to the place des Lices, where you really should reward yourself with a coffee and a well-earned rest while you watch the world go by at the renowned **Le Café** (➤ 160) – unless you can be tempted to play a game or two of *boules* on the square.

A game of pétanque in the place des Lices, St-Tropez

3 VENCE TO GRASSE

Drive

DISTANCE 44km (27.5mi)
TIME Allow a half-day with visits
START POINT Vence 186 B3 **END POINT** Grasse 186 A2

1–2
Leave Vence on the **D2210** signposted Grasse and Tourrettes-sur-Loup. After 3km (2mi), just off the road, is **Château Notre-Dame-des-Fleurs**. This magnificent 19th-century castle became a contemporary art foundation in 1993 and contains a permanent collection of works by Matisse, Dufy and Chagall.

2–3
Continue along the **D2210** to **Tourrettes-sur-Loup**. Tourrettes is a lovely medieval village on a rocky ridge. The village is popular with artists and artisans, but perhaps best known for its production of violets (► 15).

3–4
Eight kilometres (5mi) farther on, you will arrive at **Pont-du-Loup**.

TAKING A BREAK
Taverne Provençale, Gourdon
✉ Place de l'Église
☎ 04 93 09 68 22;
www.lataverneprovencale.com

From here it is worth taking a short detour to **Le Bar-sur-Loup**. Clinging to the hillside, this pretty village is surrounded by sweetly scented terraces of jasmine, roses and violets.

4–5
Return to Pont-du-Loup; follow signs to Gorges du Loup (**D6**) and Gourdon. A tortuous route winds up this spectacular gorge, through narrow twists of rock, below precipitous, chalky cliffs and past bubbling springs, gushing rapids and sparkling waterfalls. After

Picturesque alleyways crisscross the medieval village of Tourettes-sur-Loup

In imposanter Lage liegt der Ort Gourdon

7km (4mi), turn left at Bramafan bridge on to the **D3** to **Gourdon**. The village is a veritable eagle's nest, clinging to the summit of a cliff, 500m (1,640ft) above the Loup. Visitors crowd its cobbled streets, gift shops, perfumeries and medieval castle, and admire the breathtaking panorama of the entire Côte d'Azur.

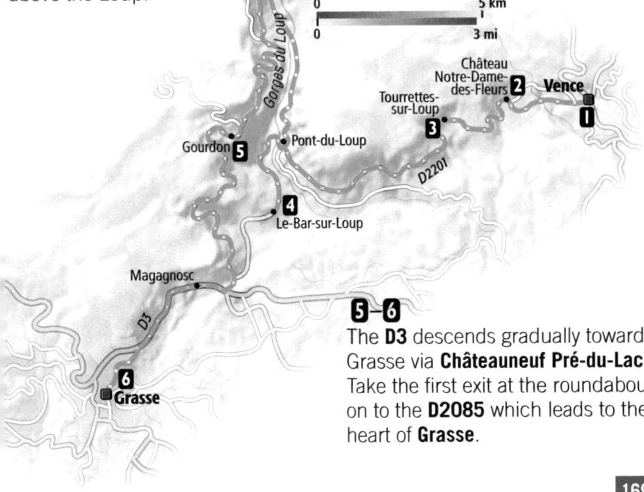

5–6

The **D3** descends gradually towards Grasse via **Châteauneuf Pré-du-Lac**. Take the first exit at the roundabout on to the **D2085** which leads to the heart of **Grasse**.

4 EXPLORING INLAND FROM THE COAST

Drive

DISTANCE 150km (93mi) **TIME** Allow a full day for this drive, and be aware that the roads inland from the coast are often winding and slow
START/END POINT Menton 187 E3

Flags flying from the tollgate on the 11th-century bridge at the heart of Sospel

This circular route into the countryside which lies behind the Principality of Monaco contrasts some of the prettiest – and busiest – villages and towns on the French Riviera with the peace and natural beauty of the Parc National du Mercantour.

1–2

Start from **Menton** (➤ 76), a pretty and curiously Italian town on the French side of the border. There's a **museum** by the waterfront to the poet, playwright and film director Jean Cocteau (1889–1963), which is worth a quick look if you have time. Pick up the road in the town centre signed **Autoroute (Nice, Italia)** and **Sospel**. Follow signs for Sospel on the winding **D2566**, passing under the A8 and through Castillon-Neuf. At **Sospel** go over the railway crossing and turn left, following signs for Moulinet and Col de Turini. The bridge at Sospel, with its central tower, was rebuilt in the 20th century after the 11th-century original was blown up during World War II.

2–3

Bear left at a bend on to the **D2204**. The road climbs to Col St-Jean, with great views back down to Sospel. Go over **Col de Braus** (1,002m/3,287ft) and descend through hairpin bends almost into L'Escarène. Just after a railway bridge turn right, signed to Lucéram and Peïra-Cava. Continue on this road to reach the jumbled medieval hilltop village of **Lucéram**.

3–4
Lucéram is known for its exhibition of nativity scenes in the winter months (Dec–Jan). The hundreds of crèches on display throughout the village come in all shapes and sizes, ranging from the tiny to the very large indeed. Visit the precious treasures in the Eglise Ste-Marguerite before heading towards Turini. There are many more hairpin bends to negotiate before you reach the superb view-point of **Peïra-Cava**. To the east, you'll see views of the magnificent Parc National du Mercantour.

4–5
Continue north from Peïra-Cava to the next viewpoint, **Col de Turini**. The mountain pass stands at 1,604m (5,262ft), and this is a good place for a break and refreshment at the hotel **Les Trois Vallées Suffien**.

5–6
Turn left on to the **D70**, following signs for La Bollène-Vésubie and Nice. Descend with care, and after about 10km (6mi), just after the Chapelle-St-Honorat tunnel, look out for a small **chapel** on the left, on a bend. There are fabulous views from the parking area here.

6–7
Continue on this road through La Bollène-Vésubie and at a T-junction (intersection) turn left on to the **D2565**, signed for Nice and St-Martin-Vésubie (Vésubie is the name of the river which runs through here). This brings you to the valley floor. Follow signs for Lantosque and Nice. Continue southwards through **St-Jean-de-la-Rivière**. About 1km (0.6mi) beyond St-Jean fork left on to the **D19**, signed Nice par Levens.

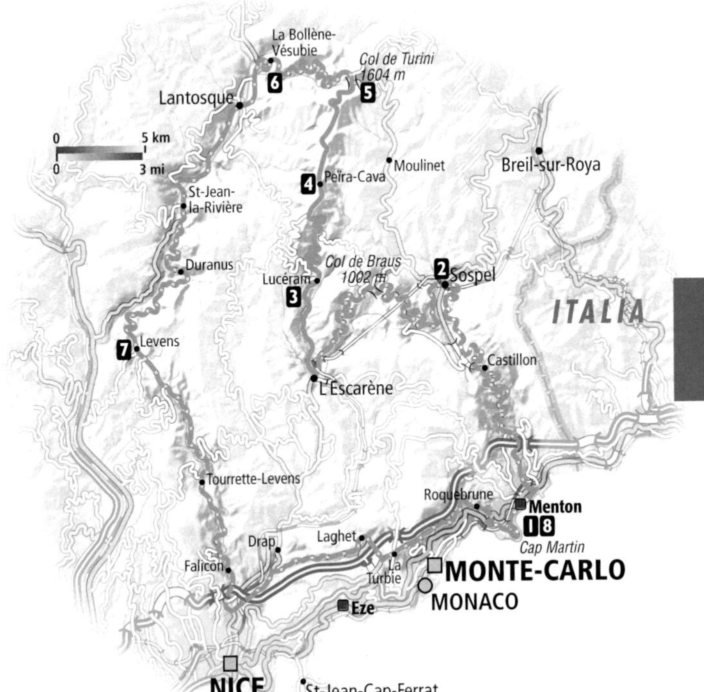

The picturesque village of La Bollène-Vésubie

This road becomes narrower as it ascends the valley. Go through a tunnel just before Duranus and look for a viewpoint on the right. The **Saut des Français** looks out from sheer cliffs. Stay on the road into **Levens**, an appealing Old town with two 18th-century chapels standing on two sides of the square, and a grand gateway – the remnant of a castle that has long since disappeared.

7–8

Leave Levens on the **D19**, following signs for Nice, and passing Tourrette-Levens. Soon after St-André the road passes under the A8. Turn left at traffic lights here, signed to Sospel. Cross a river and go straight over another set of traffic lights, passing under the A8 again. Take the next right turn, signed Route de Turin, cross the river and a level (grade) crossing, then turn left at traffic lights, signed La Trinité and Drap. At the roundabout (traffic circle) take the road signed for La Turbie and Laghet, and follow the **D2204a** up a winding valley to **Laghet**. At this point a hairpin bend takes the road sharply right.

Pass under the A8 once more, and turn left at the next junction, which is an *autoroute* slip road, then follow the signs to Menton. Turn left at the next junction, signed for La Turbie and Monaco, and stay on this road to the ancient Roman village of **La Turbie** (► 74). Its outstanding monument is the Trophée des Alpes, a triumphal arch built by Caesar Augustus around 6 BC. After La Turbie, bear left past a hotel, signed Roquebrune and Menton, and turn right at traffic lights at the bottom of the hill, signed Nice and Beausoleil. At the next traffic lights turn left, signed to Cap Martin. As it leaves the heart of the village the road veers sharp left – go straight ahead here, signed for Mayerling and Cap Martin, and you will reach the sea. Follow the coast road back to **Menton**.

TAKING A BREAK

Les Trois Vallées hotel-restaurant stands at the high point of this tour, at the Col de Turini (Tel: 04 93 04 23 23). There are also several bars and restaurants in Sospel.

Practicalities

Practicalities

BEFORE YOU GO

WHAT YOU NEED

● Required
○ Suggested
▲ Not required
△ Not applicable

Some countries require a passport to remain valid for at least six months beyond the date of entry – contact their consulate or embassy or your travel agent for details.

	UK	USA	Canada	Australia	Ireland	Netherlands
Passport/National Identity Card	●	●	●	●	●	●
Visa (regulations can change – check before your journey)	▲	▲	▲	▲	▲	▲
Onward or Return Ticket	▲	●	●	●	▲	▲
Health Inoculations (tetanus and polio)	▲	▲	▲	▲	▲	▲
Health Documentation (➤ 174, Health)	●	●	●	●	●	●
Travel Insurance	○	○	○	○	○	○
Driving Licence (national) for car rental	●	●	●	●	●	●
Car Insurance Certificate (if using own car)	●	△	△	△	●	●
Car Registration Document (if using own car)	●	△	△	△	●	●

WHEN TO GO

French Riviera

High season / Low season

JAN	FEB	MAR	APR	MAY	JUN	JUL	AUG	SEP	OCT	NOV	DEC
12°C	14°C	14°C	18°C	21°C	27°C	28°C	28°C	25°C	22°C	17°C	14°C
54°F	57°F	57°F	64°F	70°F	81°F	82°F	82°F	77°F	72°F	63°F	57°F

Sun · Sunshine & showers · Cloudy · Wet · Very wet

Temperatures are the **average daily maximum** for each month, although they can rise to 35°C (95°F) in July and August.

Spring starts in March when the mimosa and almonds come into bloom on the coast, and it is usually warm enough to sit outside on the terrace in April. Summers are hot and dry, and the coastal areas are very crowded. The autumn months (September and October) can be very pleasant, although there may be occasional thunderstorms. Colder weather arrives in November, with snow settling on high ground in December.

GETTING ADVANCE INFORMATION

Département Tourist Information:

- Alpes-Maritimes: www.cotedazur-tourisme.com
- Var: www.visitvar.fr

Tourist Offices

- www.cannes.travel
- www.monaco-tourisme.com
- www.nicetourism.com
- www.saint-tropez.st
- www.franceguide.com

Online resources with information in English:

www.provencebeyond.com;
www.provenceweb.fr
www.angloinfo.com
Route planner: www.theAA.com

GETTING THERE

By Air Nice-Côte d'Azur is the main airport in the region, but there are also international flights from within Europe to Marseille-Provence and to the smaller airport just outside St-Tropez, at La Mole.
From the UK Carriers include France's international airline, Air France (tel: 0845 084 5111 in UK; 0802 802 802 in France; www.airfrance.com), British Airways (tel: 0845 773 3377; www.ba.com), easyJet (tel: 0871 750 0100; www.easyjet.com) and Ryanair (tel: 0870 156 9569; www.ryanair.com). The flight time from London to Nice is around 2 hours.
From the US and Canada Delta Air Lines operates a few direct flights between New York and Nice-Côte d'Azur, but passengers from most US and Canadian cities will usually have to change at London (Heathrow, Gatwick or Stansted) or Paris. Delta Air Lines (tel: 1800/241 4141 in US; www.delta.com), American Airlines (tel: 1800/433 7300 in US; www.aa.com) and Air Canada (tel: 1888/247 2262 in Canada; www.aircanada.com). The flying time direct from New York to Provence is around 8 hours.
By Rail SNCF, the national carrier, operates high-speed train (TGV) services from the Gare de Lyon in Paris to Nice. The journey takes about 6 hours (www.tgv.co.uk). The Eurostar passenger train service (tel: 0870 518 6186 in UK; www.eurostar.com) from London St Pancras via the Channel Tunnel to Paris Gare du Nord takes 2.25 hours.
By Sea Several ferry companies operate regular services from England and Ireland to north and northwest France. Crossing times from England vary from 35 minutes to 9 hours, and from Ireland around 14 to 18 hours.

TIME

France is on **Central European Time**, one hour ahead of Greenwich Mean Time (GMT +1). From late March, when clocks are put forward one hour, until late October, French summer time (GMT +2) operates.

CURRENCY & FOREIGN EXCHANGE

Currency The euro (€) is the official currency of France and Monaco. Notes (bills) are issued in denominations of €5, €10, €20, €50, €100, €200 and €500 and coins are in denominations of 1, 2, 5, 10, 20 and 50 cents, and €1 and €2.
Exchange You can exchange travellers' cheques at some banks and at bureaux de change at airports, main railway stations or in some department stores, and exchange booths. All transactions are subject to a commission charge, so you may prefer to rely on cash and credit cards. Travellers' cheques issued by American Express and VISA may also be changed at many post offices.
Credit cards are widely accepted in shops, restaurants and hotels. VISA (Carte Bleue), MasterCard (Eurocard) and Diners Club cards with four-digit PINs can be used in most ATM cash dispensers. Some smaller shops and hotels may not accept credit cards – always check before you book in.

FRENCH TOURIST OFFICES AT HOME

In the UK
300 High Holborn,
London WC1V 7JH
☎ 0906 824 4123

In the US
444 Madison Avenue,
16th Floor,
New York, NY10022
☎ 212/838 7800

In Australia
Level 20,
25 Bligh Street,
Sydney, NSW 2000
☎ 02 92 31 52 44

In Canada
1981 Avenue McGill,
College Suite 490,
Montreal H3A 2W9
☎ 514/876 9881

Practicalities

WHEN YOU ARE THERE

NATIONAL HOLIDAYS

1 Jan: **New Year's Day**; 27 Jan **St Devote's Day** (Monaco only); March/April: **Easter Sunday** and **Easter Monday**; 1 May: **Labour Day**; 8 May: **VE Day** (France only); May/June **Whit Sunday** and **Whit Monday**; June **Corpus Christi** (Monaco only); 14 July: **Bastille Day** (France only); 15 Aug: **Assumption**; 1 Nov: **All Saints' Day**; 11 Nov: **Remembrance Day** (France only); 19 Nov: **Monaco National Holiday** (Monaco only); 25 Dec: **Christmas Day**

ELECTRICITY

The power supply throughout France is 220 volts AC, 50 Hz. Sockets accept two-round-pin continental-style plugs. Visitors from the UK will need a plug adaptor and US visitors will need a voltage transformer.

OPENING HOURS

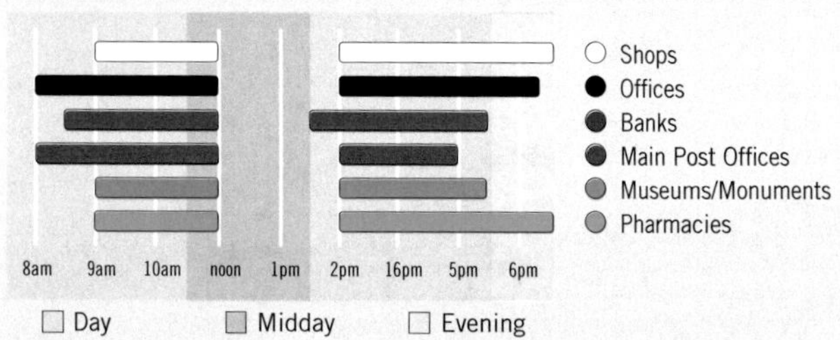

Shops In summer the afternoon opening time of shops is from 4 to 8 or 9pm. Most shops close on Sunday and many on Monday. Small food shops open from 7am and may open on Sunday morning. Large department stores do not close for lunch, and hypermarkets open 10am to 9 or 10pm but may shut on Monday morning.
Banks Banks are closed on Sunday as well as Saturday or Monday.
Museums Museums and monuments have extended summer hours. Many close one day a week; either Monday (municipal ones) or Tuesday (national ones).

TIPS/GRATUITIES

Tipping is normal for all services. As a general guide:

Taxis	Change from note (bill)
Tour guides	€3–5
Porters	€3 per bag
Chambermaids	€2 per day
Cafés/bars	Leave change
Hairdressers	Change from note (bill)
Restaurant workers	Service always included. Leave a note if service has been exemplary

TIME DIFFERENCES

Nice (CET)
12 noon

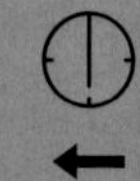

London (GMT)
11 noon

New York (EST)
6am

Los Angeles (PST)
3am

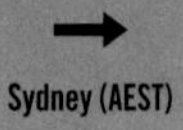

Sydney (AEST)
9pm

STAYING IN TOUCH

Post The PTT (*Poste et Télécommunications*) deals with mail and telephone services. Outside main centres, post offices open shorter hours and may close 12–2. Letter boxes are yellow. Post offices usually have an ATM.

Telephone All telephone numbers in France comprise ten digits (eight in Monaco). Public phones can only be used with (rechargeable) telephone cards (*télécarte*). You can get them from post offices, Orange stores, tobacconists and in SNCF and metro stations. Lots of public phones can receive calls – you'll spot the number written on or near the phone itself. Some cafés, bistros and post offices still have coin-operated phones.

International Dialling Codes
Dial 00 followed by

UK:	**44**	**Australia:**	**61**
USA/Canada:	**1**	**New Zealand:**	**64**
Irish Republic:	**353**	**France**	**33**

Mobile providers and services Your mobile phone should automatically connect to your provider's local partner network. Orange, Bouygues and SFR are responsible for the networks in France. Take care not to rack up high roaming charges. If you make a lot of calls, consider getting a prepaid French SIM card. You can buy them directly from mobile phone companies and at tobacconists, supermarkets and the post office. Check the tariffs in advance if you want to use your phone to get online!

WiFi & Internet Many hotels provide guests with free WiFi access. Otherwise, you can get online in internet cafés, public libraries or by purchasing a chipcard (*cyberposte* card) from the region's post offices.

PERSONAL SAFETY

The Police Municipale (blue uniforms) carry out police duties in cities and towns. The Gendarmes (blue trousers, black jackets, white belts), the national police force, cover the countryside and smaller places. The CRS deal with emergencies and also look after safety on beaches. Monaco has its own police.

To avoid danger or theft:

- Do not use unmanned roadside rest areas at night.
- Cars, especially foreign cars, should be secured.
- Beware of pickpockets.

Police assistance:
☎ 17 from any call box

TAXES AND CUSTOMS

France's VAT (*TVA*) is 19.6 per cent on most goods. Visitors from outside the EU may be entitled to tax rebates.

POLICE	**17**
FIRE	**18**
AMBULANCE	**15**

Practicalities

HEALTH

Insurance Citizens of EU countries receive reduced-cost emergency health care with relevant documentation (European Health Insurance Card), but private medical insurance is still advised, and essential for all other visitors.

Dental Services As for general medical treatment (see above, Insurance), nationals of EU countries can obtain dental treatment at reduced cost. Around 70 per cent of standard dentists' fees are refunded, but private medical insurance is still advised for all.

Weather July and August are likely to be sunny and very hot. When sightseeing, cover up, apply a good sunscreen, wear sunglasses and a hat, and drink plenty of fluids.

Medication Pharmacies – recognised by their green cross sign – have highly qualified staff able to offer medical advice, provide first-aid and prescribe a wide range of drugs, although some are available by prescription (*ordonnance*) only.

Drinking Water Tap water is safe to drink, and restaurants will often bring a carafe of water to the table, although you may prefer to buy bottled water. Never drink from a tap marked *eau non potable* (not drinking water).

TRAVELLING WITH A DISABILITY

France has made great headway in providing access and facilities for visitors with disabilities. However, some tourist offices, museums and restaurants that are in historic, protected buildings are still not fully accessible. The Association des Paralysés de France (17 blvd. Auguste Blanqui, 75013, Paris; tel: 01 40 78 69 00; www.apf.asso.fr) provides information on wheelchair access.

CHILDREN

Children are welcomed in most hotels and restaurants. Baby-changing facilities are excellent in newer museums and attractions, but limited elsewhere. Special attractions for children are marked out in this book with the logo shown above.

CONCESSIONS

Students/Youths Holders of an International Student Identity Card (ISIC) are entitled to discounted admission to museums and sights, air and ferry tickets and meals in some student cafeterias. Holders of the International Youth Travel Card (or GO 25 Card) qualify for similar discounts as ISIC holders.
Senior Citizens If you are over 60 you can get discounts (up to 50 per cent) in museums, on public transport and in places of entertainment. Purchasing a *Carte Senior* (www.senior-sncf.com; €60) can give discounts of up to 50 per cent on train travel.

RESTROOMS

Modern unisex, self-cleaning, coin-operated toilets are found on the streets of most major cities. In smaller towns and villages, free public toilets can normally be found by the market square or near tourist offices. Cleanliness varies, and some older establishments may have a squat toilet.

EMBASSIES & HIGH COMMISSIONS

UK (Marseille)

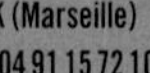

☎ 04 91 15 72 10

USA (Marseille)

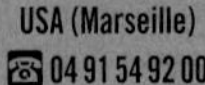

☎ 04 91 54 92 00

Ireland (Cannes)
☎ 06 77 69 14 36

Australia (Paris)
☎ 01 40 59 33 00

Canada (Nice)
☎ 04 93 92 93 22

Useful Words and Phrases

SURVIVAL PHRASES

Yes/No **Oui/Non**
Good morning/evening **Bonjour/Bonsoir**
Hello **Salut**
Goodbye **Au revoir**
How are you? **Comment allez-vous?**
Please **S'il vous plaît**
Thank you **Merci**
Excuse me **Excusez-moi**
I'm sorry **Pardon**
You're welcome **De rien/Avec plaisir**
Do you have...? **Avez-vous...?**
How much is this? **C'est combien?**
I'd like... **Je voudrais...**

DIRECTIONS

Is there a phone box around here? **Y a-t-il une cabine téléphonique dans le coin?**
Where is...? **Où se trouve...?**
...the nearest Métro **le Métro le plus proche**
...the telephone **le téléphone**
...the bank **la banque**
...the lavatory **les toilettes**
Turn left/right **Tournez à gauche/droite**
Go straight on **Allez tout droit**
The first/second (on the right) **Le premier/Le deuxième (à droite)**
At the crossroads **Au carrefour**

IF YOU NEED HELP

Could you help me, please? **Pouvez-vous m'aider, s'il vous plaît?**
Do you speak English? **Parlez-vous anglais?**
I don't understand **Je ne comprends pas**
Could you call a doctor quickly, please? **Pouvez-vous appeler un médecin d'urgence, s'il vous plaît?**

RESTAURANT

I'd like to book a table **Puis-je réserver une table?**
A table for two, please **Une table pour deux personnes, s'il vous plaît**
Do you have a fixed-price menu? **Vous avez un menu?**
Could we see the menu? **Nous pouvons voir la carte?**
Could I have the bill, please? **L'addition, s'il vous plaît**
A bottle/glass of... **Une bouteille/un verre de...**

MENU VOCABULARY

apéritifs appetisers
boissons alcoolisées alcoholic beverages
boissons chaudes hot beverages
boissons froides cold beverages
carte des vins wine list
coquillages shellfish
fromage cheese
gibier game
hors d'oeuvres starters
légumes vegetables
plats chauds hot dishes
plats froids cold dishes
plat du jour dish of the day
pâtisserie pastry
plat principal main course
potages soups
service compris service included
service non compris service not included
spécialités régionales regional specialities
viandes meat courses
volaille poultry

NUMBERS

0	**zéro**	11	**onze**	22	**vingt-deux**	110	**cent dix**
1	**un**	12	**douze**	30	**trente**	120	**cent vingt**
2	**deux**	13	**treize**	31	**trente et un**	200	**deux cents**
3	**trois**	14	**quatorze**	40	**quarante**	300	**trois cents**
4	**quatre**	15	**quinze**	50	**cinquante**	400	**quatre cents**
5	**cinq**	16	**seize**	60	**soixante**	500	**cinq cents**
6	**six**	17	**dix-sept**	70	**soixante-dix**	600	**six cents**
7	**sept**	18	**dix-huit**	80	**quatre-vingts**	700	**sept cents**
8	**huit**	19	**dix-neuf**	90	**quatre-vingt-dix**	800	**huit cents**
9	**neuf**	20	**vingt**	100	**cent**	900	**neuf cents**
10	**dix**	21	**vingt et un**	101	**cent un**	1,000	**mille**

MENU READER

agneau lamb
ail garlic
ananas pineapple
anguille eel
banane banana
beurre butter
bifteck steak
bière beer
bière pression draught beer
boeuf beef
boudin noir/blanc black/white pudding
brochet pike
cabillaud cod
calmar squid
canard duck
champignons mushrooms
chou cabbage
choucroute sauerkraut
chou-fleur cauliflower
choux de Bruxelles Brussels sprouts
citron lemon
civet de lièvre jugged hare
concombre cucumber
confiture jam
coquilles Saint-Jacques scallops
cornichon gherkin
côte/côtelette chop
couvert cutlery
crevettes grises shrimps
crevettes roses prawns
croque monsieur toasted ham and cheese sandwich
cru raw
crustacés seafood
cuisses de grenouilles frogs' legs
cuit (à l'eau) boiled
eau mineral gazeuse/non gazeuse sparkling/still mineral water
écrevisse crayfish
entrecôte sirloin steak
entrées first course
épices spices
épinards spinach
épis de maïs corn (on the cob)
escargots snails
farine flour
fenouil fennel
fèves broad beans
figues figs
filet de boeuf beef fillet
filet mignon fillet steak
filet de porc pork tenderloin
fines herbes herbs
foie gras goose liver
fraises strawberries
framboises raspberries
frit fried
friture deep-fried
fruit de la passion passion fruit
fruits de la saison seasonal fruits
gaufres waffles
gigot d'agneau leg of lamb
glace ice-cream
glaçons ice cubes
grillé grilled
groseilles redcurrants
hareng herring
haricots blancs haricot beans
haricots verts french beans
homard lobster
huîtres oysters
jambon blanc/cru/fumé smoked ham
jus de citron lemon juice
jus de fruits fruit juice
jus d'orange orange juice
lait (demi-écrémé/entier) milk (semi-skimmed/full-cream)
langouste crayfish
langoustine scampi
langue tongue
lapin rabbit
lentilles lentils
lotte monkfish
loup de mer sea bass
macaron macaroon
maïs sweetcorn
marron chestnut
menu du jour/à la carte menu of the day/à la carte
morilles morels
moules mussels
mousse au chocolat chocolate mousse
moutarde mustard
myrtilles bilberries
noisette hazelnut
noix walnut
noix de veau fillet of veal
oeuf à la coque/dur/au plat egg soft/hard-boiled/fried
oignon onion
origan oregano
pain au chocolat croissant with chocolate centre
part portion
pêche peach
petite friture fried fish (whitebait or similar)
petits (biscuits) salés savoury biscuits
petit pain roll
petits pois green peas
pintade guinea fowl
poire pear
pois chiches chick peas
poisson fish
poivre pepper
poivron green/red pepper
pomme apple
pommes de terre potatoes
pommes frites chips
poulet (blanc) chicken (breast)
prune plum
pruneaux prunes
queue de boeuf oxtail
ragoût stew
ris de veau sweetbread
riz rice
rôti de boeuf (rosbif) roast beef
rouget red mullet
saignant rare
salade verte lettuce
salé/sucré salted/sweet
saumon salmon
saucisses sausages
sel salt
soupe à l'oignon onion soup
sucre sugar
thon tuna
thym thyme
tripes tripe
truffes truffles
truite trout
truite saumonée salmon trout
vapeur (à la) steamed
venaison venison
viande hachée minced meat
vin blanc white wine
vin rosé rosé wine
vin rouge red wine
vinaigre vinegar
xérès sherry

Road Atlas

For chapters: See inside front cover

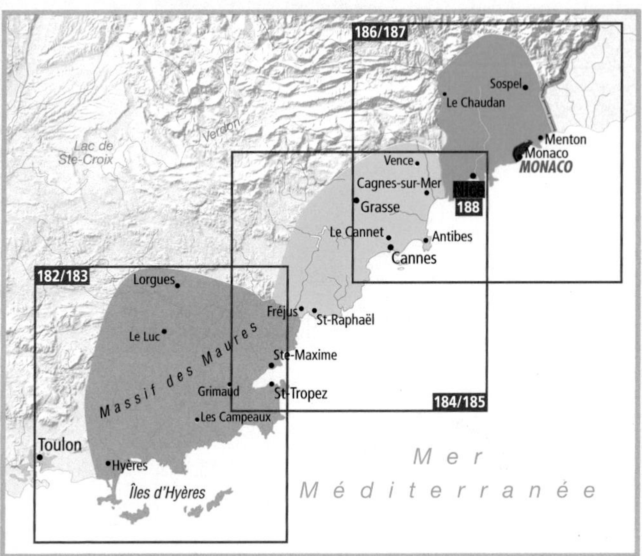

Key to Road Atlas

A 9 2	Motorway		Military airport
	Dual carriageway		Runway; glider airfield
N113	Trunk road (route nationale)		Church; chapel
907	Main road (route départementale)		Monastery; ruin
	Secondary road		Palace, castle, fortress; ruin
	Road, not surfaced	★	Place of interest
	Track		Archaeological site
	Footpath		Tower; radio mast; lighthouse
	Road under construction/planned		Waterfall; cave
	Railway		Peak; pass
	Ferry route		Campground; viewpoint
	Funicular railway		Spring; (swimming) beach
	Département boundary		Port; yacht harbour
	National park, National preserve	1	TOP 10
	Restricted area	26	Don't Miss
	International airport	22	At Your Leisure
	Regional; closed airport		

1 : 300 000

0 — 10 — 20 km

0 — 5 — 10 mi

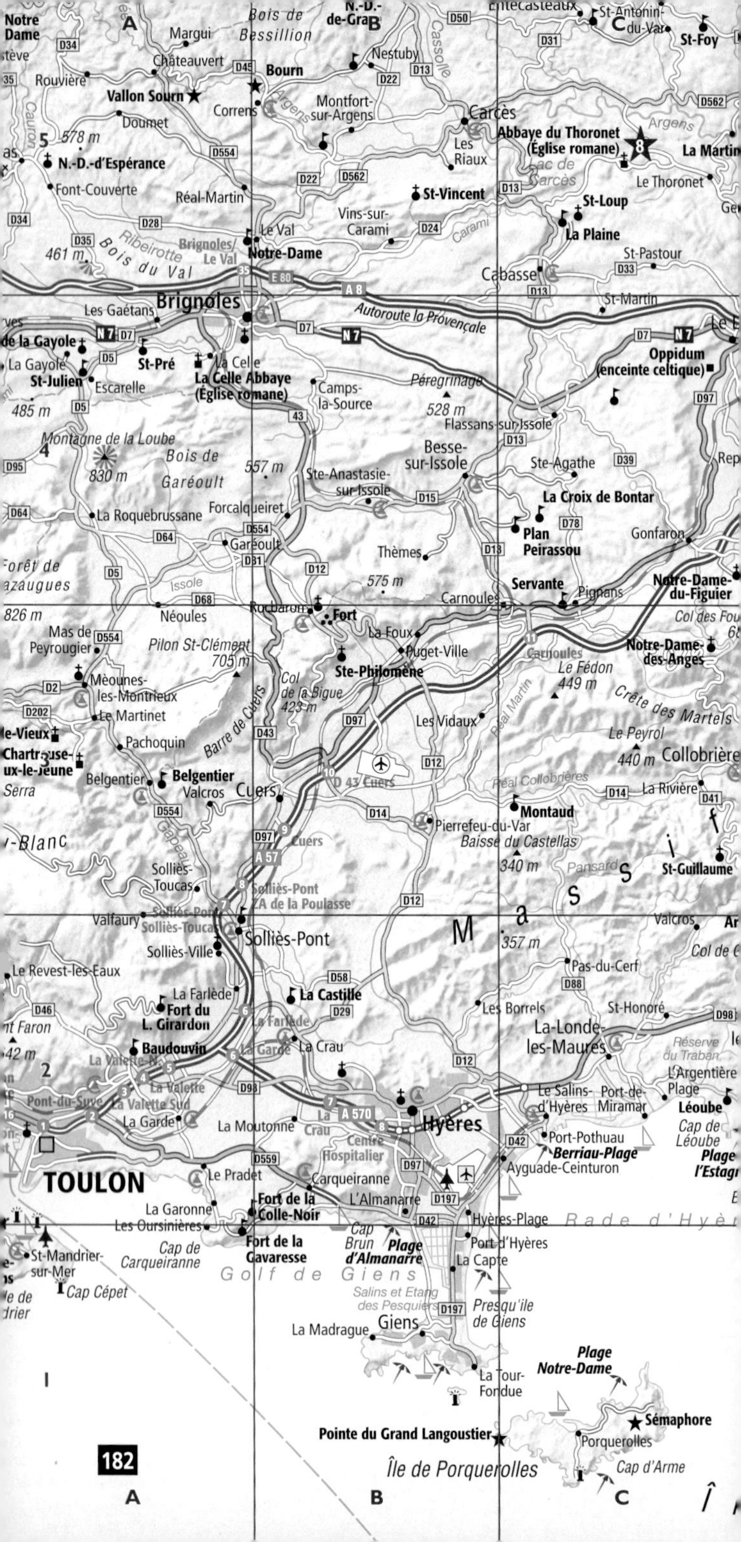

Notre Dame
Margui
Bois de Bessillion
N.-D.-de-Gra
Entrecasteaux
St-Antonin-du-Var
St-Foy
Châteauvert
Bourn
Nestuby
Rouvière
Vallon Sourn
Correns
Montfort-sur-Argens
Carcès
Doumet
578 m
Abbaye du Thoronet (Église romane)
La Martin
N.-D.-d'Espérance
Les Riaux
Lac de Carcès
Le Thoronet
Font-Couverte
Réal-Martin
St-Vincent
St-Loup
Vins-sur-Caramí
La Plaine
Le Val
Brignoles/Le Val
Notre-Dame
461 m
Bois du Val
Ribeirotte
St-Pastour
Cabasse
E 80
A 8
St-Martin
Les Gaétans
Brignoles
Autoroute la Provençale
de la Gayole
St-Pré
La Gayole
La Celle
Oppidum (enceinte celtique)
St-Julien
La Celle Abbaye (Église romane)
Escarelle
Camps-la-Source
Péregrinage
528 m
485 m
Flassans-sur-Issole
Montagne de la Loube
Besse-sur-Issole
830 m
Bois de Garéoult
557 m
Ste-Anastasie-sur-Issole
Ste-Agathe
La Croix de Bontar
La Roquebrussane
Forcalqueiret
Plan Peirassou
Garéoult
Gonfaron
Forêt de Mazaugues
Thèmes
575 m
Issole
Servante
Carnoules
Pignans
Notre-Dame-du-Figuier
826 m
Néoules
Rocbaron
Fort
Col des Fourches
Mas de Peyrougier
La Foux
Pilon St-Clément
705 m
Puget-Ville
Notre-Dame-des-Anges
Carnoules
Le Fédon
449 m
Ste-Philomène
Mèounes-les-Montrieux
Col de la Bigue
423 m
Crête des Martels
Le Martinet
Les Vidaux
Réal Martin
Le Peyrol
440 m
Collobrières
Pachoquin
Barre de Cuers
Belgentier
Chartreuse-de-Montrieux-le-Jeune
Serra
Valcros
Cuers
Réal Collobrières
La Rivière
Montaud
Pierrefeu-du-Var
Baisse du Castellas
Gapeau
Cuers
340 m
Pansard
St-Guillaume
Solliès-Toucas
Solliès-Pont ZA de la Poulasse
Massif
Valfaury
Solliès-Pont
Valcros
357 m
Col de Ca
Solliès-Ville
Le Revest-les-Eaux
Pas-du-Cerf
La Farlède
La Castille
Fort du L. Girardon
La Farlède
Les Borrels
St-Honoré
Mont Faron
La-Londe-les-Maures
Réserve du Trabari
Baudouvin
La Crau
La Garde
La Valette-N.
L'Argentière Plage
La Valette
Le Salins-d'Hyères
Port-de-Miramar
Léoube
Pont-du-Suve
La Valette Sud
La Garde
La Moutonne
La Crau
A 570
Hyères
Cap de Léoube
Centre Hospitalier
Port-Pothuau
Berriau-Plage
Plage l'Estagnol
TOULON
Le Pradet
Carqueiranne
Ayguade-Ceinturon
La Garonne
Fort de la Colle-Noir
L'Almanarre
Les Oursinières
Hyères-Plage
Rade d'Hyères
St-Mandrier-sur-Mer
Cap de Carqueiranne
Fort de la Gavaresse
Cap Brun
Plage d'Almanarre
Port-d'Hyères
La Capte
Golf de Giens
Cap Cépet
Salins et Etang des Pesquiers
Presqu'ile de Giens
La Madrague
Giens
Plage Notre-Dame
La Tour-Fondue
Sémaphore
Pointe du Grand Langoustier
Porquerolles
Île de Porquerolles
Cap d'Arme

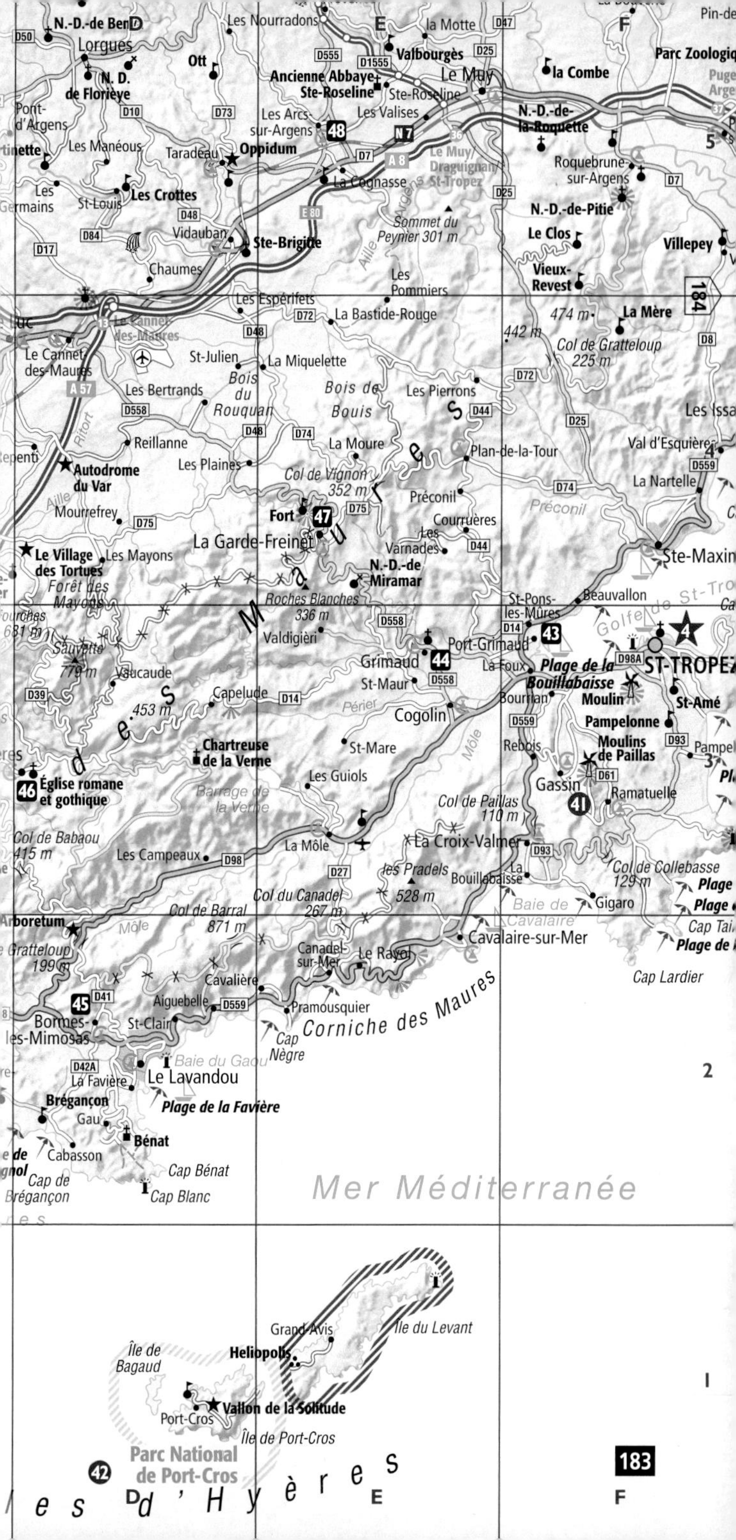

Lorgues
N.-D.-de Benva
N. D. de Florièye
Ott
Les Nourradons
la Motte
Valbourgès
Ancienne Abbaye Ste-Roseline
Le Muy
Ste-Roseline
Les Valises
Parc Zoologique
la Combe
N.-D.-de-la-Roquette
Roquebrune-sur-Argens
Les Arcs-sur-Argens
Taradeau
Oppidum
Les Manéous
Pont-d'Argens
Les Crottes
St-Louis
Les Germains
La Cognasse
Le Muy/Draguignan/St-Tropez
Sommet du Peynier 301 m
N.-D.-de-Pitie
Le Clos
Vieux-Revest
Villepey
Vidauban
Ste-Brigitte
Chaumes
Les Pommiers
Les Espérifets
La Bastide-Rouge
474 m
La Mère
442 m
Col de Gratteloup 225 m
Le Cannet-des-Maures
St-Julien
La Miquelette
Bois du Rouquan
Bois de Bouis
Les Pierrons
Les Bertrands
Reillanne
Les Plaines
La Moure
Plan-de-la-Tour
Val d'Esquières
Les Issambres
La Nartelle
Autodrome du Var
Col de Vignon 352 m
Préconil
Mourrefrey
Fort
La Garde-Freinet
Courruères
Les Varnades
N.-D.-de Miramar
Ste-Maxime
Le Village des Tortues
Les Mayons
Forêt des Mayons
Roches Blanches 336 m
Beauvallon
St-Pons-les-Mûres
Golfe de St-Tropez
Valdigièri
Port-Grimaud
Grimaud
La Foux
Plage de la Bouillabaisse
ST-TROPEZ
St-Maur
Sauvette 779 m
Vaucaude
453 m
Capelude
Cogolin
Bourrian
Moulin
St-Amé
Pampelonne
Chartreuse de la Verne
St-Mare
Rebois
Moulins de Paillas
Gassin
Ramatuelle
Église romane et gothique
Les Guiols
Barrage de la Verne
Col de Paillas 110 m
Col de Babaou 415 m
Les Campeaux
La Môle
La Croix-Valmer
Les Pradels 528 m
La Bouillabaisse
Col de Collebasse 129 m
Col du Canadel 267 m
Col de Barral 871 m
Baie de Cavalaire
Gigaro
Arboretum
Cavalaire-sur-Mer
Cap Lardier
Col de Gratteloup 199 m
Canadel-sur-Mer
Le Rayol
Cavalière
Aiguebelle
Pramousquier
Corniche des Maures
Bormes-les-Mimosas
St-Clair
Cap Nègre
Baie du Gaou
Le Lavandou
La Favière
Plage de la Favière
Brégançon
Gau
Bénat
Cabasson
Cap Bénat
Cap de Brégançon
Cap Blanc
Mer Méditerranée
Massif des Maures
Grand Avis
Île du Levant
Heliopolis
Île de Bagaud
Port-Cros
Vallon de la Solitude
Île de Port-Cros
Parc National de Port-Cros
Îles d'Hyères
D E F
184

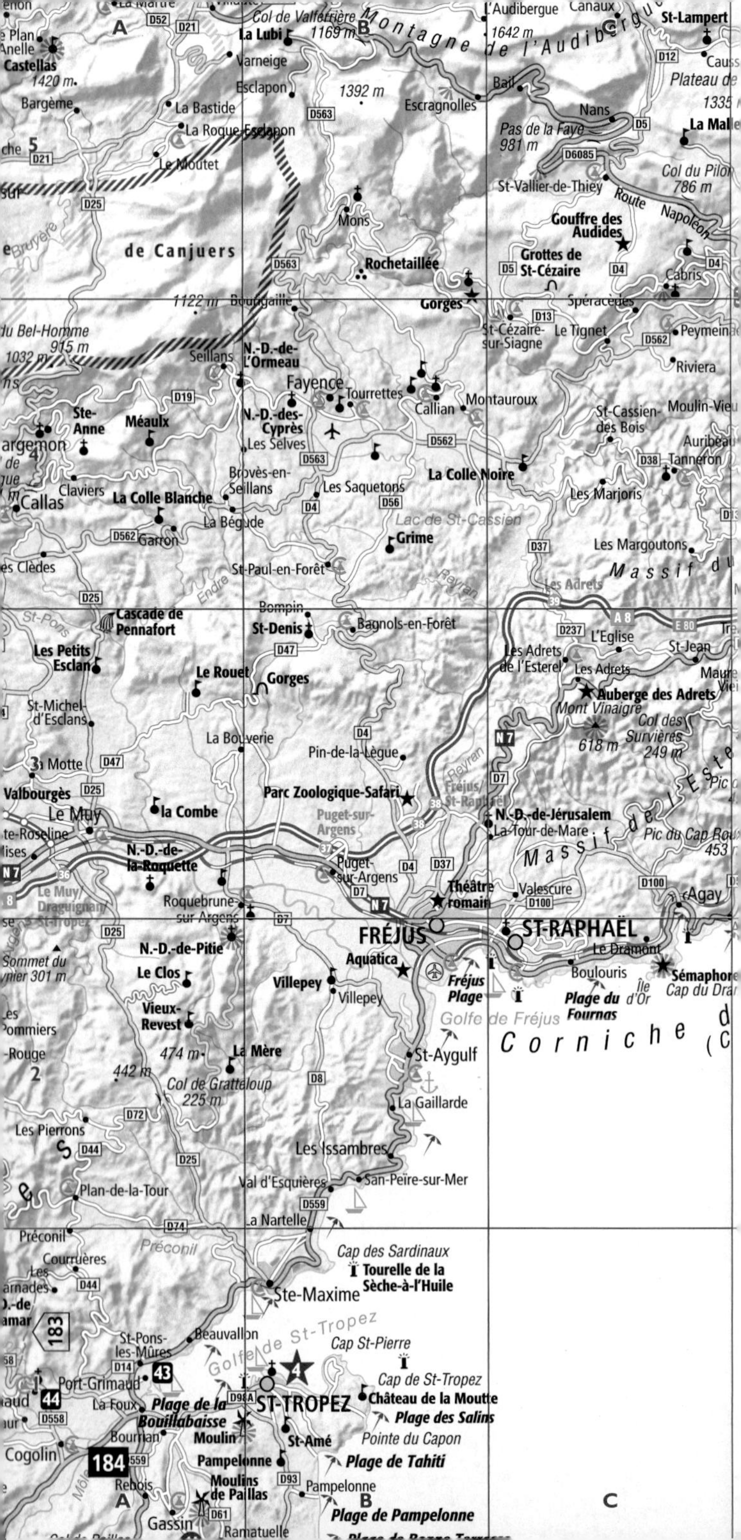

A
B
C
D52
D21
Col de Valferrière 1169 m
Montagne de l'Audibergue
L'Audibergue
1642 m
Canaux
St-Lampert
Castellas
1420 m
La Lubi
Varneige
Esclapon
1392 m
Escragnolles
Bail
Plateau de
1335
Bargème
La Bastide
La Roque-Esclapon
D563
Nans
D5
La Malle
Pas de la Faye 981 m
D21
Le Moutet
D6085
Col du Pilon 786 m
St-Vallier-de-Thiey
Route Napoléon
D25
Mons
Gouffre des Audides
de Canjuers
D563
Rochetaillée
Grottes de St-Cézaire
D5
D4
D4
Cabris
Gorges
Spéracèdes
1122 m
Bougaille
D13
St-Cézaire-sur-Siagne
Le Tignet
D562
Peymeinade
du Bel-Homme 915 m
1032 m
Seillans
N.-D.-de-l'Ormeau
Fayence
Tourrettes
Callian
Montauroux
Riviera
D19
Ste-Anne
Méaulx
N.-D.-des-Cyprès
St-Cassien-des-Bois
Moulin-Vieux
Les Selves
D562
Auribeau
D563
Tanneron
D38
Callas
Claviers
Brovès-en-Seillans
Les Saquetons
La Colle Noire
La Colle Blanche
D4
D56
Les Marjoris
La Bégude
Lac de St-Cassien
D562
Garron
Grime
D37
Les Margoutons
Les Clèdes
St-Paul-en-Forêt
Reyran
Massif du
Endre
D25
Les Adrets
39
A 8
E 80
Cascade de Pennafort
Bompin
St-Denis
Bagnols-en-Forêt
D237
L'Eglise
St-Pons
D47
Les Adrets de l'Esterel
St-Jean
Les Petits Esclans
Le Rouet
Gorges
Les Adrets
Auberge des Adrets
Mont Vinaigre
Col des Suvières
618 m
249 m
St-Michel-d'Esclans
D4
La Bouverie
N 7
Pin-de-la-Lègue
La Motte
D47
Reyran
D7
Valbourgès
D25
Fréjus/St-Raphaël
Parc Zoologique-Safari
Le Muy
la Combe
Puget-sur-Argens
38
N.-D.-de-Jérusalem
La-Tour-de-Mare
Pic du Cap Roux 453
Ste-Roseline
37
N.-D.-de-la-Roquette
Puget-sur-Argens
D4
D37
Massif de l'Esterel
D100
N 7
36
Le Muy/Draguignan/St-Tropez
Roquebrune-sur-Argens
D7
Théâtre romain
Valescure
D100
Agay
D7
N 7
D25
FRÉJUS
ST-RAPHAËL
N.-D.-de-Pitié
Le Dramont
Sommet du Rouvier 301 m
Aquatica
Boulouris
Sémaphore
Le Clos
Villepey
Fréjus Plage
Île d'Or
Cap du Dramont
Villepey
Plage du Fournas
Vieux-Revest
Golfe de Fréjus
Corniche d
La Mère
474 m
St-Aygulf
442 m
Col de Gratteloup 225 m
D8
La Gaillarde
D72
Les Pierrons
D44
D25
Les Issambres
Plan-de-la-Tour
Val d'Esquières
San-Peïre-sur-Mer
D559
La Nartelle
D74
Préconil
Préconil
Courruères
Cap des Sardinaux
Tourelle de la Sèche-à-l'Huile
D44
Ste-Maxime
183
Beauvallon
Golfe de St-Tropez
Cap St-Pierre
St-Pons-les-Mûres
D14
43
4
Cap de St-Tropez
Port-Grimaud
44
La Foux
Plage de la Bouillabaisse
D98A
ST-TROPEZ
Château de la Moutte
D558
Plage des Salins
Moulin
Bourrian
St-Amé
Pointe du Capon
Cogolin
184
D559
Pampelonne
Plage de Tahiti
D93
Rebois
Moulins de Paillas
Pampelonne
Plage de Pampelonne
Gassin
D61
Ramatuelle

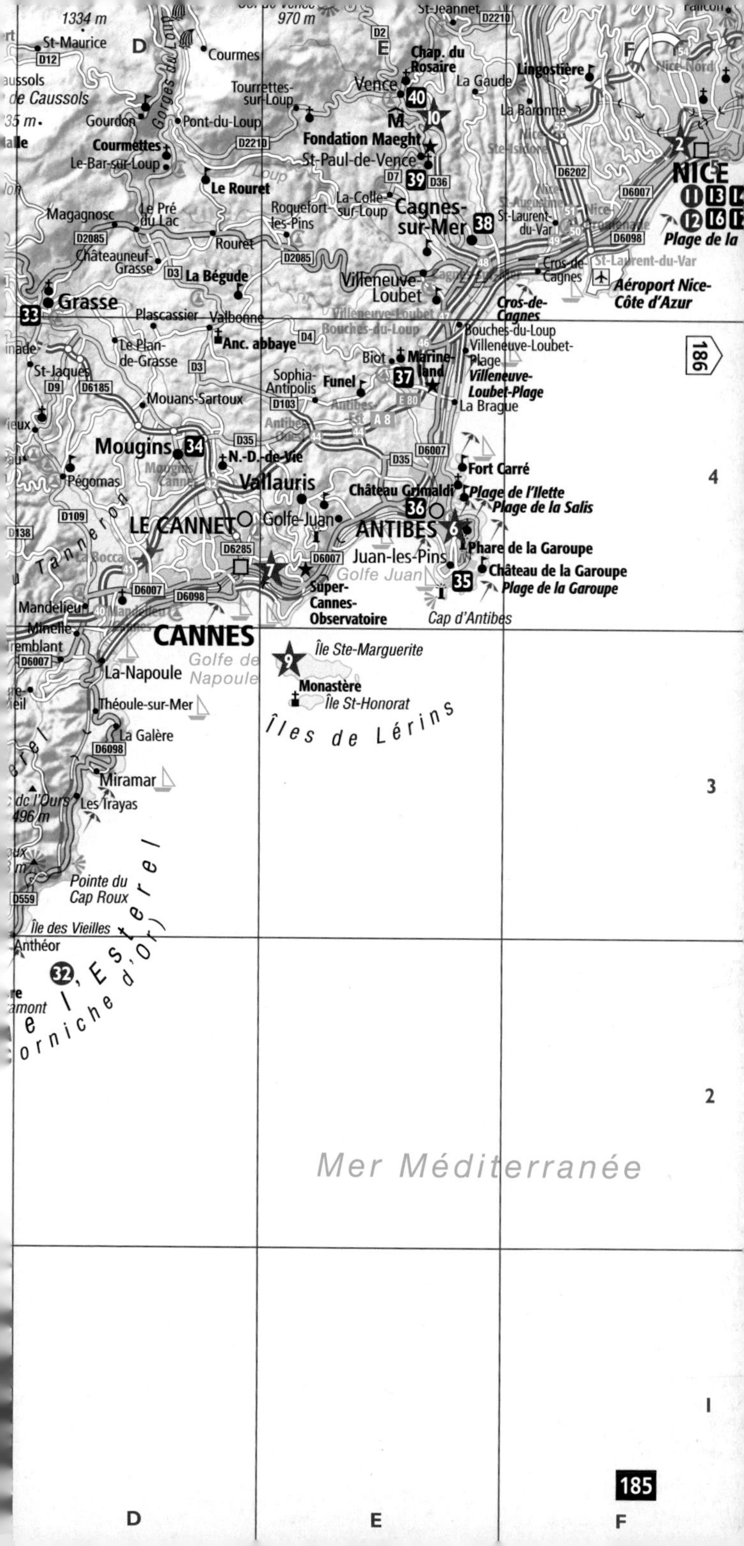

St-Maurice
Coursmes
Vence
Chap. du Rosaire
La Gaude
Lingostière
Tourrettes-sur-Loup
Gourdon
Pont-du-Loup
Courmettes
Le-Bar-sur-Loup
Fondation Maeght
St-Paul-de-Vence
Le Rouret
Magagnosc
Le Pré du Lac
Roquefort-les-Pins
La-Colle-sur-Loup
Cagnes-sur-Mer
St-Laurent-du-Var
NICE
Plage de la
Châteauneuf-Grasse
Rouret
La Bégude
Villeneuve-Loubet
Cros-de-Cagnes
Aéroport Nice-Côte d'Azur
Grasse
Plascassier
Valbonne
Anc. abbaye
Bouches-du-Loup
Villeneuve-Loubet-Plage
Le Plan-de-Grasse
St-Jaques
Biot
Marineland
Sophia-Antipolis
Funel
La Brague
Mouans-Sartoux
Mougins
N.-D.-de-Vie
Vallauris
Fort Carré
Pégomas
Château Grimaldi
Plage de l'Ilette
Plage de la Salis
LE CANNET
Golfe-Juan
ANTIBES
Phare de la Garoupe
Tanneron
Juan-les-Pins
Château de la Garoupe
Golfe Juan
Plage de la Garoupe
Super-Cannes-Observatoire
Cap d'Antibes
Mandelieu
CANNES
Île Ste-Marguerite
La-Napoule
Golfe de Napoule
Monastère
Île St-Honorat
Théoule-sur-Mer
Îles de Lérins
La Galère
Miramar
Les Trayas
Pointe du Cap Roux
Île des Vieilles
Anthéor
Massif de l'Esterel
Corniche d'Or
Mer Méditerranée
D
E
F
4
3
2
1

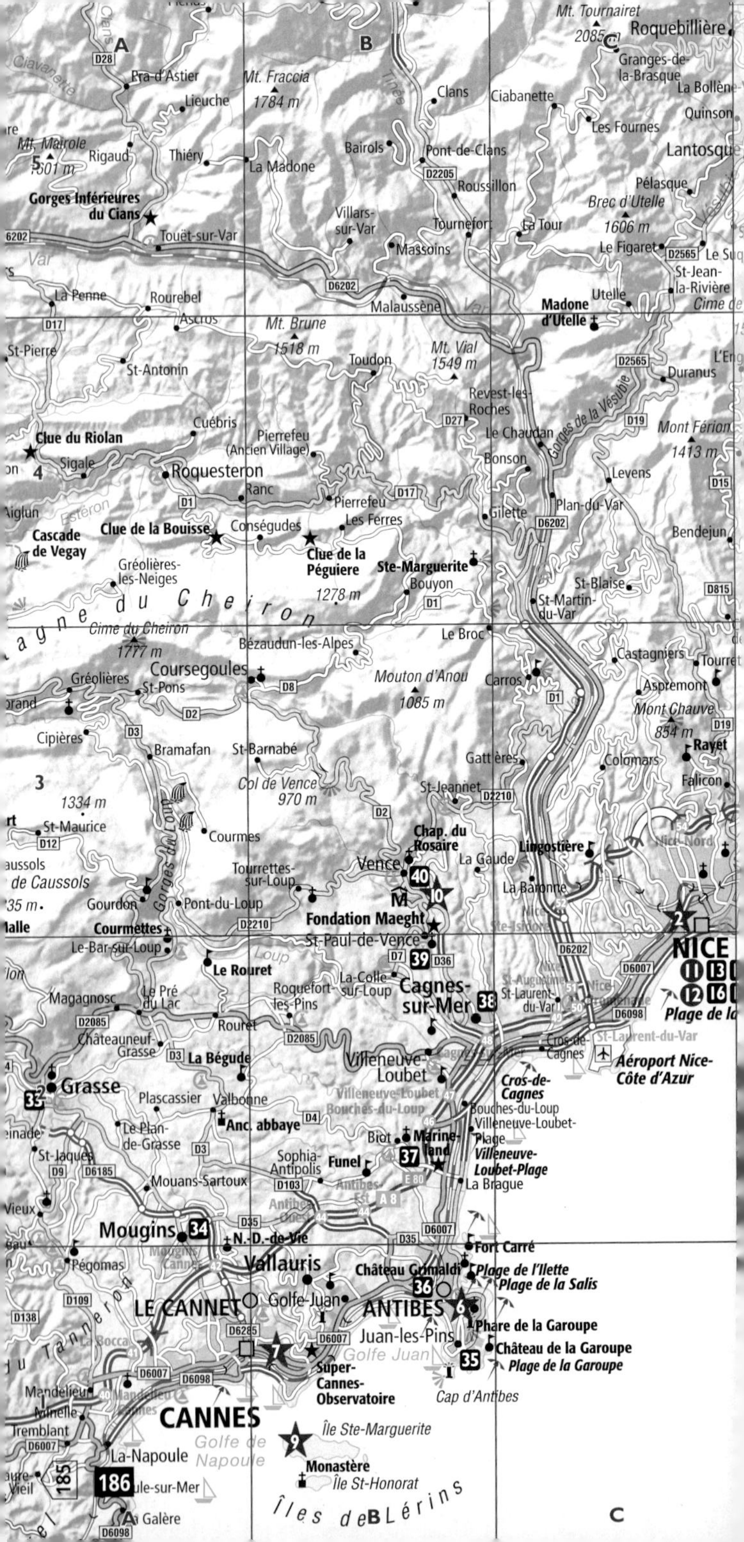

A
B
C
Mt. Tournairet
2085 m
Roquebillière
Granges-de-la-Brasque
La Bollène-V
Quinson
Lantosque
Clans
Ciabanette
Les Fournes
Pra-d'Astier
Mt. Fraccia
1784 m
Lieuche
Tinée
Mt. Mairole
1501 m
Rigaud
Thiéry
La Madone
Bairols
Pont-de-Clans
D2205
Roussillon
Pélasque
Brec d'Utelle
1606 m
Gorges Inférieures du Cians
Villars-sur-Var
Tournefort
La Tour
Le Figaret
D2565
Le Suq
Touët-sur-Var
Massoins
St-Jean-la-Rivière
Var
D6202
La Penne
Rourebel
Malaussène
Utelle
Cime de
Ascros
Madone d'Utelle
D17
Mt. Brune
1518 m
Mt. Vial
1549 m
St-Pierre
Toudon
D2565
L'Eng
St-Antonin
Duranus
Revest-les-Roches
D27
Gorges de la Vésubie
Cuébris
Pierrefeu (Ancien Village)
Le Chaudan
D19
Mont Férion
1413 m
Clue du Riolan
Sigale
Bonson
Roquesteron
Levens
Ranc
D17
D15
D1
Pierrefeu
Plan-du-Var
Aiglun
Estéron
Gilette
Les Ferres
D6202
Cascade de Vegay
Clue de la Bouisse
Conségudes
Clue de la Péguiere
Bendejun
Ste-Marguerite
Gréolières-les-Neiges
Bouyon
St-Blaise
1278 m
D1
D815
Montagne du Cheiron
St-Martin-du-Var
Cime du Cheiron
1777 m
Le Broc
Bézaudun-les-Alpes
Castagniers
Tourret
Coursegoules
Mouton d'Anou
1085 m
Carros
Gréolières
Aspremont
St-Pons
D8
D1
D2
Mont Chauve
854 m
D3
Cipières
D19
Rayet
Bramafan
St-Barnabé
Gattières
Colomars
Falicon
Col de Vence
970 m
St-Jeannet
D2210
1334 m
D2
St-Maurice
Courmes
Chap. du Rosaire
D12
Gorges du Loup
Lingostière
Nice-Nord
Caussols
Plateau de Caussols
Tourrettes-sur-Loup
Vence
La Gaude
40
10
La Baronne
Gourdon
Pont-du-Loup
Fondation Maeght
2
D2210
Cournettes
St-Paul-de-Vence
NICE
Le-Bar-sur-Loup
D7
39
D36
D6202
D6007
Loup
Le Rouret
La Colle-sur-Loup
Cagnes-sur-Mer
38
11
13
Roquefort-les-Pins
St-Laurent-du-Var
12
16
Magagnosc
Le Pré du Lac
D6098
Plage de la
D2085
Rouret
D2085
St-Laurent-du-Var
Châteauneuf-Grasse
D3
La Bégude
Cros-de-Cagnes
Villeneuve-Loubet
Aéroport Nice-Côte d'Azur
Grasse
32
Cros-de-Cagnes
Plascassier
Valbonne
Bouches-du-Loup
Anc. abbaye
D4
Villeneuve-Loubet-Plage
Le Plan-de-Grasse
Biot
Marineland
St-Jaques
D3
Sophia-Antipolis
Funel
37
Villeneuve-Loubet-Plage
D9
D6185
Mouans-Sartoux
D103
La Brague
E 80
A 8
Vieux
D35
Mougins
34
N.-D.-de-Vie
D35
D6007
Fort Carré
Pégomas
Vallauris
Château Grimaldi
Plage de l'Ilette
36
Plage de la Salis
D109
LE CANNET
Golfe-Juan
ANTIBES
6
D138
Tanneron
D6285
D6007
Juan-les-Pins
Phare de la Garoupe
7
Golfe Juan
Château de la Garoupe
D6007
D6098
Super-Cannes-Observatoire
35
Plage de la Garoupe
Mandelieu
Cap d'Antibes
Minelle
Tremblant
CANNES
9
Île Ste-Marguerite
D6007
Golfe de Napoule
La-Napoule
Monastère
185
186
Île St-Honorat
ule-sur-Mer
Îles de Lérins
A Galère
D6098

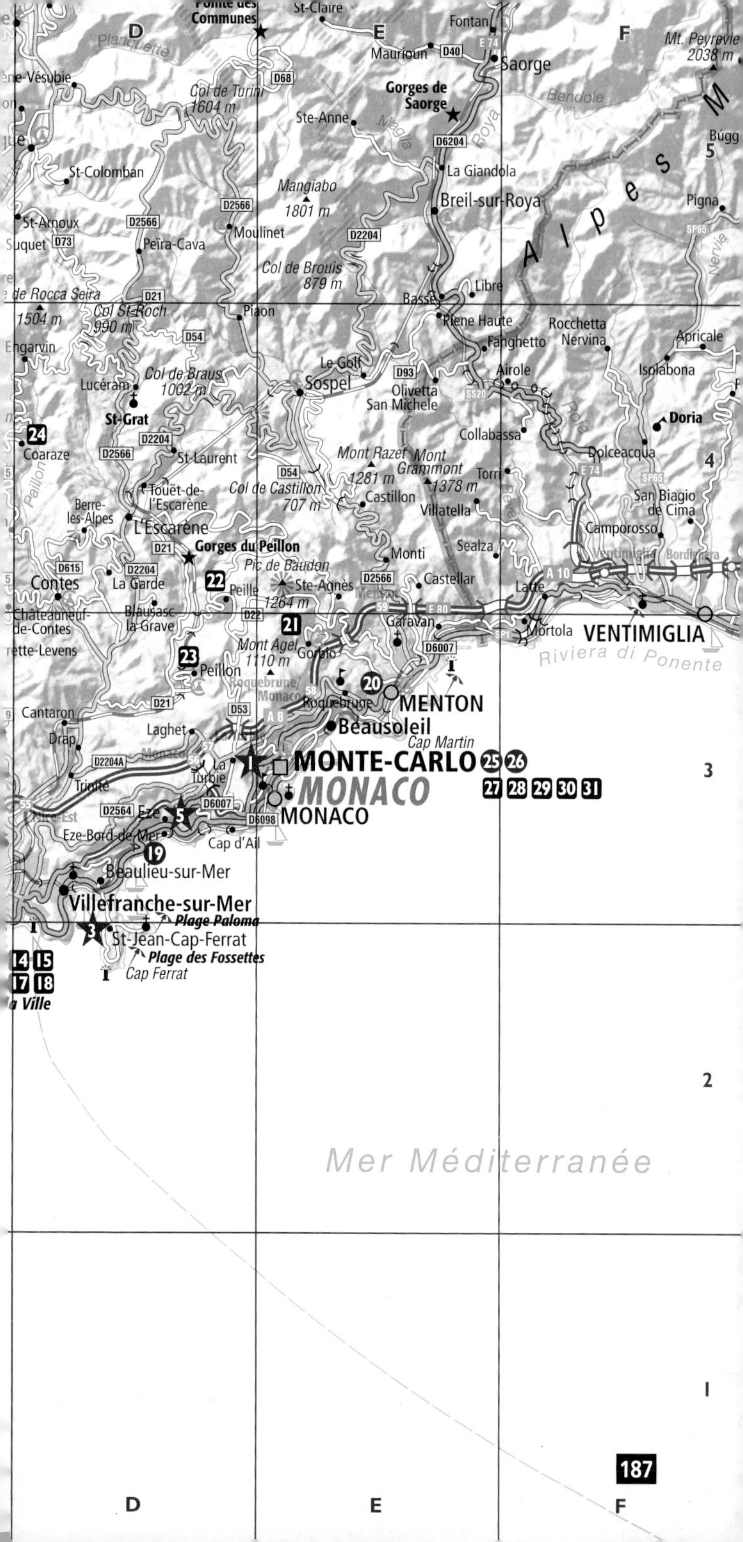
D
E
F
Pointe des Communes
St-Claire
Fontan
Mauriоun
Saorge
Mt. Peyrevie 2038 m
Planquette
Col de Turini 1604 m
Gorges de Saorge
Bendole
Ste-Anne
Roya
Bugg
St-Colomban
La Giandola
Mangiabo 1801 m
Breil-sur-Roya
Alpes
Pigna
St-Arnoux
Moulinet
Suquet
Peïra-Cava
Col de Brouis 879 m
Nervia
Libre
Basse
Piene Haute
Piaon
Col St-Roch 990 m
1504 m
Rocchetta Nervina
Apricale
Fanghetto
Engarvin
Le Golf
Airole
Isolabona
Lucéram
Col de Braus 1002 m
Sospel
Olivetta San Michele
St-Grat
Doria
Coaraze
St-Laurent
Collabassa
Mont Razet 1281 m
Mont Grammont 1378 m
Dolceacqua
Touët-de-l'Escarène
Torri
Col de Castillon 707 m
Castillon
Berre-les-Alpes
Villatella
San Biagio de Cima
L'Escarène
Camporosso
Gorges du Peillon
Monti
Sealza
Pic de Baudon
Contes
La Garde
Ste-Agnès
Castellar
Peille
1264 m
Latte
Châteauneuf-de-Contes
Blausasc la Grave
Garavan
Mortola
VENTIMIGLIA
Riviera di Ponente
Mont Agel 1110 m
Gorbio
Peillon
MENTON
Roquebrune
Cantaron
Beausoleil
Laghet
Cap Martin
Drap
MONTE-CARLO
La Turbie
Trinité
MONACO
Eze
Eze-Bord-de-Mer
Cap d'Ail
Beaulieu-sur-Mer
Villefranche-sur-Mer
Plage Paloma
St-Jean-Cap-Ferrat
Plage des Fossettes
Cap Ferrat
Mer Méditerranée
5
4
3
2
1

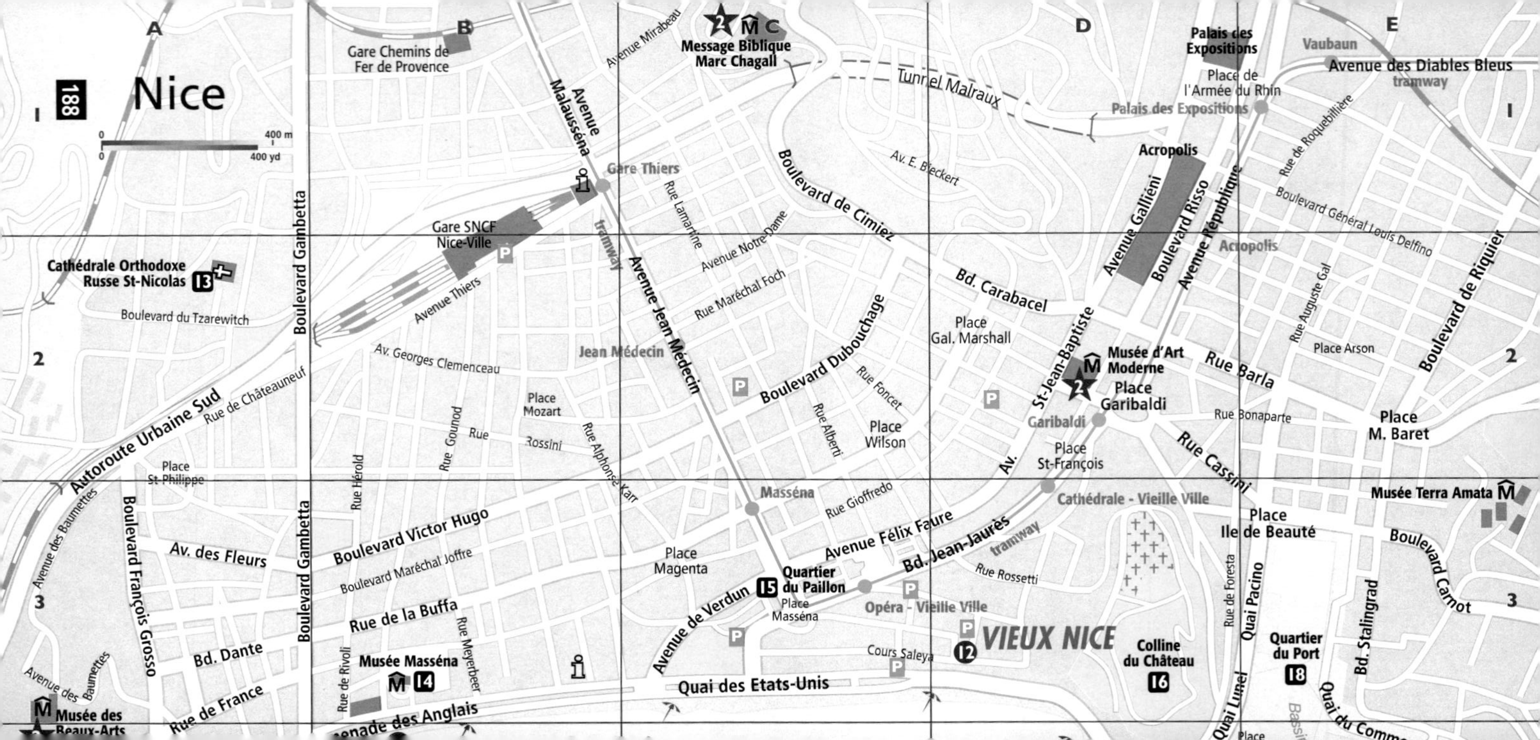
Nice
0
400 m
0
400 yd
A
B
C
D
E
1
2
3
Gare Chemins de Fer de Provence
Message Biblique Marc Chagall
Avenue Mirabeau
Tunnel Malraux
Palais des Expositions
Place de l'Armée du Rhin
Vaubaun
Avenue des Diables Bleus
tramway
Avenue Malausséna
Gare Thiers
Gare SNCF Nice-Ville
Cathédrale Orthodoxe Russe St-Nicolas
13
Boulevard du Tzarewitch
Boulevard Gambetta
Avenue Thiers
tramway
Avenue Jean Médecin
Rue Lamartine
Avenue Notre-Dame
Rue Maréchal Foch
Boulevard de Cimiez
Av. E. Bieckert
Acropolis
Avenue Galliéni
Boulevard Risso
Avenue République
Rue de Roquebillière
Boulevard Général Louis Delfino
Rue Auguste Gal
Place Arson
Boulevard de Riquier
Bd. Carabacel
Place Gal. Marshall
Av. St-Jean-Baptiste
Musée d'Art Moderne
Place Garibaldi
Garibaldi
Rue Barla
Rue Bonaparte
Place M. Baret
Jean Médecin
Av. Georges Clemenceau
Boulevard Dubouchage
Rue Foncet
Rue Alberti
Place Wilson
Autoroute Urbaine Sud
Rue de Châteauneuf
Place Mozart
Rue Gounod
Rue Rossini
Rue Alphonse Karr
Place St-François
Rue Cassini
Place St Philippe
Avenue des Baumettes
Rue Hérold
Masséna
Rue Gioffredo
Cathédrale - Vieille Ville
Musée Terra Amata
Place Ile de Beauté
Boulevard François Grosso
Av. des Fleurs
Boulevard Victor Hugo
Boulevard Maréchal Joffre
Avenue Félix Faure
Bd. Jean-Jaurès
tramway
Place Magenta
Quartier du Paillon
15
Place Masséna
Rue Rossetti
Opéra - Vieille Ville
Rue de Foresta
Quai Pacino
Bd. Stalingrad
Boulevard Carnot
Bd. Dante
Rue de la Buffa
Rue Meyerbeer
Avenue de Verdun
VIEUX NICE
12
Colline du Château
16
Quartier du Port
18
Rue de Rivoli
Musée Masséna
14
Cours Saleya
Quai des Etats-Unis
Quai Lunel
Avenue des Baumettes
Musée des Beaux-Arts
Rue de France

Nice Street Index

Index

Index

Picture Credits

AA/A Baker: 26, 64, 66, 70, 79, 88, 89, 90, 91, 100, 125, 146, 147, 150

AA/M Jourdan: 177 (centre)

AA/R Moore: 170

AA/T Oliver: 154, 172

AA/C Sawyer: 40, 41, 43, 46, 48, 49, 52, 56, 68/69, 71, 72/73 (bottom), 74, 80, 112, 115, 116/117, 118, 119, 121, 124, 126, 128, 140, 142, 144, 145, 167, 177 (top and bottom)

AA/R Strange: 12, 15, 53, 54, 55, 65, 72 (top), 76, 97, 99, 110, 122/123, 139, 143, 148, 152/153

AA/W Voysey: 165 (top)

Bildagentur Huber: Olimpio Fantuz 16/17

corbis: Massimo Borchi 25, 96, Amanda Hall 98, Grand Tour/Matteo Carassale 113, Chris Hellier 151, Sergio Pitamitz 164/165 (bottom)

DuMont Bildarchiv/Björn Göttlicher: 42, 50, 67, 92, 93, 111, 138

getty images: AFP/Alberto Pizzolil 20 (left), Loic Venance/Staff 20 (right), Patrice Coppee 127, Thomas Stankiewicz 169

laif: Yann Dolean/hemis.fr 4, Hughes Hervè/hemis.fr 7, Gamma/JDD/Eric Dessons 8, Sunset Box/Allpix 18 (left), Keystone-France 18 (right), Gamma/API 19 (left), Davide Lanzilao 19 (right), Sarnin/Madame Figaro 45, Matthieu Colin/hemis.fr 95, Gamma/Anne Nosten 156

mauritius images: Alamy 6, 13, 23, 24 (top), 155, age 10/11, 168, 149, SuperStock 24 (bottom), imagebroker 114

On the cover: huber-images.de/Carassale Matteo (top), huber-images.de/Gräfenhain (bottom), Getty Images (background)

Credits

1st Edition 2017

Worldwide Distribution: Marco Polo Travel Publishing Ltd
Pinewood, Chineham Business Park
Crockford Lane, Chineham
Basingstoke, Hampshire RG24 8AL, United Kingdom.

Authors: Beth Hall, Teresa Fisher ("The Magazine"), Peter Bausch
Editor: Bintang Buchservice GmbH (Gudrun Raether-Klünker), www.bintang-berlin.de
Revised editing and translation: Jon Andrews, jonandrews.co.uk
Program supervisor: Birgit Borowski
Chief editor: Rainer Eisenschmid

Cartography: © MAIRDUMONT GmbH & Co. KG, Ostfildern
3D-illustrations: jangled nerves, Stuttgart

Printed in China

Despite all of our authors' thorough research, errors can creep in. The publishers do not accept any liability for this. Whether you want to praise us, alert us to errors or give us a personal tip – please don't hesitate to email or post to:

MARCO POLO Travel Publishing Ltd
Pinewood, Chineham Business Park
Crockford Lane, Chineham
Basingstoke, Hampshire RG24 8AL
United Kingdom
Email: sales@marcopolouk.com

FSC®
www.fsc.org
MIX
Paper from responsible sources
FSC® C124385

10 REASONS
TO COME BACK AGAIN

1. The French Riviera is the **sunniest part of France** (so don't forget your sun cream!).
2. The region's many **art museums** are veritable treasure troves that never fail to surprise.
3. The sea is the perfect temperature for a relaxing **swim**, even as late as September!
4. The French Riviera has some of the most beautiful **parks and gardens** in the world.
5. **Mediterranean cuisine** is both delicious and good for you – it's a win-win situation!
6. The area's sun-soaked vineyards produce some truly **fantastic wines**.
7. The region's **belle époque palaces** are over a century old but still provide a feast for the eyes.
8. Such **medieval villages** as Èze and Gorbio have been lovingly restored and beautifully maintained.
9. The churches in Nice and beyond are bursting with numerous **baroque masterpieces**.
10. The **islands of Porquerolles, Port-Cros** and **Levant** are all worth a holiday in their own right.